Roasting

Roasting

Kathy Gunst

Macmillan • USA

MACMILLAN
A Simon & Schuster Macmillan Company
1633 Broadway
New York, NY 10019

MACMILLAN is a registered trademark of Macmillan, Inc.

Library of Congress Cataloging-in-Publication Data
Gunst, Kathy.
  Roasting / Kathy Gunst
  p.   cm.
  Includes index.
  ISBN 0-02-051340-2
  1. Roasting (Cookery). I. Title.
TX690.G86   1995   94-44742
641.7'1—dc20   CIP

Manufactured in the United States of America
Book Design by designLab

10 9 8 7 6 5 4 3 2

For my mother, Nancy Levy Gunst

Contents

Acknowledgments

This book was a long time in the making and involved the encouragement and assistance of many people.

First I want to thank my family, in particular my husband, John Rudolph, for all his love, support, and professional advice. Thanks also to my daughters, Maya and Emma, the best little eaters I have ever met. You two are a mother's dream come true—enthusiastic, adventurous eaters who are willing to try even the "weirdest foods." Who would have believed that a four-year-old and seven-year-old could fall in love with roasted beets with ginger butter or roasted goat cheese with olives and tomatoes or that "very yummy" roasted duck with mangoes.

My father, Lee Gunst, has given his support and love throughout all my projects—both professional and personal. Thanks to my mother-in-law, Nancy K. Rudolph, for all her good cooking, love, and help with the kids. You are a constant source of inspiration to me. I thank my grandparents, Leonard and Leona Levy, who are so full of love and encouragement. Thanks also to Alan and Nancy Rudolph for all their support and good food ideas.

Many friends and chefs contributed recipes and ideas to this book. Thanks to Larisa Yaskell for giving me the time (and peace of mind) to finish this book, and to Karen Frillmann, intrepid traveler, eater, and devoted friend. To Valerie and Ric Jorgensen for partaking of many roasted meals and being enthusiastic through it all. Thanks to Edwin Child for lending me your spectacular kitchen in France and to the many friends and family members who sat at our table over the years, sharing all this roasted food.

Thanks to my agent, Robert Cornfield, who not only makes these projects happen but also keeps me on the right track; to Deborah Melmon, whose wonderful illustrations bring my work to life; to Pam Hoenig, my first editor, for envisioning this book with me and making it such a good one; and to Jane Sigal, who edited every word of this book with a thoroughly professional touch. All your questions have shaped this into a much finer book.

Introduction

Roasting is the seductress of the culinary world. Only a few minutes after you begin the cooking process, your kitchen is enveloped in rich aromas. The scent of well-seasoned fresh ingredients being transformed by the intense heat of an oven teases you, haunts you, like the anticipation that accompanies the beginning of a love affair. You feel the same longing experienced by ancient peoples as they took in the rich smell of meat thrust into hot, white coals. Roasting was the first method of cooking; it remains one of the most beguiling.

As the roasting process continues, you're convinced that you will lose your mind if the food is not done soon. The scent could be coming from any number of dishes: a leg of lamb lightly coated in a fruity olive oil and topped with sprigs of rosemary; a fresh turkey basted with butter and generous amounts of garlic; or perhaps a more unusual choice like a stew of carrots, parsnips, and onions roasted until they are tender and their natural sweetness comes out.

Despite the sensuous appeal of roasting, many people think of it as an old-fashioned and fussy method. Nothing could be further from the truth. One newspaper food editor I talked with summed it up this way: "All my readers can make pesto and homemade pasta, but they don't know how to roast a chicken. Our mothers and grandmothers knew how to roast every cut of meat and poultry they found in a butcher shop, but this generation finds roasting scary."

The idea of cooking a roast dinner need not be intimidating, even for cooks just starting out. *Roasting* aims to demystify one of the world's greatest forms of cookery. Not only does this book prove that roasting is a simple art, but it shows that an endless variety of foods lend themselves to this process. This book offers updated versions of old standbys along with dozens of innovative new recipes. It also answers all your questions about roasting, from equipment to carving.

The term "roasting" is most often associated with poultry, beef, pork, and game, but these are just some of the foods that can be roasted successfully. In this book you'll find recipes for the best standing rib roast, a crown roast of pork, and many varieties of roast chicken, but you'll also learn how to roast peaches and mangoes to make a fabulous chutney and transform roasted eggplant and tomatoes into a simple French terrine. Soon you'll know that portobello mushrooms roasted with garlic and herbs taste and smell as hearty as roast beef, and that roasted heads of garlic add intrigue to even the simplest dishes.

For a cooking technique that yields so many satisfying and complex flavors, roasting is a surprisingly simple way to prepare food, making it ideal for both entertaining and family dinners. Most of the preparation can be done ahead of time, and once the ingredients are put in the oven, they can be left to cook virtually unattended. This gives you the luxury of time—time to prepare other foods, set the table, and be with family and friends.

A woman I know told me that on Easter Sunday she decided to roast a ham. She seasoned the pork, placed it in the oven, and spent the entire day walking around the house saying to her husband: "Shouldn't I be doing something? This seems too easy. I must be doing something wrong."

One of the great myths about roasting is that it takes forever and involves a lot of mess and confusion. But the truth is that roasting is as ideal for Tuesday night's dinner as it is for Sunday night's. There are a surprising number of recipes on these pages that can be made from start to finish in about an hour. Best of all, you can roast an entire meal in one pan. For example, surround a chicken with new potatoes, baby onions, whole heads of garlic, and thick slices of zucchini, then pop it in the oven. An hour later dinner is ready, and there's only the roasting pan to clean after the meal.

Roasting is also a low-fat method of cookery. Many roasting recipes begin with foods that are naturally juicy. So by their very nature, roasted foods, whether meat, fish, poultry, or vegetables, require the addition of little or no butter, oil, or other fat to keep the food moist and flavorful. A remarkable range of foods, from beets and bananas to duck and even chicken, may be roasted without the addition of *any* fat. A dash of wine or chicken stock keeps these foods moist just as well as butter or oil. When a recipe requires fat, I tend to rely on olive oil because it imparts such a fine flavor to foods without adding a lot of cholesterol. In cases where butter or cream is essential, I try to add only the smallest amount possible.

Working on this book presented many surprises. From the very start, I assumed that the chapters on beef and other meats would be the bulk of the project. But, in fact, it was the vegetable chapters that offered the greatest challenge and the most creative possibilities. Roasted vegetables have become a hot item in many restaurants in recent years, so I assumed that, like most trends, this one would have its limits. But an entire volume could be written on the subject. Roasting vegetables (as opposed to boiling, steaming, or sautéing them) yields intense flavors. The natural sweetness found in most vegetables (root vegetables in particular) comes shining through, and consequently the vegetables need very little adornment—whether we're talking about beets wrapped tightly in foil and roasted until perfectly sweet or a mélange of roasted winter vegetables made with leeks, onions, carrots, squash, and potatoes. Even corn, which is traditionally boiled, can be roasted in its own husk until sweet and smoky.

Don't make the mistake of thinking of roasted vegetables only as "side dishes." They can be every bit as satisfying and hearty as roasted meats. They fill you up without ever being heavy. And they are a great way to introduce vegetables to children. The natural sweetness is sure to win them over.

There are only a few beef recipes presented in this volume, but each one is memorable. I tried many experiments roasting beef with strongly flavored spices and herbs and some unusual sauces. But each time I came back to a basic truth: the best method for roasting beef is simple and straightforward. When you have good-quality beef, there isn't any reason to add much more than a grinding of fresh pepper, a few cloves of garlic, and an occasional fresh herb. And if you follow my recipe for roast beef, I think you'll find it's the best you've ever tasted.

There are very few veal recipes in this chapter. The main reason is cost: most cuts of veal have become prohibitively expensive. And I've found that, aside from veal scallops or cutlets, most supermarkets do not stock veal on a regular basis. But a book on roasting without a recipe for roast breast of veal, a surprisingly reasonably priced and tender cut, is unthinkable. And for veal lovers I've also included a recipe for a roast center-cut loin of veal with a delicious lemon-parsley sauce.

Roasting fruit was another challenge that provided some of the most interesting recipes in the book. Fresh figs roasted in orange juice and then topped with pine nuts make a quick dessert, and roasted pears combined with a sauce made from roasted pear juice, Grand Marnier, and cream are an elegant end to any meal. But roasted fruit can also be the basis for savory dishes: bananas can be roasted with brown sugar and then mixed with scallions, red bell pepper, jalapeño pepper, and fresh lime juice to form a fabulous Caribbean-style chutney. And roasted apples that have been stuffed with herbs, breadcrumbs, and garlic make a thoroughly unusual and exciting side dish for poultry, meats, or pork dishes. I found that apples, figs, peaches, bananas, and other fresh fruit are fabulous roasted, either on their own or mixed into other dishes.

Cooks all over the world have known for centuries that roasting is an easy way to produce extremely moist, delicious fish. I discovered that roasting works well with a wide variety of fish and shellfish because the high heat seals in the fish's natural flavors—whether it's shrimp in the shell buried in coarse salt and roasted until perfectly juicy and tender; littleneck clams roasted with fresh tomatoes, shallots, and wine; or a fillet of salmon roasted with thin slices of buttery avocado. See page 129 for tips about what type of fish works best for roasting.

During the two years that I worked on this book, I was obsessed by one question. What exactly is meant by the term "roasting"? Until the introduction of the modern kitchen oven, roasting had only one meaning—it involved cooking foods, often meats or poultry, skewered on a fireplace spit. Today the most common place to roast food is inside a gas or electric oven, the same place and the same heat source that is used for baking. So what does roasting mean in 20th-century culinary terms?

The term "roasting" appears over and over in cookbooks, both old and new. You'll find it in recipes for beef, veal, pork, chicken, duck, and peppers. A recipe for roast pork instructs the cook to season the meat and "bake the pork until tender." The instructions for baked apples begin with "Roast the apples for 30 minutes." I located dozens of references for roasted peppers: "Broil the peppers until charred." "Bake the peppers until soft." Or "preheat the broiler and broil the peppers. Serve the roasted peppers with olive oil."

I checked with a wide variety of chefs, cookbooks, and reference books, only to learn that everyone defines the term differently.

According to the most recent edition of *Larousse Gastronomique*, roasting, or *rôtissage,* is "Cooking meat, poultry, game, or fish by exposing it to the heat of a naked flame or grill (spit-roasting) or to the radiant heat of an oven (oven-roasting)....Whichever method is used, the meat is first exposed to a high heat, which produces a surface crust and concentrates the juices inside the meat, conserving all its flavor."

Edward Behr, author of *The Artful Eater,* states, "To roast is to cook by radiant heat, dry heat. Oven roasting is high-heat baking....The lines that distinguish one method of cooking from another are sometimes artificial, but they make the concepts clear."

In *Cordon Bleu Basic Cookery Methods,* published by the London Cordon Bleu School of Cookery, a section on roasting begins: "Roasting is the traditional—and most popular—method of cookery in this country, so it is up to every serious student of cookery to master this most important art....True roasting was always done on a revolving spit over an open fire.... If you are not lucky enough to own a spit, you can obtain equally good results by roasting meat in the oven. But extra care is needed because cooking in the oven is really baking."

At this point, my head swirling, I looked for a dictionary definition. *Webster's New Universal Unabridged Dictionary* defines the word *roast* this way: "originally, to cook (meat, etc.) over an open fire or in hot ashes, etc.," or " to cook (meat, etc.) by dry heat, as in an oven."

And then there are the definitions I got from my two daughters. The four-year-old claims it means "broiling hot, like in the summertime," and my seven-year-old tells me, with just a touch of sarcasm in her voice, that roasting is "what we eat for dinner every single solitary night."

Roasting, grilling, baking, broiling—everyone has a personal definition of these terms, and the bottom line is that this is a game of semantics. Technically, there is very little difference between baking and oven roasting. Roasting on a spit is similar to grilling and broiling. However, the recipes in this book all have several things in common. They are, in almost every case, roasted in a regular kitchen oven with dry, radiant heat. With very few exceptions, these recipes are cooked with a quick, high blast of heat to sear the food's exterior—whether it's beef, poultry, or apples; the food is then cooked at a slightly lower temperature until tender and juicy (see Box, page 115 for more on searing). Although modern kitchen ovens don't have the romantic appeal of an open fire or an old-fashioned rotisserie, they do offer temperature control, which makes it easier to produce perfectly roasted foods. What will surprise you is that when foods are roasted properly in a regular kitchen oven, they are every bit as flavorful as foods cooked over an open fire.

While I was working on this book, I was fortunate enough to witness a variety of roasting techniques. On the island of Jamaica, Jack Shapansky, the chef at Cibboney in Ocho Rios, and Walter Staib, a consultant who put together the menu at each of the resort's four restaurants, took me on a tour of the "VV Jerk

Center" in downtown Ocho Rios. People stop by this local bar throughout the day to eat foods that have been roasted in a huge pit and flavored with jerk sauce—a potent combination of Scotch bonnet peppers, thyme, onion, and local spices.

I watched as huge breadfruit (an exotic fruit that looks like an oversized coconut, but tastes like a buttery potato) and whole sides of pork smothered in sauce were buried in the blazing hot, white ash of local pimiento wood. This roasting method is the traditional way to cook breadfruit and jerked pork, singeing the fruit and the meat on the outside and letting them roast until perfectly tender and juicy on the inside. The same method is used for roasting suckling pig, yams, goat, corn, and fish.

As men use long-handled shovels to move the white ash around the pork, the aroma of chile peppers and cinnamon drifts up into the tropical air. The meat is so tender it slices easily with the dullest of knives; its flavor is a combination of smoke and tingling hot chilies that aggressively tickle your tongue. The breadfruit is cooked until the skin is completely black. When peeled, the flesh tastes of wood smoke and butter. (For more on roasted breadfruit, see Shapansky's recipe on page 94.)

"The secret to roasting," explains Staib, "is that the flavor goes inside the food instead of going away from it." This is as good a definition of the word as any you'll find.

In southern France I feasted on roasted eggplant, duck, chicken, and beef. In his restaurant, La Haute Burlière, in the Provençal village of Viens, Chef Robert Eymony roasts at least half the items on his menu in a centuries-old fireplace, as well as in his surprisingly small kitchen oven. "Roasting," explains Eymony, "is an art that has no equal." Eymony experiments with a wide variety of foods and says he never grows "restless" with the technique because it always "presents new possibilities."

This is the same feeling I am left with after roasting everything from sides of beef to bananas. The possibilities are endless. I hope you'll enjoy the recipes in this volume and find some favorites. Then you can create your own roasting classics, experimenting with vegetables, fruit, fish, and more. I think you'll find that there are few methods of cooking that satisfy the senses so completely.

Kathy Gunst

Roasting Equipment

Unlike some other forms of cookery, roasting does not require a lot of fancy, expensive equipment. If you have a decent roasting pan and a working oven thermometer, you're ready to roast. There are, however, a few pieces of equipment that can help make roasting a more accurate, reliable art.

In order to research roasting equipment, I took a trip to one of my favorite kitchen supply shops. Bridge Kitchenware, located in midtown Manhattan, is run by Fred Bridge and his two sons. This place is as irresistible to cooks as F.A.O. Schwarz is to children—a virtual fantasyland of cookware. Inside this warehouse-like shop, with its 22-foot ceilings, you'll find everything from French pastry molds and slabs of marble to copper roasting pans and trussing needles. In terms of roasting, this is one of the best places to learn about equipment.

Roasting Pans: Having a good roasting pan is key. At Bridge Kitchenware they recommend stainless-steel pans because they are highly durable and their nonreactive cooking surface allows you to make sauces directly in the pan after you cook the roast. Also, stainless steel has no coating that comes off after months or even years of use. Make sure to look for a shallow roasting pan because it allows as much of the food (meat, poultry, vegetables) as possible to be exposed to the oven's dry heat for proper roasting. Shallow roasting pans come in a wide range of materials: stainless steel, tin-lined copper, aluminum, anodized aluminum, blue steel, and enameled steel.

Whatever type of pan you buy, be sure to measure the inside of your oven and then purchase a pan that sits at least 2 inches away from the oven walls. This will give you just enough room to maneuver the pan in and out of your oven easily. Roasting pans come in an array of sizes—small enough for a quail or Cornish hen or large enough for the biggest Thanksgiving turkey. As far as price goes, you can spend as little as $20 for a small, thin stainless-steel pan or up to around $600 for a large imported copper pan.

I own a variety of pans for roasting. My favorite is a large French aluminum roasting pan that I particularly like to use for large birds, beef, and pork. It's an extra-heavy pan, constructed to last a lifetime, with sturdy handles securely riveted in place. It's well worth the price to invest in one really good large roasting pan that you can use for special occasions, holidays, and parties. I also use all sorts of unconventional pans to roast in: broiler pans, ovenproof skillets, gratin dishes, and sauté pans. You can use any of these, as long as the pan or skillet isn't particularly deep; the food won't get enough direct exposure to the heat if the sides are more than a couple of inches high. Always look for a pan that has good weight to it so that it won't warp when exposed to high temperatures. The best pans—often labeled "professional"—also have strong handles set into them to make basting and removing the pan from the oven easier.

Roasting Racks: Bridge Kitchenware highly recommends using a roasting rack to ensure proper browning on the top, sides, *and* bottom of the roast. But I have a confession to make: over 75 percent of the recipes in this book were done *without* a roasting rack. I have found that a rack is essential only when cooking very fatty foods—like goose and duck—but not necessary when cooking most other foods. In general, I find roasting racks are a nuisance and a major pain to clean. I also like roasted foods to be in direct contact with the marinade or flavoring ingredients in the bottom of the pan. I have indicated which recipes truly require a roasting rack.

Having made my confession, I do acknowledge that there are many people who always use roasting racks. And if you are looking to eliminate as much fat as possible from your diet, I would recommend that you use a rack for roasting poultry, beef, and pork.

There are essentially three types of racks: flat racks; V-shaped or adjustable raised racks; and a fairly new device, the vertical roaster.

A flat roasting rack looks like an oven rack with the wires closer together. The advantage of using a flat rack is that the meat or poultry touches the rack only on the bottom and the meat gets uniform exposure to the heat.

V-shaped racks, also referred to as adjustable racks, are good for uneven cuts of meat or poultry. The wires are on a 120-degree angle. These are the most popular types of racks and can be adjusted to suit whatever type of food you are roasting.

A vertical roaster is a wire stand for an unstuffed bird; the rack is stuffed directly into the bird's cavity. The advantage of a vertical rack is that the fat drains off while the food roasts; consequently, manufacturers refer to the rack as a "low-calorie method of cooking." The reviews on this gadget are mixed: many cooks report that the birds are overcooked on top and undercooked on the bottom; others swear by it.

If you don't want to buy a rack, you can always use an inverted baking sheet as a kind of makeshift roasting rack. Simply place a baking sheet in your roasting pan *upside down* and center the roast on top. The baking sheet will elevate the roast so that it's not touching, or cooking, in its own fat.

Bulb Basters: Although you can baste any type of roast using a large spoon, a bulb baster can make the job easier. All roasts benefit from basting. (See page 27 for more on the subject.) Find a bulb baster that is narrow enough to reach through most roasting racks so you can suck up the juices from the bottom of the pan without lifting the roast off the rack. Also look for a baster that comes with a thin brush for cleaning.

There are now combination baster/skimmers available in many shops, a device with two interchangeable tips that allow you to skim the liquid from the bottom of a roasting pan and then separate the fat from the pan juices. You can baste the roast with the pan juices and discard the fat as it accumulates.

Basting Brushes: Long, wide "paint" brushes, these tools are used to brush marinades, glazes, and natural pan juices onto roasted or barbecued foods. Look for a brush with a long handle so that you won't have to stick your whole arm into the oven in order to baste. Always buy basting brushes with flameproof natural bristles.

Cheesecloth: A lightweight, loosely woven cotton cloth, cheesecloth is excellent for placing over the breast of a turkey or other large bird to keep the breast meat moist. You can baste a bird directly through the cheesecloth. The cloth should always be removed during the last 45 minutes of roasting so that the covered area can brown along with the rest of the bird.

Meat Thermometers: Of all the tools I have in my kitchen (and I own a fair amount of gadgetry), the instant-read or rapid-response meat thermometer is my most treasured possession. The reason a good meat thermometer is so critical is that finding the internal temperature of a roast is the ultimate doneness test. It is, in fact, the only sure way to know how rare or well-done a roast is. Most kitchen ovens, even the most expensive, fanciest ovens in the world, have been known to be off by 5 or 10 degrees, which can turn a good roast into one that is sadly overcooked or just underdone. A recipe direction to "roast for 1 hour" sounds very simple and straightforward, but if your oven tends to run a few degrees high, the roast will be overcooked. In short, a meat thermometer is your most reliable friend.

When inserted into meat, poultry, or fish, this thin, pencil-like tool gives you an instant temperature reading ranging from 60 degrees to 220 degrees. Getting a proper internal-temperature reading can mean the difference between a brilliant roast and a disastrous one. For beef, lamb, or pork, the thermometer should be inserted into the center of the roast without touching the bone (if any) for the most accurate reading; the thin "needle" permits a reading without making a large opening in the roast and releasing precious juices. When roasting poultry, try to insert the thermometer into the leg "pit"—the section between the leg and the breast—or insert the thermometer in the breast (at the neck end) as deeply as possible without touching the bone. Touching the bone is to be avoided on all roasts because the bone acts as a heat conductor and causes a higher temperature reading. Always leave the thermometer in the roast for at least 10 seconds or until it stops moving.

My enthusiasm for instant-read meat thermometers may come as a surprise to some cooks who feel that meat thermometers are unreliable tools. If you are unsure about the accuracy of your thermometer (or meat thermometers in general), there are other ways to test the recipes in this book. In almost every case I give the internal temperature of the roast *as well as* the cooking time (how many minutes per pound), and tell you what color the meat or poultry's juices should be when cooked.

A regular meat thermometer is thicker and more bulbous and is left in a roast throughout the cooking time. There are a couple of problems with these thermometers: first, they tend to get cloudy from the high heat, making accurate readings difficult; and second, they pierce a large hole in the roast, causing it to lose juices.

Trussing Needles, Kitchen String, Poultry Lacers, and Kitchen Skewers: Trussing needles look like long, narrow steel knitting needles with a large hole on one end; they are available in 6- to 12-inch lengths in stainless steel. Bridge Kitchenware advises choosing one that will go "completely through the item to be trussed," meaning it's longer than the width of the roast. An 8-inch needle is ideal for stitching veal breast and small birds; a 10-inch needle works well with chicken; and a 12-inch needle is used for large capons and turkeys. Curved needles (whose tips bow 20 degrees upward) are also available and are easier to work with when you're sewing up corners. These needles should be threaded with cotton kitchen string. (For more information on trussing, see Box on page 89.)

Instead of tying the bird's cavity shut, you can use poultry lacers—thin stainless-steel skewers that are used to close up the cavity. You can also use small stainless-steel kitchen skewers. Of course, you can simply close a bird's cavity by tying the legs together with kitchen string. And in a pinch you can push a thick slice of bread, the heel of a loaf, or thick slices of potato in the cavity of a large turkey, chicken, or other bird to keep the stuffing inside.

Gravy or Grease Separator: This ingenious device is a clear measuring cup with an extra-long spout that separates the fat from the gravy or pan juices. According to Fred Bridge in *The Well-Tooled Kitchen*, "Fat rises above the heavier liquid with which it is combined, and this cup's long, low-set spout—a sleek, single-vent version of the famous French *gras-maigre* gravy boat—neatly pours off that underlying liquid layer as it retains the fatty upper one."

Carving Boards and Roasting Platters: When made of sturdy, attractive wood, thick carving boards can double as a serving platter. The most popular design features a wide groove, or moat, around the edges to catch precious juices; some also have indentations in the center of the board to secure the roast.

Whenever I think of these carving boards, I am reminded of barbecues in the suburban backyard of my childhood. I can see my father removing a thick slab of steak from the grill, placing it on the carving board, slicing into it, and then watching as the small well filled with bright red juices. I was horrified to learn that those juices were blood. But rather than turning into a vegetarian, I tasted the juice spooned over my meat and quickly understood why carving boards are designed in this way: you don't want to miss a drop of the meat's natural juices.

Carving Knives: There is a wide variety of knives that are sold as "carving knives," many of them quite expensive and fancy looking. What you want to look for is a knife with a long blade and a very sharp point, preferably made of stainless steel or high-carbon stainless steel, anywhere from 7- to 14-inches long. If you are going to buy only one carving knife, I'd suggest one around 8 inches long. And needless to say, the most effective carving knife is a *sharp* one.

Carving knives are often part of a set that also includes a carving fork (a long-handled fork), also sometimes called a carver's helper. The fork is very useful in holding a roast in place while you are carving. Another crucial tool is a sharpening steel for keeping your carving knives as sharp as possible.

Room to Spare

I call for large, medium-size, or small roasting pans or skillets in my recipes instead of specifying pan measurements. Here's what you should be looking for when you choose a roasting pan to use for a recipe. Ideally, it should be large enough to hold the roast and leave a good 2 inches on all sides. You never want to cramp a roast because the air won't circulate around it and you'll find it difficult to spoon the juices from the bottom of the pan over the roast. Just as important is the fact that if the pan is too small you won't be able to fit in all those goodies that I always like to surround roasts with. Always leave enough room to scatter cloves (or whole heads) of garlic, vegetables, potatoes, onions, and so on.

I have never mastered the "art" of using an electric carving knife. These knives were once very popular, but seem to have faded in popularity.

For more information on roasting equipment, visit Bridge Kitchenware, which is located at 214 East 52nd Street, New York, NY 10022 (between 2nd and 3rd Avenues), (212) 688-4220. They also have a mail-order catalog with many items related to roasting. The cost for the catalog is three dollars, which is refundable on the first purchase. Call (800) 274-3435 for catalog orders.

Another good mail-order source for roasting equipment is Williams Sonoma. You can write to the Williams Sonoma Mail Order Department, P.O. Box 7456, San Francisco, CA 94120-7456; call (800) 541-2233; or visit one of their many stores in major cities across the country.

Beef and Veal

Provençal-Flavored Eye of Round Roast

This is the simplest of recipes, relying only on a good piece of beef, a splash of olive oil, a few fresh herbs, and a ripe, juicy tomato. In the summer, I like to make the roast early in the morning before it gets too hot, let it chill all day, and then serve it for dinner, thinly sliced, or mixed into salads or sandwiches. But it's also wonderful served hot, topped with a spoonful of pan juices. With this roast, serve a spinach salad and broiled tomatoes.

1½ teaspoons olive oil

One 2-pound beef eye of round

Freshly ground black pepper

2 tablespoons mixed finely chopped fresh
     herbs, such as oregano, thyme, basil,
     and savory; or 1½ teaspoons dried

2 cups tomato chunks, fresh or canned
     (optional)

6 cloves garlic, peeled and left whole

⅓ cup dry white wine or sherry

Salt

Preheat the oven to 400 degrees.

Use ½ teaspoon of the oil to grease the bottom of a small flameproof roasting pan. Place the beef in the pan and rub the remaining oil all over it. Sprinkle the top liberally with pepper and the herbs. Scatter the tomatoes and garlic around the beef.

Roast the beef, basting with any juices that accumulate in the pan, until the internal temperature reaches 125 to 130 degrees for rare to medium-rare beef, 45 minutes to 1 hour.

Remove the roasting pan from the oven. Place the beef on a carving board and let sit, loosely covered with aluminum foil, if serving the beef warm—for 15 to 20 minutes before slicing. If serving cold, let the beef come to room temperature before covering with foil and refrigerating.

To make a simple sauce, remove and reserve the garlic cloves and discard any excess fat from the roasting pan, leaving the tomatoes in the pan. Place the pan over moderate heat and add the wine, scraping the bottom and sides of the pan to dissolve the browned juices. Press down on the tomatoes to release their juices. Season to taste with salt and pepper. Bring the sauce to a boil and let simmer about 5 minutes. Strain the sauce to remove the tomato skins and pour into a gravy boat or small serving bowl.

Cut the beef into thin slices on the diagonal and top with the sauce and reserved garlic. If serving the beef cold, simply reheat the sauce until warm and spoon it over the cold beef.

Makes 4 to 6 servings

Cook Until Done: Beef and Veal

In each of the recipes, I have indicated the roasting time, internal temperature, and degree of doneness that I think result in the most flavorful dish. However, I am fully aware that everyone has a personal definition of how long beef should roast.

The temperatures listed below are meant to guide you to the roasted beef and veal of your liking. These temperatures and those given in the recipes are the *final internal temperatures* of the meat; always compensate by removing the meat when it is 5 to 10 degrees below the desired temperature because the roast will continue to cook once it has been removed from the oven.

120 to 125 degrees for very rare to rare, or pink meat

130 to 140 degrees for medium-rare to medium, or slightly pink meat

150 to 160 degrees for well-done meat, or meat that is no longer pink (and meat that many people think is overcooked!)

Having stated my preferences, I feel obligated to let you know that the U.S.D.A. and the National Live Stock and Meat Board of Chicago give different parameters. Because of current scares about bacteria in rare meat, they have significantly raised their roasting temperature recommendations. They are as follows:

145 degrees for medium-rare meat

160 degrees for medium meat

170 degrees for well-done meat

(Note that there is no recommendation for rare meat.)

How Much Meat Per Person: Beef and Veal

As my butcher likes to tell me, it's hard to know exactly how much meat to serve unless you know whom you are serving. If 200-pound Uncle Fred is coming to dinner, you're going to need a lot more than if 80-pound (eats-like-a-bird) Aunt Bessie is invited. In other words, consider the size of your guests' appetites and shop accordingly.

For a rib roast: $3/4$ pound per person.

For a tenderloin or boneless roast: about $1/2$ pound per person.

For ribs: about $1/2$ to 1 pound per person.

For veal breast (bone in): $3/4$ to 1 pound per person.

Roast Top Round
with Sweet Potatoes and Shallots

For those who claim they come home from work too tired to cook, this is the ideal recipe. You can walk in the door at 5:30, preheat the oven, season the meat (top round is an exceptionally tender cut of beef and very modestly priced), slice the sweet potatoes, and sit down to eat (it's actually close to feasting) by 6:45!

2 teaspoons flavored oil (pages 198 and 236) or good-quality olive oil

One 2- to 3-pound beef top round

1 tablespoon chopped fresh thyme; or 1 teaspoon dried

1 tablespoon chopped fresh sage; or 1 teaspoon dried

3 cloves garlic, peeled and thinly sliced

4 medium-size shallots, peeled and thinly sliced

Freshly ground black pepper

2 large sweet potatoes, scrubbed and cut crosswise into 2-inch-thick slices

Salt

$1/2$ to $3/4$ cup dry red or white wine

Preheat the oven to 350 degrees.

Use 1 teaspoon of the oil to grease the bottom of a large roasting pan. Place the beef in the pan and rub the remaining oil all over it. Sprinkle the top of the beef with half of the thyme, sage, garlic, and shallots. Season with a generous grinding of pepper. Surround the beef with the potato slices; sprinkle the remaining herbs, garlic, and shallots on the sweet potatoes, and season with salt and pepper. Pour $1/2$ cup of the wine around (not on top of) the beef.

Roast the beef and sweet potatoes, basting every 20 minutes or so and adding the remaining $1/4$ cup of wine if necessary, until the internal temperature reaches 125 degrees for rare beef, 45 minutes to 1 hour.

Remove the roasting pan from the oven and let the beef and sweet potatoes sit in the pan, loosely covered with aluminum foil, for 10 to 15 minutes before slicing.

Transfer the beef to a carving board and the sweet potatoes to a warm bowl. Cut the meat into thin slices. Remove any excess fat from the pan and pour the pan juices and bits of garlic and shallots on top of the beef. Pass the sweet potatoes separately.

Makes 4 to 6 servings

Best Cuts for Roasting: Beef and Veal

When you roast meat you generally want the most tender, least-exercised section of the animal. The following cuts are your best bets for tender, juicy roasts:

Beef: Tenderloin, rib roast (standing rib or boneless), top round, rump roast (also called sirloin tip roast), top loin, eye of round, ribs.

Veal: (Many of these cuts are prohibitively expensive; see veal recipes on pages 30 to 33 for specific recommendations.) Rib roast, loin (or sirloin) roast, eye of round, top round, breast, or crown roast.

The Art of Roast Beef

Edward Behr, an elegant essayist who lives in northern Vermont, writes about roast beef in his book *The Artful Eater.* "The meat is seared first for the compelling reason of the deliciousness of the deeply browned crust." Behr goes on to say that "the essence of roasting, what defines it, is a deeply caramelized, richly flavored outer crust encasing a succulent and, one hopes, tender interior—always cooked to rare. The juxtaposition of qualities can only be achieved with high heat."

Standing Rib Roast

The recipe for roasting a standing rib roast is as simple and straightforward as can be: stud the beef with garlic, sprinkle it with freshly ground pepper, surround it with potatoes and onions, and stick it in the oven. But it's also one of those dishes that's very easy to miscalculate.

What makes the difference between a perfectly cooked, juicy roast and a dry, unappealing one? There are several factors to consider. Starting with a piece of beef of the highest quality is essential. This is one of those show-stopper dishes, something to make when there's a special occasion. So don't settle for second-rate supermarket beef. This dish requires a visit to the finest butcher around; you want top-quality prime beef. Figure on $^3/_4$ pound of beef per person. Leftovers are definitely desirable.

There is endless controversy over the correct method and temperature for roasting beef; every cookbook and recipe you check will tell you something different. What works best for me is searing the beef in the oven at a high temperature (I like 450 degrees rather than 500 degrees because I've found that the extra 50 degrees can sometimes burn the meat) and then reducing the temperature for the duration of the roasting.

Serve the beef with a simple green vegetable (string beans with slivered almonds, Brussels sprouts, or creamed or sautéed spinach). Of course, the classic accompaniments are Yorkshire Pudding (page 246), Herbed Pepper Popovers (page 248), and ground horseradish or a luscious concoction called Horseradish Cream (page 232). For directions on carving a standing rib roast, see page 20.

On the subject of gravy I am a purist: nothing but the natural juices that accumulate as you carve the meat should top the beef. When you're eating prime beef, there is no need to disguise flavors; this is not the time for fancy sauces or a lot of complicated seasonings. Keep it simple. This is also the occasion for an extraordinary, full-bodied red wine.

The Beef:

One well-aged 5-pound beef standing rib roast, about 3 ribs, trimmed of excess fat and tied

2 cloves garlic, peeled and very thinly sliced

Freshly ground black pepper

Sweet Hungarian paprika

The Accompaniments:

20 small to medium-size new potatoes; or 8 to 10 baking potatoes, peeled and cut into quarters

About 20 small white boiling onions, peeled and left whole

Salt and freshly ground black pepper

1 tablespoon chopped fresh thyme; or 1 teaspoon dried

Preheat the oven to 450 degrees.

Using a small sharp knife, make several small slits in the fat along the top of the beef and gently insert the garlic slices. Season the top of the beef liberally with the pepper and paprika. Place the beef on a rack in a large flameproof roasting pan. (The rack is optional, as roasting beef directly in the pan doesn't result in less flavorful meat.) Surround the beef with the potatoes and onions and season the vegetables with the salt, pepper, and thyme.

Roast the beef for 15 minutes. Reduce the oven temperature to 325 degrees. Continue roasting until the internal temperature reaches 125 degrees for rare beef, about 20 minutes per pound, or 1 hour to 1 hour 15 minutes total roasting time. Baste the beef and the vegetables every 20 minutes or so and turn the vegetables over so they brown evenly, being careful not to leave the oven door open for too long.

Remove the roasting pan from the oven and let the beef and vegetables sit in the pan, loosely covered with aluminum foil, for 15 to 20 minutes before carving. Use this time to prepare Yorkshire Pudding if you like.

Transfer the beef to a carving board and the vegetables to a warm bowl. Remove any excess fat from the pan.

Carve the beef. You can either serve the bone with the meat still on it (to a very hungry diner) or cut the meat off the bone. Serve the beef with the pan juices poured on top. Pass the vegetables separately.

Makes 6 servings

How to Carve a Standing Rib Roast

These carving instructions are for right-handed carvers. Lefties should simply reverse the following instructions.

1. Place the roast on a carving board, resting on the bones with the rib bones facing away from you. Let rest.

2. Place the fork in your left hand and insert in the top of the roast.

3. Place the knife in your right hand and, starting at the right end of the roast, simply cut the meat vertically, across the grain, into thick or thin slices.

4. The individual ribs can be separated easily. Just cut vertically between them.

How Old's the Beef?

The term "well-aged" frequently appears in connection with beef, in particular, with roast beef. In order to better understand the term "well-aged," I spoke with John Bruno, the third-generation owner of the famous steak restaurant Pen and Pencil, on East 45th Street in Manhattan.

Bruno explains that meat can be eaten when it's freshly slaughtered, but it lacks "finesse, or interesting taste." At Pen and Pencil they age their roast beef for four weeks, as opposed to many other butchers and steak houses, which age their beef for only two weeks. The reason, says Bruno, is simple: "When you age beef, the natural enzymes stay active and help to break down any toughness in the meat. Aging can take place in the open air [also called dry aging] or sealed in plastic [wet aging]." Bruno says that a well-aged piece of beef is comparable to a well-aged wine; it develops character, grace, and subtlety.

The only thing to watch out for with well-aged beef is mold. "Within two weeks of aging a piece of beef," explains Bruno, "mold begins to appear." Always make sure to cut off any sign of mold, or have the butcher cut it out for you. Make sure you cut off *all* the mold. "Cut until you see clean white fat," says Bruno, "or until you see bright red meat."

Sirloin Tip Roast
with Provençal Eggplant Topping

In the tiny village of Viens in southern France, Robert Eymony runs La Haute Burlière, a charming restaurant located in the living room of his centuries-old stone house. While guests enjoy an aperitif on the terrace, looking out on fields of lavender and a spectacular view of the Luberon Mountains, Robert is busy in the kitchen putting the finishing touches on the day's specialties. There are only about six tables here and a very limited menu, but you can always be assured that there will be several types of roasted meat, poultry, or fish served.

Roasting is what Robert Eymony likes to do best, a skill that has earned him a place in the esteemed Chaîne des Rôtisseurs, an international organization that honors the fine art of roasting. The centerpiece of his dining room is a huge stone fireplace where Robert experiments with a variety of roasting methods. There I tasted a delicious roast beef dish topped with the flavors of Provence. It was the inspiration for this recipe.

The beef can be roasted in a regular kitchen oven or over an open fire. It is roasted with a simple dusting of pepper and rosemary and then topped with slices of roasted eggplant that have been briefly sautéed with anchovies, black olives, and fresh basil. The beef is delicious served with roasted potatoes. Open a bottle of wine from Provence (a red from Bandol would be ideal) and enjoy.

1 large eggplant

2 tablespoons olive oil

1½ pounds sirloin tip roast (rump roast) or another beef roast

Salt and freshly ground black pepper

4 cloves garlic, peeled and finely chopped

1½ tablespoons chopped fresh rosemary; or 1 teaspoon dried

Preheat the oven to 400 degrees.

Trim the stem end off the eggplant and discard it. Wrap the eggplant tightly in aluminum foil. Roast it until soft and tender but not falling apart when prodded with a finger, about 1 hour. Remove the eggplant from the oven and let it cool slightly. Cut the eggplant crosswise into 8 thick slices. Do not remove the skin.

Grease the bottom of a medium-size roasting pan with 1 tablespoon of the oil. Place the beef in the pan and rub the salt, pepper, half of the garlic, and all of the rosemary over it. Surround it with the potatoes, if using, and season them with salt and pepper.

Roast the beef, basting occasionally and stirring the potatoes, until the internal temperature reaches about 130 degrees for medium-rare beef, about 1 hour.

12 small new potatoes, scrubbed and left whole or cut in half if large (optional)

6 cured anchovy fillets

$1/2$ cup pitted black olives, preferably the small Niçoise variety

2 tablespoons very thinly sliced fresh basil or parsley

In a large skillet, heat the remaining 1 tablespoon oil over moderate heat. Add the eggplant slices, anchovies, and the remaining garlic and cook, turning the eggplant once, until the eggplant turns golden brown and the anchovies begin to dissolve, about 3 minutes on each side. Remove the skillet from the heat and add the olives and basil.

Remove the roasting pan from the oven. Let the beef and potatoes, if using, sit in the pan, loosely covered with aluminum foil, for 10 to 15 minutes before slicing.

Transfer the beef to a carving board and the potatoes, if desired, to a warm bowl. Discard any excess fat from the roasting pan and pour the remaining pan juices over the eggplant. Carve the beef into thin slices and top each slice with a piece of eggplant and some of the pan juices.

Makes 4 servings

A Passion for Roasting

To listen to Chef Eymony talk about roasting is to hear a man speak with passion. His voice rises with excitement as he explains the "basics" of good roasting. According to Chef Eymony, when you are roasting over fire it is essential that you use the right type of wood. "For beef," he claims, "the wood must be oak; for lamb you use vine stock; and for pork and veal you must use wood from a pine tree. This can make the difference between a good dish and a great one."

Whether you roast over an open fire or in a kitchen oven, the heat must be very hot, "hot enough to 'burn' the surface of the meat so the juices don't run out." How do you know when the meat is ready? Eymony points to his nose. "You must smell or touch," he explains. "I know with my nose. But you can also touch. If the meat is very soft, it is rare. The firmer it is on the outside, the more well done it is on the inside."

Chanukah Brisket with Roasted Vegetables

On the first night of Chanukah, tradition dictates that potato pancakes (latkes) be served. In my family, tradition also dictates that the latkes be accompanied by a beef brisket cooked in a casserole on top of the stove, where it slowly simmers for hours and hours.

But one year I decided to do things differently. Instead of using the stove-top method, I placed the meat in a shallow roasting pan, surrounded it with a generous supply of onions, leeks, carrots, celery, parsnips, and shallots, and roasted it in a low oven. (Strictly speaking, this is an example of pot roasting, as opposed to dry-heat roasting.) We gathered around the table and ate far too many potato pancakes while the scent of the roasting meat and sweet root vegetables filled the house.

Toying with tradition, especially on a holiday, can be risky business, but the brisket glistened in the roasting pan, the vegetables looked perfectly caramelized, and my hopes rose. The knife slid through the meat like it was butter, and we all feasted on the juiciest, most tender brisket I have ever tasted.

The other trick I learned that holiday was that roasted brisket can be cooked up to three days before serving. Simply roast the meat, cool it thoroughly, cover, and refrigerate. The night you plan to serve the brisket, remove the meat from the refrigerator and reheat it in a low oven until warm throughout. With the brisket, serve potato pancakes, fresh horseradish, sour cream, and applesauce.

About 1 cup all-purpose flour

Salt and freshly ground black pepper

One 5- to 6-pound beef brisket, excess fat trimmed

2 tablespoons mild vegetable oil, such as safflower

10 medium-size onions, peeled and cut in half

2 large leeks, trimmed, cut lengthwise in half, and cut crosswise into 3-inch pieces

2 medium-size shallots, peeled and cut in half

3 cloves garlic, peeled and coarsely chopped

8 medium-size carrots, peeled and cut into thick 3-inch matchstick strips

6 ribs celery, trimmed and cut into thick 3-inch matchstick strips

3 large parsnips, peeled and cut into thick 3-inch matchstick strips

1 cup chopped fresh parsley

2 bay leaves

3 tablespoons tomato paste

About 1 cup water

About 1 cup dry red wine

Preheat the oven to 400 degrees.

Place the flour on a large plate and season well with the salt and pepper. Coat the meat with the seasoned flour, shaking off any excess.

In a large flameproof roasting pan or large, shallow, flameproof casserole, heat 1 tablespoon of the oil over moderately high heat. Add the meat and cook until it turns a nice brown color on one side, about 5 minutes. Add the remaining oil and brown the meat on the other side, 3 to 5 minutes.

Remove the pan from the heat and place the onions, leeks, shallots, garlic, carrots, celery, parsnips, parsley, and bay leaves around the meat. Using a spoon, spread the tomato paste on top of the meat (fat-side up) and pour 1 cup of the water and 1 cup of the wine around (not on top of) the meat. Season with salt and pepper and cover the pan with aluminum foil if you don't have a lid.

Roast the meat and vegetables for 10 minutes. Reduce the oven temperature to 325 degrees and roast the meat and vegetables, basting with the juices every half hour or so, for $2^1/_2$ to $3^1/_2$ hours total roasting time. The meat should be very tender.

The meat and vegetables can then be cooled thoroughly and placed, covered, in the refrigerator for 1 to 3 days. Reheat them in a 250-degree oven until a knife inserted in the center of the meat is warm to the touch when withdrawn after 30 seconds, about 20 minutes.

Remove the roasting pan from the oven. Let the meat and vegetables sit in the pan, loosely covered with aluminum foil, for 10 minutes. Transfer the meat to a carving board and cut it into $^1/_4$-inch slices on the diagonal. Arrange the slices on a warm platter and surround with the vegetables.

Discard any excess fat in the roasting pan. Place the pan over moderately high heat and bring to a boil, scraping up the browned roasting juices. Taste for seasoning and serve the juices in a gravy boat or drizzled over each serving.

Makes 6 to 8 servings

Roasted Beef Ribs in Maple-Barbecue Sauce

You can use "Texas beef ribs" or short ribs in this recipe. Plan on letting the ribs marinate for 48 hours and serve with coleslaw, corn bread, and plenty of ice-cold beer. But the ribs will still be delicious if they marinate for only 8 hours.

This barbecue sauce can be as mild or as spicy as you like; add hot pepper sauce accordingly. It also works well with pork, chicken, or shrimp.

The Barbecue Sauce:

1³/₄ cups ketchup

¹/₂ cup pure maple syrup

3 tablespoons balsamic vinegar

2 tablespoons Worcestershire sauce

1 tablespoon Dijon mustard

¹/₂ cup chopped scallions or fresh chives

1 teaspoon ground cinnamon

¹/₂ teaspoon ground allspice

Dash hot pepper sauce

Salt and freshly ground black pepper

The Ribs:

3¹/₂ to 4 pounds beef ribs, cut into individual ribs

Prepare the barbecue sauce: In a medium-size bowl, mix all the ingredients for the barbecue sauce and taste for seasoning. The sauce should have a good balance of sweet and savory, with the flavor of the spices present. Adjust as needed.

Place the ribs in a large bowl and coat the top, bottom, and sides with the sauce. Cover and refrigerate, turning the ribs and basting every few hours or so, for 8 or up to 48 hours.

Preheat the oven to 325 degrees.

Remove the ribs from the sauce, reserving the sauce, and place them in a large shallow roasting pan, bone-side down. Brush the ribs with a bit of the sauce.

Roast the ribs for 30 minutes. Turn the ribs over, baste with additional sauce, and roast another 30 minutes. Turn the ribs again, baste with the remaining sauce, and roast, basting every 15 minutes or so, until tender, another 45 minutes to 1 hour. If the sauce begins to dry out in the bottom of the roasting pan, add ¹/₄ to ¹/₂ cup water to dilute the sauce and keep it from burning. Most of the sauce will caramelize directly on the ribs. Serve hot or at room temperature.

Makes 4 servings

Basting Instinct

You'll quickly notice that many of the recipes in this book ask you to "baste," then "baste," and then "baste again." Basting is the simple act of moistening a dish while it's roasting by spooning the cooking juices or melted fat over the dish. There are several reasons why basting is so crucial when roasting: Basting can prevent roasted foods, particularly the surface of the food, from drying out. In other words, basting can help a food stay moist. Basting also helps give foods—particularly poultry and meat— an attractive and highly desirable golden brown color and crispy exterior.

To Salt or Not?

In general, *don't* add salt to a roast (meat, in particular) before roasting, as it tends to draw the juices out. Season the meat toward the end of the cooking time or after it has been removed from the oven.

Composed Salad of Roast Beef, Roasted Shallots, and Caramelized Honey Walnuts

Thin slices of cold roast beef are topped with savory roasted shallots, honeyed walnuts, and a mustardy vinaigrette. This is an ideal light dinner for a warm summer's night, accompanied by French rolls and a cold bottle of rosé wine.

The Shallots:

6 small shallots, peeled and left whole

1 teaspoon olive oil

1 tablespoon balsamic vinegar

Salt and freshly ground black pepper

The Beef Salad, Walnuts, and Vinaigrette:

4 cups mixed salad greens, thoroughly washed and dried

12 thin slices cold rare roast beef, made from any of the recipes in this chapter

1 cup Caramelized Honey Walnuts (page 249)

Salt and freshly ground black pepper

1 tablespoon Dijon mustard

2 tablespoons balsamic or red or white wine vinegar

¼ cup good-quality olive oil

Preheat the oven to 350 degrees.

Prepare the shallots: Place the shallots in an ovenproof skillet or gratin dish just large enough to hold them in one layer and toss with the oil. Pour the vinegar on top and season liberally with salt and pepper. Roast, tossing the shallots every 5 minutes or so, until they are golden brown and tender, about 15 minutes. Remove the skillet from the oven, let cool slightly, and cut the shallots in half. Reserve the cooking juices.

Meanwhile, place the greens on a large platter. Arrange the roast beef around or over the greens and top with the roasted shallots. Sprinkle the salad with the Caramelized Honey Walnuts.

In a small bowl, mix the salt, pepper, and mustard together. Add the vinegar and then whisk in the oil. Add the reserved cooking juices from the shallots and taste for seasoning. Pour this vinaigrette over the salad or pass it separately.

Makes 2 to 4 servings

Ultimate Roast Beef Sandwich

My mouth waters just thinking about this summer sandwich—thin slices of roast beef on homemade bread topped with a thick slice of garden tomato, a sprinkling of blue cheese, and a drizzle of a piquant sauce made with peppers, parsley, and capers.

8 fairly thin slices homemade or good-quality store-bought bread

8 thin slices cold rare roast beef, made from any of the recipes in this chapter

4 thick slices large ripe tomato

About 1/2 cup crumbled Roquefort or other blue cheese

Freshly ground black pepper

About 1/2 cup Green Sauce (page 227)

Place 4 slices of the bread on a work surface. Place 2 slices of roast beef on each, top with a slice of tomato, 2 tablespoons of the blue cheese, and a generous grinding of black pepper.

Place the remaining 4 slices of bread on a work surface and drizzle each one liberally with the Green Sauce. Place the bread with the Green Sauce on top of the meat and slice in half.

Makes 4 servings

Stuffed Breast of Veal

This is an absolutely delicious cut of meat that is surprisingly inexpensive. Ask the butcher to keep the bones on the roast and cut a small pocket between the bones and the meat that you can use for a light herbed-bread stuffing. It may seem odd to have the stuffing on the bottom of the roast, but the meat juices drip down while roasting and give the stuffing an unbelievably good flavor.

In most cases a breast of veal needs to be specially ordered from a good butcher. If you have trouble finding a breast of veal, you can substitute a veal brisket. Fresh herbs really make a difference in this dish. With the veal, serve any spinach dish and roast potatoes or orzo.

The Stuffing:

1 tablespoon olive oil

1 large Vidalia or other onion, chopped

Salt and freshly ground black pepper

1 cup fresh or dried plain breadcrumbs

1/4 cup chopped fresh parsley

1/2 cup chopped fresh chives

3 tablespoons chopped fresh thyme

2 tablespoons chopped fresh rosemary

Preheat the oven to 400 degrees.

Prepare the stuffing: In a large skillet, heat the oil over moderate heat. Add the onion and cook, stirring, about 5 minutes. Add the salt and pepper to taste and remove from the heat. In a medium-size bowl, mix the breadcrumbs, cooked onions, parsley, chives, thyme, and rosemary.

Stuff the veal: Using your hands or a small spoon, push the stuffing into the pocket, pressing down lightly. (Be careful not to overstuff the veal. If there is too much stuffing, simply place the extra in a lightly oiled or buttered casserole and heat it separately.) Close up the opening with poultry lacers or small kitchen skewers, making sure the stuffing won't spill out.

Place the veal in the center of a large flameproof roasting pan and sprinkle the top with the thyme, rosemary, and a generous grinding of pepper. Pour 1 cup of the wine on top and surround the veal with the tomatoes. Sprinkle the top of the veal with paprika.

Roast the veal for 15 minutes. Reduce the oven temperature to 325 degrees. After 30 minutes, add another 1/2 cup wine and baste the veal thoroughly. After another 30 minutes add another 1/2 cup wine, basting again. Repeat every 30 minutes, roasting the veal until the juices run clear yellow, not pink, and the internal temperature reaches 160 degrees, about 2 hours total roasting time.

The Veal:

One 7¹/₂-pound bone-in breast of veal, small pocket cut

2 tablespoons chopped fresh thyme

2 tablespoons chopped fresh rosemary

Freshly ground black pepper

2 to 2¹/₂ cups dry white wine

2 large tomatoes, cut into 1-inch cubes (see Note)

Sweet Hungarian paprika

1 tablespoon all-purpose flour

About ¹/₂ cup water, homemade chicken stock or low-sodium canned chicken broth, or additional dry white wine

¹/₄ cup chopped fresh parsley

Remove the roasting pan from the oven. Place the veal on a carving board, cover loosely with aluminum foil, and let sit 15 minutes before carving.

Discard any fat from the roasting pan. Place the pan over two burners. Bring to a boil over moderate heat, scraping up any browned pan juices. Whisk the flour into the pan juices and let cook for about 1 minute. Slowly whisk in the water, stock, or additional wine and let it simmer until flavorful and somewhat thickened, 5 to 8 minutes. Season to taste and sprinkle in the parsley.

Carve the veal into individual ribs, cutting directly through the cartilage that joins the ribs and making sure each portion has a good amount of stuffing. (The cartilage softens with roasting, so it's not difficult to cut.) Top with the pan gravy.

Makes 6 serving

> Note: *If you can't find good ripe tomatoes, simply omit them.*

Roast Veal with Lemon-Parsley Sauce

There are few cuts of meat as tender and moist as a veal roast. This dish is for a celebration or special party, a time when you won't flinch at the prohibitive cost of a center-cut veal roast.

As with good roast beef, the flavorings added to roast veal are best left simple, such as garlic, lemon zest, and white wine. When the roast is done, white wine, chicken stock or broth, parsley, and lemon juice are stirred into the pan juices to create a quick, satisfying sauce. The fresh lemon flavor—from both the grated zest and the juice—highlights the meat's own taste without overwhelming it in any way.

The veal needs to "marinate" for at least 1 hour, or preferably overnight, so plan your time accordingly.

I also like to surround the roast with small white boiling onions, new potatoes, and wedges of fresh zucchini. Instead of potatoes, you could also try this dish with pasta—*stelline,* or star-shaped pasta, is particularly good—tossed with olive oil, pepper, and grated Parmesan cheese. A good dry white wine is crucial.

The Veal and Vegetables:

About 1¹/₂ tablespoons olive oil

One 3- to 4-pound veal roast (see Note)

2 cloves garlic, peeled and thinly sliced

1¹/₂ tablespoons grated lemon zest

1¹/₂ teaspoons dried thyme

Freshly ground black pepper

1 to 1¹/₂ cups dry white wine

18 small white boiling onions, peeled and left whole (optional)

18 small new potatoes, scrubbed clean and left whole, peeled or unpeeled (optional)

2 large zucchini, ends trimmed, cut lengthwise into quarters (optional)

Grease the bottom of a large flameproof roasting pan with the half of the oil. Place the veal in the pan. Using a small sharp knife make small slits around the top and sides of the veal. Gently insert the garlic and press about 1 tablespoon of the lemon zest into the slits. Rub the remaining oil, the thyme, the remaining ¹/₂ tablespoon lemon zest, and the pepper all over the veal. Pour ¹/₂ cup white wine around the veal. Refrigerate, covered, for at least 1 hour, preferably overnight.

Preheat the oven to 400 degrees.

Place the onions, potatoes, and zucchini around the roast if desired. Roast the veal for 20 minutes. Remove the roasting pan from the oven, add ¹/₂ cup wine, and baste well. Reduce the oven temperature to 325 degrees. Place the pan back in the oven and continue roasting, basting the veal every 20 minutes and adding the remaining wine as needed, until the internal temperature of the veal reaches 140 degrees for slightly pink meat, about 1¹/₂ hours total roasting time.

Remove the roasting pan from the oven. Place the veal on a carving board and cover loosely with aluminum foil.

Place the vegetables and potatoes in a warm serving bowl, cover, and keep warm.

Prepare the lemon-parsley sauce: Discard any excess fat from the roasting pan. Place the pan on the stove over two burners. Add the wine and stock or broth and bring to a boil over moderately high heat, scraping up any browned juices. Reduce the heat to low and simmer for 5 minutes. Strain the sauce to remove any bits of lemon zest and return the sauce to the pan. Add the lemon juice to taste and then the salt, pepper, and parsley. Let simmer until the sauce is flavorful and somewhat reduced, 2 to 3 minutes.

Cut the kitchen string from the roast and separate the bones from the meat. (The bones can be saved for a stock or for lunch the next day; there will be some meat left on them.) Thinly slice the veal and serve with the onions, potatoes, and zucchini. Pass the lemon-parsley sauce separately.

Serves 4 to 6

The Lemon-Parsley Sauce:

1½ cups dry white wine

½ cup homemade chicken stock or low-sodium canned chicken broth

1 to 2 tablespoons lemon juice

Salt and freshly ground black pepper

½ cup chopped fresh parsley

> Note: *Ask your butcher for a center-cut loin veal roast (the tenderloin and top loin tied together) with the bones removed and then tied back on the roast. This allows you to simply remove the string when the roast is done and easily carve the meat but also lets the bones contribute good flavor to the roast. If you don't mind carving through bones, you can opt to have them left on. Make sure the roast is neatly tied with kitchen string.*

Lamb

Leg of Lamb with Soy–Balsamic Vinegar Glaze

The tart sweetness of balsamic vinegar balances the richness of the lamb beautifully. Count on letting the lamb marinate at least 1 hour or up to 24 hours. I like to surround this roast with red new potatoes.

One 6½-pound whole or half leg of lamb

3 cloves garlic, peeled and thinly sliced

1 tablespoon olive oil or flavored oil
    (pages 198 and 236)

⅓ cup balsamic vinegar

¼ cup low-sodium soy sauce

3 tablespoons chopped fresh rosemary;
    or 2 teaspoons dried

2 tablespoons chopped fresh thyme;
    or 1 teaspoon dried

Freshly ground black pepper

24 small red new potatoes, scrubbed and
    left whole

Place the lamb in a large flameproof roasting pan. Using a small sharp knife, make thin slits all along the top of the lamb. Stud the top with the slices of garlic, inserting them about ½ inch into the flesh so they stick out. Rub the top of the lamb with the oil, half of the vinegar, and half of the soy sauce. Let marinate, covered and refrigerated, for at least 1 hour or up to 24 hours.

Preheat the oven to 450 degrees.

Sprinkle the lamb with half of the herbs and a generous grinding of pepper. Arrange the potatoes and whole garlic around the lamb. Pour the remaining vinegar and soy sauce over the potatoes and garlic and stir to coat. Sprinkle the vegetables with the remaining herbs.

Roast the lamb for 15 minutes. Reduce the oven temperature to 350 degrees and continue roasting the lamb until the internal temperature reaches 125 degrees for rare meat, about 12 minutes per pound, or about 1 hour 20 minutes total roasting time.

After about 45 minutes of cooking, add ¾ cup of the wine around the lamb, basting it. Turn the vegetables over so they brown on all sides.

Remove the roasting pan from the oven. Transfer the lamb to a carving board and let the lamb sit, loosely covered with aluminum foil, for 15 to 20 minutes before carving. Transfer the vegetables, leaving a few cloves of garlic in the pan, to a serving bowl or platter and keep warm.

10 cloves garlic, peeled and left whole

1 cup dry white wine

½ cup water

1 bunch watercress (optional)

Discard any excess fat from the roasting pan. Place the pan over two burners. Add the remaining wine and the water and bring to a boil over medium-low heat, scraping up any browned juices. Let the pan juices simmer until thickened and reduced slightly, 5 to 10 minutes. Mash any bits of garlic left in the pan into the pan juices. Taste for seasoning.

Cut the lamb into thin slices and serve with the potatoes, garlic, and pan juices. Garnish with a bunch of watercress if desired.

Makes 6 servings

Cook Until Done: Lamb

In each of the recipes, I have indicated the roasting time, internal temperature, and degree of doneness that I think result in the most flavorful dish. However, I am fully aware that everyone has a personal definition of how long lamb should roast.

The temperatures listed below are meant to guide you to the roasted lamb of your liking. These temperatures and those given in the recipes are the *final internal temperatures* of the meat; always compensate by removing the meat when it is 5 to 10 degrees below the desired temperature because the roast will continue to cook once it's been removed from the oven.

125 degrees for rare, or pink meat

130 to 135 degrees for medium-rare, or slightly pink meat

140 degrees for medium meat, or meat that is pink/gray

150 to 155 degrees for well-done, or meat that shows no signs of pinkness

Having stated my preferences, I feel obligated to let you know that the U.S.D.A. and the National Live Stock and Meat Board of Chicago give different parameters. Because of current scares about bacteria in rare meat, they have significantly raised their roasting temperature recommendations. They are as follows:

145 degrees for medium-rare lamb

160 degrees for medium lamb

170 degrees for well-done lamb

(Note that there is no recommendation for rare meat.)

Roast Leg of Lamb with Middle Eastern–Style Yogurt Sauce

There aren't many ways to roast lamb that produce meat this exceptionally tender and juicy. The lamb is marinated in a spicy, herb-filled yogurt sauce for at least 24 hours and then roasted. The yogurt acts as a tenderizer and creates a delicious creamy sauce.

When I first created this recipe, I wanted to marinate the lamb in a Middle Eastern–style sauce—full of cumin, cinnamon, pepper, and yogurt. But my garden was producing an abundant supply of basil. So I chopped a bunch of basil, garlic, and pine nuts (or pignoli)—the basis of the well-loved Italian sauce pesto—and then added the yogurt, cinnamon, cumin, and a dash of hot pepper sauce. The result is an incredible blending of flavors, the kind of sauce food writers like to refer to as "bold" and "assertive."

Roast the lamb with potatoes cut into quarters and serve with a fresh tomato and basil salad and warm pita bread.

This recipe is for half a leg of lamb (about 4 pounds); if you're using an entire leg, simply double the ingredients for the yogurt sauce.

One 4-pound half leg of lamb

1½ cups plain low-fat yogurt

½ cup fresh basil leaves

4 cloves garlic, peeled and chopped

¼ cup pine nuts

1 tablespoon olive oil

1½ teaspoons ground cumin

1 teaspoon ground cinnamon

Salt

Dash hot pepper sauce

4 large baking potatoes, cut into quarters (optional)

¼ cup homemade chicken stock or low-sodium canned chicken broth (optional)

Place the lamb in a large bowl.

Place the yogurt, basil, garlic, pine nuts, oil, cumin, cinnamon, and salt in a blender or food processor and process until smooth. (The sauce will be fairly thin at this point and will thicken while it roasts.) Taste for seasoning and add hot pepper sauce to taste. The sauce should have a bit of a punch. Pour the sauce over the lamb, cover, and refrigerate, turning the lamb every 12 hours, for at least 24 hours and up to 48 hours.

Preheat the oven to 450 degrees.

Place the lamb in a large flameproof roasting pan, pour the sauce on top, and surround with the potatoes if desired.

Put the lamb in the oven and reduce the temperature immediately to 350 degrees. Roast the lamb, basting it every 15 minutes, until the internal temperature reaches 125 degrees for rare meat, 10 to 12 minutes a pound, or about 1 hour total roasting time.

Remove the roasting pan from the oven. Place the lamb on a carving board and let sit, loosely covered with aluminum foil, for about 10 to 15 minutes before carving. Place the potatoes in a warm serving bowl and cover to keep warm.

The sauce, which will be quite thick and coagulated, can be drizzled over the lamb. If you like a smoother sauce, heat the roasting pan over moderate heat, scraping up any browned roasting juices from the bottom. Whisk in the stock or broth and season to taste.

Cut the meat into thin slices. Serve with the sauce and pass the potatoes separately.

Makes 4 to 6 servings

Ric's Birthday Leg of Lamb
with Caramelized Eggplant and Garlic

When my friend Ric Jorgensen turned fifty, I asked him what he would like for a birthday present. I had visions of a new Swiss Army knife or a silk shirt. But his request was specific. "Please," he begged, "roast me a leg of lamb."

This version marinates the lamb in dry sherry and sherry vinegar, tops it with a generous supply of fresh rosemary sprigs and garlic, and surrounds it with chunks of baby Italian eggplant. The eggplant are coated with the marinade and become caramelized, creating a perfect topping for the rare lamb slices. Plan on marinating the lamb for at least 24 hours. It makes a great birthday present.

With the lamb, serve couscous, Three-Onion Roast (page 181), and Carrot and Parsley Salad (page 244).

One 8- to 9-pound whole leg of lamb

4 cloves garlic, peeled and sliced into thin slivers

1½ tablespoons olive oil or flavored oil (pages 198 and 236)

About 1½ cups dry sherry

½ cup low-sodium soy sauce

⅓ cup sherry vinegar or balsamic vinegar

¼ cup fresh rosemary sprigs, chopped; or 1 tablespoon dried

2 tablespoons chopped fresh thyme; or 2 teaspoons dried

Using a small sharp knife, make small slits all along the top and sides of the lamb and insert the garlic slivers. Spread the oil on the bottom of a large roasting pan and place the lamb, rounded, meaty side up, in the pan. Pour the sherry, soy sauce, and vinegar on top. Sprinkle half of the rosemary and half of the thyme on top and cover. Refrigerate for at least 24 hours and up to 48 hours.

Preheat the oven to 450 degrees.

Surround the lamb with the eggplant and heads of garlic. Sprinkle the remaining rosemary and thyme on top. Season with salt, pepper, and a generous sprinkling of paprika.

Roast the lamb for 15 minutes. Reduce the oven temperature to 350 degrees and roast until the internal temperature reaches 130 to 135 degrees for medium–rare meat, another 1 hour 45 minutes. Baste the lamb and eggplant every 20 minutes or so, adding an additional ½ cup of sherry if necessary.

14 small Italian eggplant, ends trimmed, cut in half lengthwise

6 whole heads garlic, unpeeled

Salt and freshly ground black pepper

Sweet Hungarian paprika

Remove the roasting pan from the oven. Place the lamb on a carving board and let sit, loosely covered with aluminum foil, for 15 minutes before slicing. Place the eggplant and garlic in a serving bowl and cover loosely with aluminum foil to keep warm, or keep them warm in a 200-degree oven.

Discard any excess fat from the roasting pan and scrape up any browned roasting juices. Cut the lamb into thin slices and serve with the warm pan juices, eggplant, and garlic. (The garlic can be "squeezed" out of the skin directly onto the lamb as a kind of paste or "jam.")

Makes 8 to 12 servings

How to Carve a Leg of Lamb

These carving instructions are for right-handed carvers. Lefties should simply reverse the following instructions.

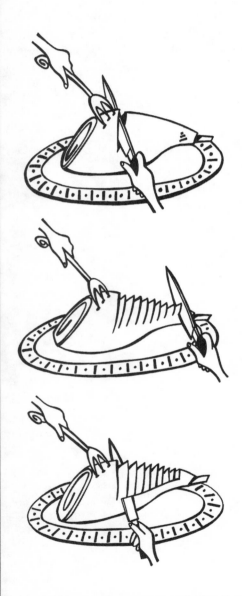

1. Place the leg of lamb on a carving board or serving platter with the round, meaty side up and the shank bone (the thin, narrow bone that juts out) facing to your right. Let rest.

2. Place the carving fork in your left hand and firmly spear the meat in the large, meaty end, called the sirloin end.

3. Holding the knife in your right hand, make the first cut vertically down to the bone, about an inch to the right of the fork.

4. Working from left to right, continue making slices parallel to the original cut, at whatever thickness you desire. All cuts should be sliced down to the bone.

5. On the final slice, when the blade hits the bone, turn the blade 90 degrees toward the fork and slice along the bone to loosen all the slices. The slices of meat can then be easily lifted with your fork.

6. To carve the bottom of the lamb, turn it over and thinly slice the lamb sideways, parallel to the leg bone.

A Flavorful Little Gravy

When making a gravy directly in the roasting pan, you should keep these tips in mind: Always remove the roast, place it on a carving board, and cover loosely with aluminum foil. Remove any excess fat from the bottom of the roasting pan, being careful not to take up any of the precious brown pan juices. If the roasting pan is large, place it over two burners so that the heat will reach all parts of the pan. In any case, set the pan over moderate heat. Add your stock, wine, or water and herbs or seasonings, scraping up any brown particles sticking to the bottom and sides of the pan. Let the gravy simmer until slightly thickened and flavorful, about 5 to 10 minutes. If the gravy seems weak or lacking in flavor, raise the heat and simmer a few more minutes. If the gravy seems too strong, add some additional stock, water, or wine.

Rolled Butterfly of Lamb with Spinach-Pesto Filling

Although this recipe involves several steps—marinating the lamb for at least 24 hours, making the pesto, stuffing the meat, and then rolling it up—there is nothing difficult about it. Most of the work is done ahead of time.

The spinach pesto complements the flavor of the lamb beautifully, as do the new potatoes and fennel spears that surround the meat. Be sure to leave some meat for leftovers; the lamb is excellent thinly sliced and served cold with a green salad or steamed asparagus tossed in a simple vinaigrette.

The Lamb:

One 6- to 7-pound leg of lamb, butterflied (see Note)

2 tablespoons olive oil

Sprigs fresh rosemary and/or thyme

Freshly ground black pepper

The Marinade:

1 cup dry red wine

$^1\!/_2$ cup low-sodium soy sauce or tamari

$^1\!/_3$ cup balsamic vinegar

$^1\!/_2$ cup fresh rosemary sprigs

Trim the lamb: Place the lamb on a work surface and trim off the excess fat and any small side pieces; reserve the meat trimmings for making stock or soup along with the bone. In order to roll the meat into a uniform shape, you need to trim the meat into an even shape.

Marinate the lamb: Place the lamb in a large nonreactive bowl. Add the marinade ingredients, cover, and refrigerate for at least 24 hours and up to 48 hours. Turn the lamb every 12 hours or so.

Make the pesto: Heat 1 tablespoon of the oil in a small saucepan over moderate heat. Add the garlic and cook, stirring, for about 30 seconds, being careful not to let it brown. Remove the pan from the heat and reserve. Place the spinach with the water clinging to the leaves in a large pot, set over high heat, and cook, covered, until soft, 5 to 6 minutes. Drain the spinach and rinse it under cold running water. Drain again and press all the water out of it. Process the spinach in a food processor until coarsely chopped. Add the cream, pine nuts, the remaining 2 tablespoons of oil, the cooked garlic and oil, salt, and pepper and process until pureed.

The Pesto:

3 tablespoons olive oil

2 cloves garlic, peeled and chopped

10 ounces fresh spinach, stemmed and thoroughly washed but not dried (about 8 cups)

1 tablespoon heavy cream

$\frac{1}{4}$ cup pine nuts

Salt and freshly ground black pepper

The Vegetables and Gravy:

About 16 small to medium-size new potatoes

Salt and freshly ground pepper

1 large bulb fennel; or 2 small bulbs, cut into eighths

$\frac{1}{4}$ cup dry red wine or water

Fill and roll the lamb: Remove the lamb from the marinade, reserving the marinade. Pat dry with paper towels. Using a small thin-bladed spatula or knife, spread the pesto over the inside surface of the lamb, making sure to leave a 1-inch border on all sides. (If you add too much pesto or spread it too close to the edges, it will ooze out once you roll it up.) Reserve any remaining pesto to drizzle over the meat after roasting. Roll the lamb tightly, forming a long, thin cylinder. Using kitchen string, tie the lamb at intervals about 1 to 2 inches apart.

Grease the bottom of a large flameproof roasting pan with 1 tablespoon of the oil. Place the rolled lamb in the pan, and rub the remaining tablespoon of oil over it. Add half of the marinade and scatter the rosemary and/or thyme sprigs on top. Season with a generous grinding of black pepper. (You can prepare the dish up to this step about 8 hours before roasting. Keep it covered in the refrigerator.)

Preheat the oven to 450 degrees.

Scatter the potatoes around the lamb and sprinkle them with salt and pepper.

Roast the lamb for 15 minutes. Reduce the heat to 350 degrees. Add the fennel to the pan and continue roasting until the internal temperature of the lamb reaches 125 degrees for rare meat, about 1 hour more. After the lamb has cooked for about 1 hour, add the remaining marinade basting the meat.

Remove the roasting pan from the oven. Place the lamb on a carving board and let sit, loosely covered with aluminum foil, for 15 to 20 minutes before slicing. Place the potatoes and fennel in a heatproof serving bowl, and keep warm in a 250-degree oven.

Discard any excess fat from the roasting pan. Set the pan over medium-low heat. Add the wine or water and bring to a boil, scraping to dissolve the browned roasting juices. Season to taste with salt and pepper.

Discard the string from the lamb. Cut the lamb into slices about $\frac{1}{2}$ inch thick. Serve with the hot gravy and drizzle the warm lamb with any remaining pesto. Pass the roasted potatoes and fennel separately.

Makes 8 servings

Note: *Have the butcher butterfly the leg for you. Be sure to save the bones to use for stocks and soups. See page 52.*

Rack of Lamb with Sun-Dried Tomato–Garlic–Rosemary Crust

There are few meals more elegant or satisfying than a roasted rack of lamb. In this version the chops are marinated in a touch of olive oil and fresh rosemary, and then a topping of fresh breadcrumbs, garlic, rosemary, and sun-dried tomatoes is pressed on the meat. When roasted, this aromatic topping becomes a kind of crispy, crunchy crust—the ideal foil to the tender, still-pink meat.

With the lamb, serve polenta or roasted potatoes and Sautéed Escarole (page 239).

1 tablespoon plus 1 teaspoon olive oil

One 1½-pound rack of lamb, about 8 chops, trimmed of excess fat

2 tablespoons chopped fresh rosemary

About ¼ cup coarse fresh breadcrumbs (see Note)

¼ cup sun-dried tomatoes, chopped (see Note)

2 cloves garlic, peeled and chopped

Salt and freshly ground black pepper

1 tablespoon Dijon mustard

Grease a medium-size roasting pan with 1 teaspoon of the oil. Place the lamb, bone side down, in the pan and rub the remaining oil all over it. Rub 1 tablespoon of the rosemary all over the lamb, cover, and refrigerate for at least 30 minutes or overnight.

Preheat the oven to 400 degrees.

Place the breadcrumbs, remaining tablespoon of rosemary, sun-dried tomatoes, garlic, salt, and pepper in a food processor or blender and process until well mixed. Using the back of a spoon, spread the mustard along the fatty side of the lamb, and sprinkle on some black pepper. Press the breadcrumb-tomato topping on top of the mustard, pressing down firmly with your fingers or the back of a spoon.

Roast the lamb until the internal temperature reaches 125 degrees for rare meat, about 30 minutes.

Remove the roasting pan from the oven and let the lamb sit in the pan, loosely covered with aluminum foil, for 5 minutes before carving. Cut vertically between the chops to separate them, season with salt and pepper and serve 4 per person.

Makes 2 servings

Note: *This recipe works best with freshly made breadcrumbs. Place a 2-inch heel of a crusty French or Italian bread in a food processor or blender and process until you have coarse breadcrumbs.*

If using sun-dried tomatoes in oil, be sure to drain off the oil on paper towels before chopping. If using dry tomatoes, place them in a cup of boiling water until soft, about 5 minutes. Drain and dry thoroughly before chopping.

Bone Up on Bones

A roast with the bone in cooks faster than a boneless cut of meat. The bone conducts heat to the meat's center and cuts down on the cooking time.

Roast Shoulder of Lamb with Spinach-Parmesan Stuffing

Shoulder of lamb is a relatively inexpensive cut of meat that is ideal for stuffing. In this recipe the shoulder is boned (you could also substitute a boned or butterflied leg of lamb) and marinated with garlic, olive oil, and grated lemon zest. The lamb is then stuffed with spinach and thin shavings of Parmesan cheese, rolled up into a thick log shape, and roasted. A quick sauce is made using the pan juices and a touch of white wine. Surround the lamb with potatoes and onions and whole heads of garlic; the roasted garlic is fabulous squeezed out onto thin slices of the meat.

There are a few essential ingredients to make the most of this dish: fresh (not dried) rosemary, and real Parmigiano-Reggiano. Although this cheese is costly, you don't need much, and its flavor adds a great deal to the final taste and texture of the lamb.

The Lamb and Marinade:

One 5-pound boneless shoulder of lamb, excess fat trimmed; or one 5-pound butterflied (boneless) leg of lamb, trimmed

4 cloves garlic, peeled and chopped

1 tablespoon chopped fresh rosemary

Juice of 1 large lemon

Grated zest of 1 large lemon

Freshly ground black pepper

2 tablespoons olive oil

$^1/_2$ cup white wine

Marinate the lamb: Place the lamb cut side (inside) up on a clean work surface, and rub the top with half of the garlic, $^1/_2$ tablespoon of the rosemary, half of the lemon juice, and half of the lemon zest. Sprinkle liberally with pepper. Place the lamb in a large nonreactive bowl and rub the outside with the remaining garlic, lemon juice, and lemon zest and another $^1/_2$ tablespoon of rosemary. Pour the oil and wine on top, cover, and refrigerate for at least 4 hours or up to 48 hours.

Preheat the oven to 400 degrees.

Prepare the stuffing: Place the spinach with the water clinging to the leaves in a large pot, set over high heat, and cook, covered, until soft, 5 to 6 minutes. Drain the spinach and rinse it under cold running water. Drain again and press all the water out of it. Chop the spinach finely.

In a small skillet, heat the oil over moderate heat. Add the garlic and cook, stirring, about 2 minutes; do not let the garlic burn. Add the spinach and a generous pinch of salt and pepper to taste. Let cool.

The Stuffing:

1 pound fresh spinach, stemmed and thoroughly washed but not dried

1 teaspoon olive oil

1 clove garlic, peeled and chopped

Salt and freshly ground black pepper

1 tablespoon chopped fresh rosemary

About 1 cup or 20 shavings of Parmigiano-Reggiano cheese from a 1/2-pound piece (see Note)

The Accompaniments and Sauce:

20 new potatoes, scrubbed; or 10 roasting potatoes, scrubbed and cut in half

4 whole heads garlic, unpeeled

24 small white boiling onions, peeled and left whole

1 tablespoon chopped fresh rosemary

Salt and freshly ground black pepper

1 1/2 cups dry white wine

1/2 cup water or homemade chicken stock or low-sodium canned chicken broth

Remove the lamb from the marinade, reserving the marinade. Pat the meat dry with paper towels. Place the lamb on a clean work surface. Sprinkle 1 tablespoon of the rosemary on the inside of the lamb along with salt and pepper. Place the spinach on top of the rosemary and spread over the surface of the lamb, making sure to leave at least a 1-inch border. Top with the cheese shavings and roll the lamb up. Using kitchen string, tie the lamb lengthwise and then at 1-inch intervals crosswise, so that the meat is held together tightly.

Place the lamb in a large flameproof roasting pan, seam-side down, and surround with the potatoes, garlic, and onions. Sprinkle the top of the lamb and the vegetables with the rosemary and the salt and pepper. Pour 1 cup of the white wine around the lamb.

Roast the lamb for 30 minutes. Reduce the oven temperature to 325 degrees. Baste the lamb, turn over the potatoes and onions so they brown well on both sides, and continue roasting until the internal temperature reaches 125 degrees for rare, about 30 minutes more.

Remove the roasting pan from the oven. Place the lamb on a carving board, cover loosely with a piece of aluminum foil, and let sit for 15 to 20 minutes before slicing. Place the vegetables in a warm bowl, cover loosely, and keep warm.

Discard any excess fat from the roasting pan. Place the roasting pan over two burners. Add the remaining 1/2 cup white wine and the water, stock, or broth and bring to a boil over moderate heat, scraping up any browned pan juices. Let simmer until slightly thickened, 5 to 10 minutes. Season to taste.

Remove the strings from the lamb and thinly slice. Serve with the roasted potatoes, onions, and garlic. Pass the pan juices separately.

Makes 6 to 8 servings

Note: *Use a vegetable peeler to get thin, uniformly shaped shavings of cheese.*

Lamb Hash

Leftover lamb is one of the great treats of roasting. There are curries to be made and richly flavored soups and stocks that can result. But one of my favorite ways to transform leftover lamb is to make a simple hash and accompany it with poached eggs and toast. Make sure to serve an assortment of hot sauces along with the hash.

1 teaspoon vegetable oil

1 teaspoon butter or margarine

1 cup peeled and chopped onions

1 cup cooked and diced potatoes

1 cup roasted and diced lamb

1 teaspoon chopped fresh thyme;
   or $^1/_2$ teaspoon dried

About 2 tablespoons leftover gravy
   (optional)

Salt and freshly ground black pepper

Dash hot pepper sauce, or to taste

$^1/_3$ cup chopped fresh parsley

In a medium–large skillet, heat the oil and butter or margarine over moderate heat. Add the onions and cook, stirring, until soft, about 5 minutes, being careful not to let them burn. Add the potatoes, lamb, thyme, and gravy and cook, stirring, 1 minute. Add the salt, pepper, hot sauce, and parsley and press the mixture down into the pan to create a kind of pancake. Let cook until the edges look crispy and, using a large flat spatula, flip the hash over, pressing down again to create the pancake. If you like your hash very crisp, you may want to turn up the heat until it really browns. Serve hot.

Makes 4 servings

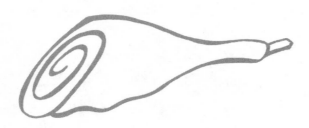

Roast Lamb Salad with Curry-Yogurt Dressing

This is a simple way to use leftover roast lamb in a light, refreshing salad. The light curry flavor mixed with yogurt and scallions wakes up the flavor of the roasted lamb. You can use any combination of vegetables and greens you like in this dish. With the salad, serve warm triangles of pita bread.

The Salad:

About 2 cups mixed salad greens, thoroughly washed and dried

10 to 12 very thin slices cold cooked roast lamb

1 large ripe tomato or 10 cherry tomatoes, diced (see Note)

1/2 cup peeled and thinly sliced cucumber

1 cup large croutons

The Dressing:

3 tablespoons thinly sliced scallions

1 teaspoon curry powder

1/8 teaspoon ground cumin

Pinch cayenne or red pepper flakes

2 tablespoons plain low-fat yogurt

2 tablespoons red or white wine vinegar

5 tablespoons olive oil

Salt and freshly ground black pepper

Place the greens on a serving plate. Arrange the lamb slices across the middle and scatter the tomatoes, cucumber, and croutons around the lamb.

In a small bowl, mix the scallions, curry, cumin, cayenne, and yogurt. Stir in the vinegar and oil and season to taste with salt and pepper. Drizzle a little dressing on top of the lamb and serve the rest separately.

Makes 2 servings

> Note: *If the only tomatoes around resemble pinkish baseballs, do without.*

Roasted Lamb Stock

The secret to good soup and rich sauce is really good homemade stock. The traditional way to make stock is simply to place meaty bones, vegetables, and seasonings into a stockpot, cover with cold water, and simmer until flavorful. But if you want a really rich, beautifully colored, flavorful stock, the secret is roasting. When you roast meaty bones with fresh vegetables, stir a touch of wine into the pan, scraping up the browned juices, and then simmer the roasted mixture with water, you get a spectacular stock. There's a little bit more effort involved in making a roasted stock, but it's well worth it.

This is a master recipe for any type of "roasted" stock. Instead of using lamb bones, you can substitute 4 pounds of veal breast for a veal stock, 6 pounds of chicken (backs, bones, and necks work best) for a rich chicken stock, or 6 pounds of beef bones for a beef stock, and proceed with the recipe as directed below. The stock can be frozen for several months and defrosted as needed. Use this stock when you want a meaty flavor in soups and sauces.

4 pounds lamb shanks or shoulder chops or other meaty bones

2 onions, peeled and cut into quarters

1 leek, trimmed and chopped

1 large carrot, peeled and chopped

1 rib celery, trimmed and chopped

4 sprigs fresh thyme; or 1 teaspoon dried

About 1 cup dry white or red wine

About 2 quarts water

1 bay leaf

6 black peppercorns

Salt

Preheat the oven to 425 degrees.

Place the meaty bones, onions, leek, carrot, celery, and thyme in a large roasting pan and roast, stirring once or twice, until the meat and vegetables are well browned, about 45 minutes. Remove from the oven and discard any excess fat. Add the wine to the pan, scraping up any browned roasting juices.

Transfer the contents of the roasting pan to a large stock or soup pot and cover with the water, bay leaf, peppercorns, and a sprinkling of salt. (There should be enough water in the pan to cover the meat completely.) Bring the stock to a boil over high heat, reduce the heat to moderately low, partially cover, and gently simmer until it is well flavored, 2 to 3$^{1}/_{2}$ hours. Skim off any fat or white froth that floats to the top of the pan as the stock is simmering. If the flavor of the stock becomes too concentrated, add more water and/or wine as needed.

Remove the pot from the heat and let the stock cool. Strain the stock and discard any excess fat that has floated to the top. Let the stock cool at room temperature or it may sour. Refrigerate or freeze until needed.

Makes about 2 quarts

Pork

Roast Pork with Sweet Red Peppers and Cinzano

The idea for this dish came from Edwin Child, an old friend who is a wonderful cook. Years ago Edwin invited my husband and me to dinner, and we roasted a fresh-killed duck with Cinzano (sweet vermouth) and whole cloves of garlic over an open fire. It was one of the greatest duck dishes I'd ever tasted.

Recently Edwin suggested trying to roast *pork* with Cinzano, and this is what I came up with. The sweetness of the Cinzano and the red peppers, mixed with fresh thyme, chives, and garlic, is a vibrant contrast to the mild pork. The Cinzano blends with the natural pork juices and creates an unforgettable—and utterly simple—pan sauce. This is an ideal dish for a party as it marinates for 1 hour before cooking and is roasted for just 1½ hours. Accompany the pork with Spinach Soufflé Roll Stuffed with Roasted Red Peppers (page 240) and mashed or roasted potatoes.

One 3-pound boneless pork loin, cut in half lengthwise

2 cloves garlic, peeled and thinly slivered

2 tablespoons chopped fresh thyme; or 2 teaspoons dried

2 tablespoons chopped fresh chives or thinly sliced scallions

2 large red bell peppers, cored and thinly sliced

1 large onion, peeled and thinly sliced

Lay the two halves of the pork out on a clean work surface. Press the slivers of garlic and half of the thyme and chives or scallions into the cut surface of the meat. Place the two pork halves back together and tie well with kitchen string in several places to hold it together securely.

Place the pork in a large roasting pan and surround with the bell peppers, onion, and whole garlic cloves. Season with the remaining thyme and chives and salt and pepper to taste. Pour the Cinzano over the pork and sprinkle the paprika on top of the meat. Let marinate for 1 hour.

Preheat the oven to 400 degrees.

Roast the pork for 15 minutes. Baste the pork and reduce the oven temperature to 325 degrees. Continue roasting the pork, basting every 15 to 20 minutes, until the juices run clear yellow and not pink when the meat is pierced, and the internal temperature of the meat reaches 155 to 160 degrees, about 30 minutes per pound, or about 1½ hours total roasting time.

8 cloves garlic, peeled and left whole

Salt and freshly ground black pepper

1 cup Cinzano or dry red wine or sherry

Sweet Hungarian paprika

Remove the roasting pan from the oven. Place the pork on a carving board and let sit, loosely covered with aluminum foil, for 15 minutes before removing the string. Place the vegetables in a bowl, loosely covered with foil to keep warm.

Cut the pork into thin slices and serve topped with the peppers, onions, garlic, and pan juices.

Makes 4 servings

Cook Until Done: Pork

The temperatures listed below and in the recipes are the *final internal temperatures* of the meat; always compensate by removing the meat when it is 5 to 10 degrees below the desired temperature because the roast will continue to cook once it's been removed from the oven.

The big fear with pork is trichinosis; according to the National Pork Producers Council, trichinosis is killed off at 137 degrees. However, they recommend that pork always be cooked until it reaches an internal temperature of 155 to 160 degrees.

A cured bone-in ham (which needs only reheating) is safe to eat when it reaches a final internal temperature of 140 degrees.

How Much Meat Per Person: Pork

For a boneless pork loin: about $1/2$ pound per person.

For ribs: about $1/2$ to $3/4$ pound per person.

For a crown roast: about 2 chops per person, or $3/4$ to 1 pound.

For chops: about 1 to 2 chops per person, depending on the thickness of the chop.

For bone-in whole ham: about $1/2$ to $3/4$ pound per person, closer to a pound with leftovers.

Roast Loin of Pork with Portobello Mushroom Sauce

This is a delicious, elegant way to roast a boneless loin of pork. The meat is marinated in Madeira, garlic, and fresh thyme and roasted for about an hour. Fresh portobello (or regular white) mushrooms are roasted along with the pork, and a sauce is made in the pan with the pan juices, broth, and a touch of cream and parsley.

One 3-pound boneless pork loin, rolled and tied

2 cloves garlic, peeled and thinly sliced

1¼ cups Madeira or dry sherry

2 tablespoons chopped fresh thyme

2 large fresh portobello mushrooms, stems trimmed, cut into eighths; or 3 large shiitakes or 6 regular white mushrooms, stems trimmed, cut into quarters

Place the pork in a medium-size flameproof roasting pan. Using a small sharp knife, make small slits in the thin layer of fat that covers the top of the pork. Insert the sliced garlic. Pour ¹/₂ cup of the Madeira over the pork and sprinkle with 1 tablespoon of the thyme. Cover and marinate at room temperature, basting occasionally, for at least 1 hour, or refrigerate up to 24 hours.

Preheat the oven to 350 degrees.

Roast the pork, basting occasionally, for 30 minutes. Add another ¹/₂ cup of the Madeira and baste the meat. Roast another 30 minutes. Remove the roasting pan and discard any excess fat. Add the mushrooms to the pan and season them with ¹/₂ tablespoon of the thyme, salt, and pepper. Continue roasting until the juices run clear yellow and not pink when the meat is pierced and the internal temperature of the pork reaches 155 to 160 degrees, another 20 to 30 minutes.

Remove the roasting pan from the oven. Place the pork on a carving board, loosely covered with foil, for 15 minutes before slicing. Place the mushrooms in a warm serving bowl, loosely covered with foil to keep warm.

Salt and freshly ground black pepper

1 cup homemade chicken stock or low-
sodium canned chicken broth

3 tablespoons heavy cream

$^1/_2$ cup finely chopped fresh parsley

Discard any excess fat from the roasting pan. Place the pan over two burners on the stove and heat the pan juices over moderately high heat. Add the stock or broth and the remaining $^1/_2$ tablespoon of thyme and bring to a boil, scraping up any browned juices. Add the cream, parsley, and remaining $^1/_4$ cup Madeira. Let simmer vigorously until slightly thickened and flavorful, 5 to 10 minutes. Season the sauce to taste.

Thinly slice the pork and pour any juices that are released into the sauce. Serve with the hot sauce on top. Pass the mushrooms separately.

Makes 6 servings

Best Cuts for Roasting:
Pork

Center-cut (bone in or boneless) pork loin roast, tenderloin, leg, crown roast, chops, ribs.

How to Take a Roast's Temperature

When using a meat thermometer to gauge the internal temperature of a roast, always insert the thermometer into the thickest part of the meat and make sure it's not touching the bone. (For more information on using meat thermometers, see page 10.)

Is Room Temperature Better?

When I first learned to cook, I was always taught that meat and poultry should be brought to room temperature before roasting. Those were the good old days, when "salmonella" and "bacteria" weren't household words. Although the temperature and length of cooking time for a roast can be affected if a piece of meat or poultry is not at room temperature, it does not mean that your roast is going to be ruined.

The safest bet is to *allow meats and poultry to sit on the counter, outside the refrigerator, for a maximum time of 10 to 15 minutes.* In that time the temperature of the meat will rise, but you won't run the risk of developing harmful bacteria.

Keep in mind that removing meat or poultry from the refrigerator and getting it ready to roast (sprinkling on spices, garlic, wine, etc.) easily takes 10 to 15 minutes.

Roast Loin of Pork with Garlic-Chipotle Crust

I'm not sure where the roots of this dish originate. The chipotle peppers are definitely Mexican, but it's more honest to say that I simply put together a few strongly flavored ingredients to create a "dry" marinade for this roast. Using a mortar and pestle, I crush several cloves of garlic with dried red chile peppers, a few chipotle peppers in adobo sauce (tomato, paprika, vinegar, and sesame oil), cinnamon, fresh thyme, and a touch of olive oil. Then I spread this rich, spicy red paste on the meat and allow it to marinate for at least 6 hours. The chile and garlic permeate the meat, creating a wonderfully flavored roast.

This dish is definitely spicy but can be altered according to your capacity for heat. I like to surround the roast with medium-size red new potatoes and small white boiling onions, but it would also be delicious served with a rice pilaf or warm tortillas. A refreshing orange and watercress salad would balance the strong flavors of this roast.

The Chile Paste:

4 cloves garlic, peeled and chopped

Pinch salt

1 to 3 small dried red chile peppers
  (see Note)

1 to 3 tablespoons chipotle peppers in
  adobo sauce (see Note)

1¹/₂ tablespoons chopped fresh thyme;
  or 1¹/₂ teaspoons dried

1¹/₂ teaspoons ground cinnamon

1 tablespoon olive oil

The Roast:

One 3-pound boneless pork loin

About 1 cup dry white wine

12 medium-size potatoes, scrubbed and left
  whole

20 small white boiling onions, peeled and
  left whole

Salt and freshly ground black pepper

About ¹/₂ cup cold water

Prepare the chile paste: Using a mortar and pestle, crush the garlic with the salt to a paste. Add the dried chile peppers and the chipotle peppers and crush until fairly smooth. Add the thyme, cinnamon, and oil.

Place the pork in a large bowl and spread the paste all over the meat, gathering most of the paste on the top. Cover and let marinate in the refrigerator for at least 6 hours, preferably overnight.

Preheat the oven to 425 degrees.

Place the pork with the paste in a large flameproof roasting pan. Add a few tablespoons of wine to the pan.

Roast the pork for 15 minutes. Turn the pork over and roast an additional 15 minutes.

Remove the roasting pan from the oven and reduce the oven temperature to 325 degrees. Turn the pork over again and surround with the potatoes and onions. Pour ¹/₂ cup wine on the vegetables and season them with salt and pepper. Continue roasting the pork, basting frequently and adding the remaining wine, until the juices run clear yellow and not pink when the meat is pierced and the internal temperature of the meat reaches 155 to 160 degrees, about 1¹/₂ hours total roasting time. Stir the potatoes and onions every 15 minutes so they brown on all sides.

Remove the roasting pan from the oven. Place the pork on a carving board and let sit, loosely covered with aluminum foil, before slicing. Place the potatoes and onions in a warm small serving bowl and keep warm.

Discard any excess fat from the roasting pan. Place the pan over moderate heat and let the juices in the pan simmer, scraping up any browned juices. Add a few tablespoons of water and let the pan juices cook down until slightly thickened and full of flavor, 5 to 8 minutes.

Cut the pork into thin slices and drizzle with the spicy sauce. Serve the potatoes and onions on the side.

Makes 4 to 6 servings

Note: *One small dried chile will create a mildly spicy paste, and 3 will give you a paste with a real wallop.*

Canned chipotle peppers in adobo sauce are available in Latin American shops and gourmet food shops.

Roast Pork with Rum and Vidalia Onions

Hot, sweet, and sour is how I would describe the flavors found in this pork dish. A boneless pork roast is marinated in orange juice, rum, chile pepper sauce, dried ginger, and a touch of brown sugar. The pork is then roasted with sweet Vidalia onion chunks. Plan on letting the pork sit in the marinade for at least 24 hours. If you let it marinate for 48 hours, you will find the pork is so tender you can practically cut it with a fork.

Serve this pork roast with a favorite rice dish, a bowl of thinly sliced oranges, and a salad of strongly flavored or pleasantly bitter mixed greens.

³/₄ cup orange juice, fresh-squeezed or "old-fashioned" type with pulp

¹/₄ cup dark rum

2 tablespoons low-sodium soy sauce

About 2 tablespoons hot pepper sauce (see Note)

2 tablespoons light brown sugar or honey

1¹/₂ teaspoons ground ginger

One 3-pound boneless pork roast, tied

2 large Vidalia or other sweet onions, peeled and cut into eighths

2 oranges, peeled, thinly sliced, and seeded

A variety of hot sauces

In a large nonreactive bowl, mix the orange juice, rum, soy sauce, hot pepper sauce, sugar or honey, and ginger. Add the pork and spread the marinade on all sides. Cover and refrigerate for 24 to 48 hours, turning the pork every 12 hours or so.

Preheat the oven to 350 degrees.

Remove the pork from the marinade, reserving the marinade, and place in a medium-size flameproof roasting pan or in a large ovenproof skillet. Surround the pork with the onions and top with 2 tablespoons of the marinade. Roast the pork for 30 minutes.

While the pork is roasting, pour the remaining marinade into a small saucepan and simmer over moderately low heat until somewhat thickened, about 20 minutes.

Remove the roasting pan from the oven and pour half the reduced marinade on top of the pork and onions. Roast another 30 minutes. Remove from the oven and, using a pastry brush, paint the top of the pork with the remaining marinade. Continue roasting until the juices run clear yellow and not pink when the meat is pierced and the internal temperature of the meat reaches 155 to 160 degrees, about 15 to 20 more minutes, for a total roasting time of about 1 hour 20 minutes.

Remove the roasting pan from the oven. Place the pork on a carving board and let sit, loosely covered with aluminum foil, for 10 minutes before carving. Place the onions in a small bowl and cover loosely with foil to keep warm.

Discard any excess fat from the roasting pan. Place the pan over two burners on the stove. Bring the juices and marinade to a simmer over moderate heat and cook, scraping up any browned pan juices, until intensely flavorful and somewhat thickened, about 5 minutes.

Thinly slice the pork and top with the onions and sauce. Serve the oranges and hot sauces on the side.

Makes 6 servings

Note: *Two tablespoons of hot pepper sauce will give the pork a "bite." If you'd like the meat spicier, add more, or if you want it mild, add only 1 tablespoon.*

Where's the Fat?

Once your roast is cooked, you'll want to discard some or all of the fat that has collected in the bottom of the roasting pan. You can use a spoon, a bulb baster, or a gravy or grease separator (for more information on this equipment, see pages 9 and 11).

If you're using a spoon or bulb baster, first tilt the pan to collect all the fat and pan juices in one corner. Remove the clear yellow fat, leaving the darker meat juices. It is this darker juice that is the essence of the sauce or gravy to come. This is "liquid gold" and should *never* be discarded.

Depending on how you feel about fat (in the pan and on your body), you may or may not want to leave a bit in with the pan juices. Fat can add enormous flavor, but it is not required to make a good sauce or gravy.

Roast Pork and White Beans, French-Style

The Beans:

2 cups dried white beans

1 medium-size onion, peeled and left whole

2 bay leaves

Salt and freshly ground black pepper

2 cloves garlic, peeled and left whole

The Meat and Vegetables:

2 bay leaves

1½ pounds boneless pork loin, tied

¼ cup slab bacon, rind discarded, cut into 1-inch cubes

1 large leek, trimmed and cut crosswise into thin slices

2 medium-size ripe tomatoes, cut into 1-inch cubes; or 1½ cups canned whole tomatoes, drained and chopped

4 cloves garlic, peeled and left whole

1 cup homemade chicken stock or low-sodium canned chicken broth; or ½ cup stock or broth and ½ cup reserved bean liquid

Freshly ground black pepper

1 teaspoon chopped fresh rosemary; or ½ teaspoon dried

1 teaspoon chopped fresh sage; or ½ teaspoon dried

Prepare the beans: Place the beans in a large bowl and cover with cold water. Cover and let soak overnight. Drain the beans and place in a medium-size saucepan. Cover with fresh cold water. Add the onion, bay leaves, salt, pepper, and garlic, and bring to a boil over high heat. Reduce the heat to moderate and let simmer until the beans are barely soft but not overly tender (they need to hold up to another hour of cooking), about 1 hour. Drain the beans, reserving the liquid, if desired. Discard the onion, bay leaves, and garlic.

Preheat the oven to 400 degrees.

Place the drained beans in the bottom of a medium-size roasting pan or shallow casserole. Add the bay leaves. Place the pork in the middle, pressing it into the beans. Press the bacon into the beans. Place the leek, tomatoes, and garlic around the pork and pour the stock over the beans. Generously grind black pepper over the pork and sprinkle the rosemary and sage on top.

Roast the pork and beans, uncovered, for 15 minutes. Reduce the oven temperature to 325 degrees and continue roasting until the beans are tender and the pork is soft when prodded with a finger and the internal temperature reaches 155 to 160 degrees, another 30 to 50 minutes.

Makes 4 to 6 servings

Roast Pork Tenderloin with Mustard-Maple-Sage Glaze

The tenderloin is considered by many to be the most tender cut of pork; it also happens to be one of the leanest. Here it is coated in a thick glaze made with mustard, maple syrup, and fresh sage leaves and surrounded with potatoes. It makes an elegant and utterly simple meal that can be completed, from start to finish, in about an hour.

1 teaspoon vegetable or pure olive oil

One 1- to 1½-pound pork tenderloin

2 tablespoons Dijon mustard

2 tablespoons pure maple syrup or honey

1½ tablespoons chopped fresh sage; or 1½ teaspoons dried

4 medium-size baking potatoes, peeled and quartered

Salt and freshly ground black pepper

Sweet Hungarian paprika

About ⅓ cup dry sherry or white wine

1½ teaspoons all-purpose flour

About 1 cup homemade beef or chicken stock or canned low-sodium broth

Preheat the oven to 400 degrees.

Lightly grease the bottom of a medium-size or large flameproof roasting pan or ovenproof skillet with the oil and put the pork in it. In a small bowl, mix the mustard, maple syrup or honey, and 1 tablespoon of the sage. Spread the top and sides of the pork with the glaze.

Surround the pork with the potatoes and sprinkle them with salt, pepper, and paprika. Add pepper and paprika to the top of the pork and pour the sherry or wine around (not on top of) it.

Roast the pork for 10 minutes. Reduce the oven temperature to 325 degrees. Turn the potatoes over and baste the pork. Continue roasting until the internal temperature reaches 155 degrees, 30 to 40 minutes. Add more sherry or wine if the pan dries out.

Remove the roasting pan from the oven. Place the pork on a carving board, cover loosely with aluminum foil, and let sit for 5 to 10 minutes. Place the potatoes in a warm bowl and cover loosely.

Discard any excess fat in the roasting pan. Place the pan on the stove over moderate heat. Sprinkle in the flour and stir to make a paste. Cook, stirring, until it turns golden brown, about 1 minute. Slowly whisk in the stock or broth, add the remaining sage, plus salt and pepper, and let simmer until slightly thickened and flavorful, about 5 minutes.

Thinly slice the pork and serve it with the roast potatoes and the gravy.

Makes 4 to 6 servings

Roast Smoked Country Ham with Apple Cider Glaze

My youngest daughter, Emma, loves ham. On her third birthday I roasted a huge smoked country ham with a thick, gooey glaze made from apple cider and cloves. The cider creates a wonderfully sweet foil for the rich meat, without the addition of sugar.

One 16-pound fully cooked whole smoked bone-in country ham

$^1/_4$ cup whole cloves

About 3 cups apple cider without preservatives

About $1^1/_2$ cups dry sherry

Place the ham in a large roasting pan. Stud the ham all over with the cloves by inserting them into the skin. Pour $1^1/_2$ cups of the apple cider and $^3/_4$ cup of the sherry over the ham. Let marinate, covered and refrigerated, for at least 2 hours and preferably overnight, turning the meat over once or twice.

Preheat the oven to 350 degrees.

Roast the ham until hot throughout and the internal temperature reaches 140 degrees, about 12 minutes per pound, or about 3 hours 15 minutes total roasting time. A knife inserted in the ham should be warm to the touch when withdrawn after 30 seconds.

After 1 hour of roasting, pour the remaining $1^1/_2$ cups apple cider and $^3/_4$ cup sherry over the ham and baste every 15 minutes. If the marinade dries up, add more apple cider or sherry.

Remove the roasting pan from the oven. Place the ham on a carving board and let sit, loosely covered with aluminum foil, for 10 to 15 minutes before carving.

Remove any excess fat from the roasting pan. Heat the pan juices over a moderately low heat.

Cut the ham into thin slices and top with the warm pan juices.

Makes 10 to 12 servings

The Fat Advantage

In this world of low-fat cooking and calorie-counting, many cooks are tempted to remove all the fat from a roast before cooking. *Don't!* A layer of fat acts as a natural baster and causes a roast to obtain its golden brown color. Always cook a roast with the fat side up to take full advantage.

Edward Behr, author of *The Artful Eater*, explains: "Some fat is important because it bastes the sides [of the roast] as it melts and so aids in browning. This fat won't fatten you unless you help yourself to a nice crisp piece. After roasting, the juices that accumulate in the dripping pan can be degreased and spooned over the meat."

Smokehouse Hams

There are many places throughout the country that sell wonderful smoked hams, but I have never tasted a ham as good as the ones smoked at Calef's Country Store, an old-fashioned country grocery store in Barrington, New Hampshire. Their hams are smoked the traditional way in a smokehouse using hickory wood. They contain no preservatives and have a subtle smoky taste. They are some of the juiciest, most flavorful hams you'll find anywhere. Calef's hams can be ordered from Calef's Country Store, P.O. Box 57, Barrington, New Hampshire 03825, phone (603) 664-2231.

How to Carve a Whole Ham

These carving instructions are for right-handed carvers. Lefties should simply reverse the following instructions.

1. Place the ham on a carving board or serving platter with the round, meaty side up and the shank bone (the thin, narrow bone that juts out) facing to your right. Let rest.

2. Place the carving fork in your left hand and firmly spear the meat in the large meaty end, called the sirloin or butt end.

3. Holding the knife in your right hand, make the first cut vertically down to the bone about 4 inches from the shank end.

4. Working from right to left, continue making slices parallel to the original cut, at whatever thickness you desire. All cuts should be sliced down to the bone.

5. After the final slice, place the knife in the first cut. Turn the blade 90 degrees toward the fork and slice along the bone to loosen all the slices. The slices of meat can then be easily lifted up with your fork.

6. To carve the bottom of the ham, turn it over and repeat the same process as with the top.

7. Cut the remaining meat off in slices horizontally, following the contours of the bone.

Easter Ham with Orange-Shallot Glaze

This ham can be served at any time of year, for any type of special occasion. The citrus-filled flavor of fresh-squeezed orange juice mixed with Madeira wine, cloves, and a touch of cranberry juice creates a thick, gooey glaze for a smoked ham. This recipe is for a whole smoked bone-in ham (anywhere from 12 to 16 pounds), but if you're roasting half a ham, you can simply reduce the cooking time and glaze.

One 12- to 18-pound fully cooked whole smoked bone-in country ham

1 cup whole cloves

About 4¼ cups orange juice, fresh-squeezed or "old-fashioned" type with pulp

2 cups Madeira or dry sherry

1 cup sugarless cranberry juice

12 medium-size shallots, peeled and cut lengthwise in half

½ cup water (optional)

Place the ham in a large flameproof roasting pan. Insert about ½ cup of the cloves into the top of the ham (the side with the most fat) at about 2-inch intervals. Scatter the remaining ½ cup cloves in the bottom of the pan. Pour 2 cups of the orange juice, the Madeira or sherry, and the cranberry juice over the ham and let marinate, covered and refrigerated, for at least 12 hours and up to 48 hours, turning the ham once or twice.

Preheat the oven to 325 degrees.

Add the shallots to the roasting pan and roast the ham until the internal temperature reaches 140 degrees, 12 minutes per pound; a knife inserted in the ham should be warm to the touch when withdrawn after 30 seconds. The marinade should now be a thick, gooey glaze. Baste the ham about every 15 minutes, making sure the glaze is not drying out. Add 2 cups of orange juice throughout the cooking time. If the glaze appears to be burning, add the water.

Remove the roasting pan from the oven. Place the ham on a carving board and let sit, loosely covered with aluminum foil, for 10 to 15 minutes before carving. Place the shallots in a small bowl and cover loosely to keep warm.

Discard any excess fat from the pan. Place the roasting pan over two burners on the stove. Heat the sauce over moderately low heat and bring to a gentle simmer, scraping up any browned juices. Add the remaining ¼ cup orange juice (or water) if necessary to thin the sauce a bit.

Carve the ham into thin slices. Serve topped with the sauce and roasted shallots.

Makes 12 to 16 servings

Crown Roast of Pork with Summer Fruit Stuffing

A crown roast is a show-off dish, the kind of meal that elicits oohs and aahs when you bring it to the table. The crown is made up of the center loin of the pork, partially cut into chops and then connected into a large ring, or "crown." It is the pork equivalent of a rack of lamb. The center of the crown is empty, an opening just waiting to be stuffed.

One cool and breezy evening in July, I stuffed the crown with this blend of ripe summer peaches, plums, Vidalia onions, and a small handful of breadcrumbs for a filling that tasted like a Caribbean-style fresh chutney. And I tucked new potatoes and patty pan squash (a turban-shaped summer squash) in the pan around the roast.

But there are several winter alternatives to this recipe. When you crave heartier, fuller flavors, the pork can be stuffed with a combination of wild rice, apples, and chopped pecans or walnuts. This is an ideal holiday dish. Serve it with Savory Roasted Apples (page 220). You could also surround the roast with potatoes, carrots, and Brussels sprouts and then spoon the roasted vegetables and potatoes into the center before serving.

The Pork:

1 tablespoon plus 1 teaspoon olive oil

One 6-pound crown roast of pork, about
    10 chops (see Note)

3 cloves garlic, peeled and thinly sliced

3 tablespoons chopped fresh rosemary;
    or 3 teaspoons dried

2 tablespoons chopped fresh thyme;
    or 1½ teaspoons dried

Freshly ground black pepper

Grease a large flameproof roasting pan with the 1 teaspoon of oil. Place the crown roast in the pan and tuck a few slices of garlic between each chop, making sure to save a few slices to stuff into the center of the roast. Rub the inside and outside surface of the roast with the herbs and the remaining 1 tablespoon oil and sprinkle liberally with pepper. Press the remaining garlic on the inside of the roast. Let marinate at room temperature for about an hour.

Prepare the stuffing: In a medium-size skillet, heat the oil over moderate heat. Add the onion, salt, and pepper and cook, stirring, until soft, about 5 minutes. If the fruit you are using is very ripe, remove the skillet from the heat and add the remaining ingredients, stirring well to mix everything together. If the fruit is less than ripe, add the fruit to the skillet, and cook, stirring, until slightly softened, 2 to 3 minutes. Remove the skillet from the heat and stir in the remaining ingredients. (The recipe can be made up to this point up to 5 hours ahead of time and kept, covered, in the refrigerator.)

The Stuffing:

$1^1/_2$ tablespoons olive oil

1 large Vidalia or other onion, peeled and chopped

Salt and freshly ground black pepper

1 large ripe peach, peeled if you like, pitted and chopped

2 ripe plums, peeled if you like, pitted and chopped

1 tablespoon chopped fresh thyme; or 1 teaspoon dried

$2^1/_2$ tablespoons plain dry breadcrumbs

About 2 tablespoons honey (optional)

The Vegetables and Gravy:

About 20 small new potatoes, left whole; or 4 large baking potatoes, scrubbed and cut into $1^1/_2$-inch chunks

About 20 baby patty pan squash, ends trimmed; or 6 small zucchini (or a mixture of zucchini and summer squash), ends trimmed, cut lengthwise and then into thick strips about 3 inches long

1 tablespoon olive oil

1 tablespoon chopped fresh rosemary; or 1 teaspoon dried

1 tablespoon chopped fresh thyme; or 1 teaspoon dried

Salt and freshly ground black pepper

About 1 cup dry white wine

About 1 tablespoon all-purpose flour

About $^3/_4$ cup water

Preheat the oven to 450 degrees.

Place the stuffing inside the crown roast, pressing down so all of it fits. Surround the roast with the potatoes and squash and drizzle them with the oil, herbs, salt, and pepper.

Roast the pork for 15 minutes. Reduce the oven temperature to 350 degrees and continue roasting for about $1^1/_2$ hours. After 30 minutes of roasting time add $^1/_2$ cup of the white wine, basting the meat every 20 minutes or so and stirring the squash and potatoes so they brown evenly. Add another $^1/_4$ cup wine if the bottom of the pan seems to be drying out. Roast the pork until the juices run clear yellow and not pink when the meat is pierced and the internal temperature of the pork reaches 155 to 160 degrees.

Remove the roasting pan from the oven. Place the pork on a carving board, loosely covered with aluminum foil, for about 15 minutes before carving. Place the potatoes and squash in a warm bowl, loosely covered with foil to keep warm.

Make the gravy: Discard any herb twigs and any excess fat from the roasting pan. (There shouldn't be much.) Place the pan over two burners on the stove. Bring the pan juices to a boil over moderate heat. Stir in the flour and cook until the mixture begins to turn golden brown, 3 to 4 minutes. Add the remaining $^1/_4$ cup of wine and the water and bring to a boil, scraping up any browned juices. Add salt and pepper to taste and let simmer until the gravy is well flavored, 5 to 8 minutes; the more you reduce the gravy, the stronger flavored it will be.

Be sure to present the crown roast at the table before cutting into individual chops because it's such a great sight. Scoop out the stuffing before carving and place in a warm serving bowl. Hold the roast in place with a large carving fork and, using a sharp carving knife, slice down on each side of the bone to cut into individual chops. Serve with the fruit stuffing, potatoes, and squash. Pass the gravy separately.

Makes 5 or 6 servings

Note: *Have your butcher prepare the crown for you ahead of time.*

Pan-Roasted Pork with Milk, Sage, and Potatoes

This is an adaptation of one of my favorite pork recipes, Pork Loin Braised in Milk, from Marcella Hazan's *The Classic Italian Cookbook*. In Hazan's dish the pork cooks slowly on top of the stove, allowing the milk to mingle with the pork juices and create a rich sauce. In my version the pork is browned and then slowly roasted in the oven, surrounded by leaves of fresh sage, garlic, and chunks of potato all topped with milk. I *know* it sounds weird, but trust me, it works. The milk not only tenderizes the pork so that it is fall-off-the-fork tender but also creates a creamy, sage-enhanced sauce and the most buttery-tasting potatoes you've ever had. Try it—you'll see.

¹/₂ tablespoon butter

¹/₂ tablespoon olive oil

One 3-pound boneless loin of pork, tied

3 cloves garlic, peeled and chopped

In a large flameproof casserole or roasting pan, heat the butter and oil over moderately high heat. Add the pork and brown on all sides, 3 to 5 minutes. Remove the pork and thoroughly clean out the pan.

Place the pork back into the casserole and scatter the garlic, potatoes, sage, salt, and pepper around it. Pour 1¹/₂ cups milk on top of the meat and cover the casserole. (The dish can be prepared to this point up to 3 hours ahead of time and refrigerated until ready to roast.)

Preheat the oven to 300 degrees.

8 medium-size potatoes, peeled and cut into quarters

2 tablespoons fresh sage leaves, coarsely chopped; or 2 teaspoons dried

Salt and freshly ground black pepper

About 1½ cups milk

Place the casserole over high heat and bring the milk to a simmer. Cover the casserole and place in the oven. Roast the pork until very tender when pierced with a fork, 1 hour 45 minutes to 2 hours. Baste the pork every 20 minutes or so, adding ½ cup more milk (or water) if the casserole appears to be drying out.

Place the pork on a carving board. Discard the string and cut the pork into thin slices. Top with the pan juices. Pass the potatoes separately.

Makes 6 servings

Roasting 101

Before you put a roast in the oven, there are a few steps you can take to make the process easier. Make sure your roasting pan fits on the oven shelf. There's nothing worse than having a roast ready to go, oven preheated, and then finding out that it won't fit. Always position the shelf in the middle of the oven so that the roast is exposed to heat on the top and the bottom, unless otherwise indicated. And always preheat the oven to the desired temperature before you roast.

Roast Pork Chops with Smothered Apples

This is an ideal family meal, easy to make and full of the soothing flavors of fall. Thin slices of tart apples line the bottom of a shallow roasting pan, pork chops are placed on top, sprinkled with fresh sage and thyme, and a touch of apple cider is poured over the whole thing. The chops cook until tender, and the pork juices mingle with the apples and sweet cider to make a delicious roasted "applesauce."

Serve this dish with a good dry red wine or sparkling cider, a green salad, roasted sweet potatoes, and a crusty loaf of bread—preferably in front of a warm fire.

$^1\!/_2$ tablespoon butter or margarine

4 large tart apples, such as Macintosh, peeled, cored, and sliced

4 pork chops, about $^3\!/_4$ inch thick

1 tablespoon chopped fresh sage; or 1 teaspoon dried

1 tablespoon chopped fresh thyme; or 1 teaspoon dried

Freshly ground black pepper

$^1\!/_2$ cup apple cider with no preservatives

Preheat the oven to 400 degrees.

Spread the butter or margarine on the bottom of a medium-size roasting pan or ovenproof skillet. Arrange the apples in the bottom, layering as needed. Place the pork chops directly on top of the apples, sprinkle with half of the herbs and a generous grinding of pepper, and pour the cider on top.

Roast the chops for 15 minutes. Turn the chops over and sprinkle with the remaining herbs. Roast another 15 minutes.

Preheat the broiler and broil the chops until well browned, 8 to 10 minutes.

Makes 2 to 4 servings

Roasted Pork Ribs in Spicy Barbecue Sauce

These ribs are roasted long and slow until they just about fall off the bone. The combination of tomato, spices, soy sauce, and Chinese chile paste creates a thick, gooey glaze that is positively addictive.

These ribs are best made with a really spicy punch. But if you're serving kids or those who prefer mild foods, add only a touch of chile paste. Or you can divide the marinade in half and make one batch for the weak-hearted and the other with a real POW. Marinate and roast the two batches of ribs separately.

Plan on letting the ribs marinate for at least 8 hours. Serve with mashed potatoes (as a soothing counterpoint to the heat), coleslaw, Spider Corn Cake (page 247), and lots of napkins and ice-cold beer.

The spicy sauce is also excellent with chicken or turkey wings or drumsticks; use half the marinade recipe for a pound of poultry, marinate for at least 8 hours, and roast at 325 degrees for about $1^1/_2$ hours, or until the meat is almost falling off the bone.

The Marinade:

2 cups ketchup

$^1/_4$ cup soy sauce

$^1/_4$ cup Worcestershire sauce

3 tablespoons honey

1 teaspoon ground cinnamon

1 teaspoon ground cumin

1 to 3 tablespoons Chinese chile paste (see Note)

The Ribs:

4 pounds pork ribs, cut into individual ribs

$^1/_4$ cup water or dry white wine (optional)

In a large bowl, mix all the ingredients for the marinade, adding 1 tablespoon of chile paste for a somewhat mild taste and 3 tablespoons for super spicy. Add the ribs and coat well all over. Cover and refrigerate for 8 to 48 hours.

Preheat the oven to 400 degrees.

Place the ribs and half the marinade in a large roasting pan. Roast for 10 minutes, reduce the heat to 300 degrees, and continue roasting, turning the ribs once or twice, for $1^1/_2$ hours. Baste the ribs, adding more marinade every 20 to 30 minutes. If the sauce begins to dry out, add the water or wine.

Makes 4 servings

Note: *Chinese chile paste is available in Asian markets.*

Chinese-Style Pork Ribs with Black Bean Sauce

These intensely flavorful ribs have a distinct Asian flavor—the sauce is made from soy sauce, rice wine, fresh ginger, and fermented Chinese black beans—but they pair beautifully with mashed potatoes and corn bread. The ribs can marinate for as little as an hour, but they'll be even more succulent if they sit for up to 48 hours.

2 teaspoons toasted sesame oil

¹/₃ cup low-sodium soy sauce

3 tablespoons peeled and finely chopped ginger

1¹/₂ teaspoons chile paste with soybeans (see Note)

¹/₂ cup Chinese rice wine, dry sherry, or dry white wine

2 tablespoons honey or maple syrup

1 tablespoon balsamic vinegar

3 scallions, thinly sliced

12 country-style pork ribs, about 3¹/₂ to 4 pounds, cut into individual ribs

3 tablespoons fermented Chinese black beans, thoroughly rinsed and chopped

In a small bowl, mix the sesame oil, soy sauce, ginger, chile paste, rice wine, honey or maple syrup, vinegar, and half of the scallions.

Place the ribs in a large bowl and pour the marinade on top. Marinate the ribs, covered and refrigerated, for as little as 1 hour or as much as 48 hours. Turn the ribs once or twice during that time.

Preheat the oven to 350 degrees.

Place the ribs and marinade in a large flameproof roasting pan. Roast the ribs for 1 hour. Turn them over, add the remaining scallions and all the black beans, and continue roasting until the meat is so tender it is just about falling off the bone, another 45 minutes to 1 hour.

Remove the roasting pan from the oven and place the ribs on a warm platter. Discard any excess fat in the roasting pan. Set the pan over moderate heat and bring the pan juices to a simmer, scraping up the browned pan juices. Serve 2 ribs per person with the warm pan juices drizzled on top.

Makes 6 servings

Note: *This amount makes the ribs slightly spicy. Add or subtract the chile paste according to your taste. Chile paste with soybeans is available at Asian and gourmet food shops.*

Roasted Ribs with Cinnamon-Salsa Glaze

The flavors in this rib dish—chunky salsa, ground cinnamon, a touch of hot pepper sauce, and rich flowery honey—are reminiscent of a succulent pork dish I once ate in Oaxaca, Mexico. The spicy flavors mingle with the richness of the pork to create an unforgettable taste sensation.

Try these ribs served with Mexican-style rice pilaf, a tomato and avocado salad, and ice-cold Mexican beer with lime wedges. Serve extra salsa or hot pepper sauce for those who like their ribs with a real bite. The cilantro is optional because it's a flavor you either love or hate.

1½ cups chunky-style salsa, homemade or bottled

½ cup ketchup

3 tablespoons flower-scented honey

1½ teaspoons ground cinnamon

Few dashes hot pepper sauce

1½ tablespoons sweet Marsala or sherry

½ cup chopped fresh cilantro (optional)

3 pounds country-style pork ribs, cut into about 8 ribs

Mix the salsa, ketchup, honey, cinnamon, hot pepper sauce, Marsala, and, if desired, ¼ cup of the cilantro in a large nonreactive bowl. Add the ribs and coat all over. Cover and refrigerate for 8 to 48 hours.

Preheat the oven to 325 degrees.

Roast the ribs, basting with the sauce every 30 minutes or so, until the meat is thoroughly tender and practically falling off the bone, 2 to 2½ hours. Turn the ribs after about 1 hour, and then again during the last 15 minutes of roasting. Serve hot or at room temperature.

Makes 4 servings

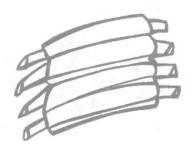

Pea Soup with Smoked Ham

After roasting a smoked ham, I always save the bone for a rich, thick pea soup. This particular rendition is loaded with carrots, celery, and thinly sliced leeks and is thickened with a combination of dried yellow and green peas. It's best to make this a day ahead of time because the flavors really come together when the soup is allowed to sit overnight.

1 meaty roasted ham bone, meat cut off and diced

4 medium-size onions, peeled and chopped

4 medium-size carrots, peeled and chopped

4 ribs celery, trimmed and chopped

1 large leek, trimmed, cut lengthwise in half, and very thinly sliced

6 black peppercorns, tied in a piece of cheesecloth

Salt

2 bay leaves

2$^{1}/_{2}$ cups mixed green and yellow dried split peas

1 cup dry sherry

Freshly ground black pepper

About 1$^{1}/_{2}$ cups small croutons

Place the ham bone in a pot large enough to hold it in one piece. Add the onions, carrots, celery, leek, peppercorns, salt to taste, and bay leaves and cover completely with cold water. (The water should reach just to the top of the bone.)

Bring to a boil over high heat, reduce the heat to moderately low, and skim off any foam that rises to the top. Add the split peas and sherry and simmer, partially covered, until the soup is thick and full of flavor, about 2 hours. Discard the peppercorns. Stir in any diced ham and season to taste with pepper. Serve hot, topped with the croutons.

Makes 6 servings

Minestrone Soup with Garden Vegetables

1 tablespoon olive oil

2 cloves garlic, peeled and finely chopped

2 medium-size leeks, trimmed and thinly sliced

2 medium-size zucchini, ends trimmed, diced or thinly sliced

4 carrots, peeled and diced or thinly sliced

3 ribs celery, trimmed and diced or thinly sliced

4 ripe tomatoes, cut into 1-inch cubes; or 3 cups canned whole tomatoes, drained and chopped

3 tablespoons chopped fresh basil

1 tablespoon chopped fresh thyme

1/2 cup chopped fresh parsley

Salt and freshly ground black pepper

1 cup dry white wine

6 1/2 cups Roasted Ham Bone Stock (recipe follows)

1/2 cup tiny star-shaped pasta or orzo

One 19-ounce can cooked white beans, rinsed and drained

1 cup fresh or canned corn kernels (optional)

1 cup grated Parmesan cheese (optional)

In a large soup pot, heat the oil over moderately low heat. Add the garlic and leeks and cook, stirring, until soft, about 6 minutes. Add the zucchini, carrots, and celery and cook, stirring, until slightly softened, about 5 minutes. Stir in the tomatoes, basil, thyme, half of the parsley, and salt and pepper to taste. Add the wine and bring to a boil over high heat. Let boil for 1 minute. Add the stock, reduce the heat to low, and let the soup simmer, partially covered, about 15 minutes.

While the soup simmers, bring a medium-size saucepan of water to a boil over high heat. Add the pasta or orzo and cook until just tender, about 10 minutes. Drain.

Add the cooked pasta to the soup along with the beans and corn and let cook until all the vegetables are tender and the soup is flavorful, about 5 minutes longer. Taste for seasoning. Serve with the remaining parsley and the cheese if desired.

Makes 10 servings

Roasted Ham Bone Stock

This is an ideal way to use a leftover ham bone from a roasted ham. There is so much flavor left in the bone after roasting that a stock is just waiting to happen. The stock is best made a day ahead of time and chilled so you can easily skim off the fat before using. It can also be used as the base of a sauce or gravy for pork dishes or to cook risotto.

1 roasted ham bone

1 large onion, peeled and cut into quarters

1 large leek, trimmed and thinly sliced

1 large carrot, trimmed and chopped

1 large rib celery, trimmed and chopped

6 black peppercorns

1 bay leaf

Salt

Place the bone in a large soup pot. Add the onion, leek, carrot, celery, peppercorns, bay leaf, and salt (go easy on the salt—most smoked hams are very salty). Cover with cold water and bring the mixture to a boil over high heat. Reduce the heat to moderately low and simmer, partially covered, until the stock is flavorful, 1 to 1 1/2 hours.

If the stock still tastes weak, raise the heat to moderately high and let it simmer vigorously until the flavor intensifies. Season to taste. Strain the stock and let cool. Refrigerate, covered, overnight. Skim off any fat floating on the top of the stock and refrigerate for up to 3 days or freeze for several months until you are ready to use the stock.

Makes about 8 to 16 cups

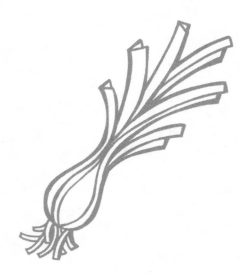

Poultry

Roast Chicken
with Lemon and Herbs

What could be more satisfying than a well-roasted chicken? Roast chicken is undoubtedly one of the most basic recipes in the world, but it seems to be one that very few cooks have mastered. I have often thought that this is the dish culinary students should have to present upon graduation. Why is it that so many roast chickens served in restaurants are thoroughly tasteless and overcooked?

The trick with roast chicken, like all roasts, is having the very best ingredients and being careful not to overcook or dry out the bird. Free-range chickens have been the source of many jokes over the past few years, but they really can be much better than your average supermarket bird. And fresh herbs make all the difference in this dish. Constant basting is also key to a perfectly golden roast. With the chicken, serve roasted potatoes and vegetables, a green salad, and a loaf of French bread—then feast!

1 teaspoon olive oil

One 3- to 4-pound chicken

Salt and freshly ground black pepper

1 medium-size lemon, with a small "X" cut
    into the side

4 sprigs fresh rosemary or tarragon;
    or 1¹/₂ teaspoons dried

8 cloves garlic, peeled and left whole

¹/₂ cup dry red or white wine or dry sherry

Preheat the oven to 450 degrees.

Grease the bottom of a large roasting pan with the oil. Place the chicken, breast-side up, in the pan and sprinkle the cavity and skin lightly with salt and pepper. Push the lemon into the bird's cavity. Sprinkle the rosemary or tarragon on the chicken and scatter the garlic around it. Pour the wine or sherry over the chicken.

Roast the chicken for 15 minutes. Reduce the oven temperature to 325 degrees. Continue roasting, basting every 15 minutes, until the juices run clear yellow and not pink when the inside of a thigh is pierced, about 1 hour to 1 hour 10 minutes.

Remove the roasting pan from the oven. Place the chicken on a carving board and let sit, loosely covered with aluminum foil, for 10 to 15 minutes before carving. Discard any excess fat from the juices in the roasting pan and heat over a moderately low heat. Cut the chicken into serving pieces. Serve the chicken topped with the pan juices and roasted garlic.

Makes 4 servings

How Much Meat Per Person: Poultry

About $^3/_4$ to 1 pound per person for a whole bone-in bird.

For turkey, figure on 1 pound per person so you will have leftovers.

Chinese-Flavored Roast Chicken with Roasted Vegetables

If you're not convinced that roasting is one of the simplest methods of cooking, consider this story: One evening I arrived home from work at 5:00, and was greeted by two exhausted and hungry children. I put this chicken together in less than 10 minutes, and we were at the table eating in just over an hour. So much for fussy preparations.

The combination of soy sauce, sesame oil, and mirin (Japanese rice wine) gives this chicken a slightly sweet, sticky glaze. You can use any combination of vegetables you like in this dish, but young parsnips, scallions, and red bell pepper work particularly well. With the chicken, serve rice or couscous and a watercress salad.

One 3- to 4-pound chicken

$^{1}/_{2}$ cup fresh basil leaves

1 medium-size lemon, with a small "X" cut into the side

4 small young parsnips, peeled and cut lengthwise in half

4 scallions, trimmed and cut lengthwise in half

1 large red bell pepper, cored and sliced lengthwise into 8 strips

$^{1}/_{3}$ cup low-sodium soy sauce

$^{1}/_{3}$ cup mirin (Japanese rice wine) or dry sherry

2 tablespoons toasted sesame oil

Freshly ground black pepper

$^{1}/_{3}$ cup chopped fresh chives (optional)

Preheat the oven to 450 degrees.

Place the chicken in a large roasting pan, breast-side up. Using your fingers, separate and loosen the breast skin from the chicken breast. Slip a few leaves of basil under the breast skin and place the rest inside the cavity of the chicken, along with the lemon. Scatter the parsnips, scallions, and bell pepper around the chicken. Pour the soy sauce, mirin, and sesame oil on top of the chicken and vegetables. Stir the vegetables to make sure they are all well coated with the sauce. Sprinkle black pepper and chives over all.

Roast the chicken and vegetables for 15 minutes. Reduce the oven temperature to 350 degrees and continue roasting until the juices run clear yellow and not pink when the thigh is pierced with a fork, 50 to 55 minutes. Toss the vegetables and baste the chicken once or twice while roasting.

Remove the roasting pan from the oven. Place the chicken on a carving board and let sit, loosely covered with aluminum foil, for 10 to 15 minutes. Place the vegetables in a warm bowl and cover loosely with foil to keep warm.

Discard any excess fat from the roasting pan and bring the juices to a simmer over moderate heat. Simmer for 5 minutes and season to taste. Carve the chicken into serving pieces and serve topped with warm pan juices and the roasted vegetables.

Makes 4 servings

Four Ways to Test a Chicken or Turkey for Doneness

Here are four no-fail ways to tell when a chicken or turkey is fully cooked:

1. Pierce the inside of the thigh; if the juices run yellow, not pink, it's ready.

2. Wiggle the drumstick. If it feels loose, the bird is done!

3. The thighs are tender when you press down on them.

4. Poultry is the one exception to the rule about the internal temperature being the ultimate test in telling whether a roast is done. You can gauge how well done poultry is by taking its internal temperature, but it should be your last test. To test a chicken, place a meat thermometer in the inner thigh; the internal temperature should be at least 160 degrees and up to 180 degrees for well-done meat. For turkey, place the thermometer into the thickest part of the breast, near the armpit; the internal temperature should be between 162 and 170 degrees, depending on how well done you like your turkey meat.

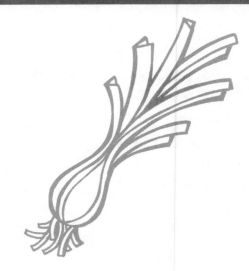

Tarragon Chicken with Roast Pears and Potatoes

I am often asked how I make up a recipe. One friend recently asked if I had ever dreamed a recipe. (The answer is yes, but that's another story.) Sometimes a recipe is developed in a methodical fashion—I set out to create the best roast chicken tarragon ever—but other dishes happen haphazardly, based on ingredients found in the refrigerator.

This wonderful chicken dish happened by chance. In this case, I had just arrived at a friend's house in the south of France with a small basket of groceries. I had bought a chicken at the local *boucherie*, or butcher's shop; there were fresh pears from a neighbor's tree; and a few leeks, potatoes, and garlic from the market. The tarragon was snipped from the 3-foot-high bush growing outside the door, and the bay leaves picked from a neighbor's tree. I never would have come up with this dish at home, but sometimes an unlikely combination of ingredients leads to memorable results. This is one of my favorite chicken recipes.

2 tablespoons fruity olive oil

1 large leek, trimmed and cut into 3-inch strips

One 3- to 4-pound chicken

3 tablespoons chopped fresh tarragon; or 2^1/$_2$ teaspoons dried

1 tablespoon peeled and chopped garlic

Salt and freshly ground black pepper

2 bay leaves

Preheat the oven to 400 degrees.

Grease the bottom of a large flameproof roasting pan with 1 tablespoon of the oil. Arrange the leek strips in a single layer in the pan. Place the chicken, breast-side up, on top of the leek. Stuff 1 tablespoon of the tarragon and the chopped garlic, salt, pepper, and bay leaves inside the cavity. Surround the chicken with the potatoes, pears, whole garlic, and shallots. Sprinkle the remaining tarragon over the chicken. Drizzle with the remaining tablespoon of oil.

Roast the chicken for about 30 minutes and then pour the Cognac or wine on top of the chicken. Reduce the oven temperature to 325 degrees. Continue roasting, basting every 15 minutes until the juices run clear yellow and not pink when the inside of a thigh is pierced, 30 to 40 more minutes.

4 large baking potatoes, peeled and cut into quarters (or in half if the potatoes are not very large)

2 large ripe pears, cored and cut lengthwise into quarters; peeling is optional

8 cloves garlic, peeled and left whole

2 shallots, peeled and cut in half

$^1/_2$ cup Cognac or dry white wine

Remove the roasting pan from the oven. Place the chicken on a carving board and let sit, loosely covered with aluminum foil, for 10 to 15 minutes. Place the pears and vegetables in a warm bowl, loosely covered with foil to keep warm.

Discard any excess fat from the roasting pan and bring the juices to a simmer over moderate heat. Simmer for 5 minutes and season to taste. Carve the chicken into serving pieces and serve topped with warm pan juices and the pears and vegetables.

Makes 4 servings

Low-Fat Chicken

One of the easiest ways to reduce the amount of fat you eat in your chicken dishes is to simply pull off any excess fat found at the opening of the cavity. There is generally a small "flap" of fat that can simply be pulled or cut off. It won't reduce the flavor of the chicken in the slightest, and it will make your chicken (as well as your sauces, gravies, and pan juices) a lot less fatty.

Roast Chicken with Herb-Garlic Butter

The technique here is to rub fresh herb-garlic butter over the chicken breast under the breast skin and all over the outside of the chicken. What happens is that the bird is continually basted throughout the roasting time, particularly on the breast meat, which is most prone to drying out. Any assortment of herbs or spices will work in the butter mixture.

This chicken is particularly good when roasted with carrots (cut into thick, long strips), whole baby onions, and zucchini (also cut into thick, long strips). With the chicken, serve polenta.

One 3- to 4-pound chicken

1 lemon, with a small "X" cut into the side

4 tablespoons (¹/₂ stick) butter, at room temperature

3 cloves garlic, peeled and very finely chopped

2 tablespoons chopped fresh basil; or 2 teaspoons dried

2 tablespoons chopped fresh tarragon; or 1 teaspoon dried

Preheat the oven to 450 degrees.

Place the chicken, breast-side up, in a large flame-proof roasting pan and stuff the lemon in the cavity.

In a small bowl, mix the butter, garlic, basil, tarragon, and pepper until smooth.

Using your fingers, separate and loosen the breast skin from the chicken breast. Spread 1 to 1¹/₂ tablespoons of the flavored butter mixture under the breast skin, rubbing (almost massaging) it evenly across the entire breast. Spread the remaining butter all over the chicken skin, top and bottom. Add ¹/₂ cup of the wine to the pan.

Roast the chicken for 15 minutes and then reduce the oven temperature to 325 degrees. Continue roasting until the juices run clear yellow and not pink when an inner thigh is pierced, about 45 minutes longer. Baste the chicken every 15 minutes with the wine and juices in the bottom of the pan, adding more wine if the pan seems dry.

Freshly ground black pepper

About 1 cup dry white wine

Remove the roasting pan from the oven. Place the chicken on a carving board and let sit, loosely covered with aluminum foil, for 10 to 15 minutes.

Discard any excess fat from the roasting pan and bring the juices to a simmer over moderate heat. Simmer for 3 to 5 minutes and season to taste. Carve the chicken into serving pieces and serve topped with warm pan juices.

Makes 4 servings

There's a Lemon in My Chicken

When you put a whole lemon inside the cavity of a chicken or any bird, it performs culinary miracles. The lemon permeates the cavity and very subtly flavors and moistens the bird's flesh. Simply carve a small "X" through the lemon's peel and place inside the cavity. The lemon will do the rest while the bird roasts.

Hoisin- and Orange-Glazed Chicken

Fresh Asian flavors permeate both the inside and the outside of this roasted chicken. Chinese hoisin sauce—a thick, sweet, chocolate-brown sauce made from soybeans, garlic, and chiles—is rubbed inside the cavity of the chicken and all over the skin. Chunks of fresh orange and ginger are placed inside the bird, and chopped ginger, soy sauce, and orange juice are poured over the outside. The bird is then roasted at a high temperature to produce a mahogany-glazed chicken that is bursting with flavor. With the chicken, serve steamed rice and stir-fried vegetables.

One 3- to 4-pound chicken

³/₄ cup hoisin sauce

¹/₂ orange, peeled and cut into small pieces

One 1-inch piece ginger, peeled

¹/₂ to ³/₄ cup orange juice, fresh-squeezed or "old-fashioned" type with pulp

1 tablespoon low-sodium soy sauce

1 teaspoon toasted sesame oil

1 tablespoon ginger, peeled and chopped

1 orange, peeled and cut into thin slices

Place the chicken, breast-side up, in a large flameproof roasting pan. Using a pastry brush, spread a bit of the hoisin sauce on the inside of the cavity and the rest of it all over the outside. Place the orange pieces and the 1-inch piece of ginger inside the cavity. Pour ¹/₂ cup orange juice, the soy sauce, and sesame oil on the chicken and sprinkle the chopped ginger on top. Let marinate, covered and refrigerated, for at least 1 hour or up to 24 hours.

Preheat the oven to 450 degrees.

Roast the chicken for 15 minutes, reduce the oven temperature to 400 degrees and roast, basting every 15 minutes or so, another 30 to 45 minutes, depending on the size of the chicken. If the juices in the bottom of the pan dry up, tip the chicken so the juices from the cavity spill out, or add another ¹/₄ cup orange juice or water.

Remove the roasting pan from the oven and tilt the remaining juices out of the chicken's cavity into the pan. Place the chicken on a carving board and let sit, loosely covered with aluminum foil, for 10 to 15 minutes.

Discard any excess fat from the roasting pan. Scrape up any browned bits clinging to the bottom of the pan, and gently heat the juices over low heat. Cut the chicken into serving pieces. Drizzle the hot pan juices over the chicken and serve garnished with the orange slices.

Makes 4 servings

Trussing: Pretty or Petty?

According to Julia Child, in her authoritative book *The Way to Cook*: "To truss means to hold in place, and when you want a chicken to look its best, you truss it to keep the legs and wings close to the body. But trussing is not only for looks. It also makes for more even roasting. Untrussed drumsticks will stick up and dry out; untrussed legs can gape away from the body and even fall off." She goes on to describe the look of a well-trussed chicken: "Its drumsticks rest nicely in place against the tip of the breast-bone; the wing tips are folded back beneath the shoulders. All is made neat and chic for its roasting and its grand entrance."

One of my primary goals in writing this book was to simplify the roasting process, making it an accessible technique for every day of the week. So I did some experiments and I found that, in most cases, trussing a bird does not add significantly to its taste. Yes, it may provide a neater-looking bird, but it rarely made a difference in the final outcome of the dish. When I roast a chicken or duck that is not stuffed, I almost never bother to truss it.

There are, however, some times when trussing or tying up a bird *is* helpful. You'll notice that many of the stuffed chicken and turkey recipes in this book are trussed or tied in some way. The reason is primarily to hold in the stuffing and keep it from spilling out all over the roasting pan. With large birds, like a holiday turkey, it can also be helpful to keep the drumsticks in closer to the breast to prevent them from drying out. It is also beneficial to tie up an uneven cut of meat (like the Rolled Butterfly of Lamb with Spinach-Pesto Filling, page 44) to promote even cooking.

For information on trussing needles and poultry lacers, see page 10. For a simple, step-by-step discussion of how to truss a chicken, see page 91.

Honey-Glazed Roast Chicken with Savory Couscous Stuffing

This exotic-flavored bird, with a wine-and-honey glaze, roasts with chunks of zucchini and needs only a red onion, orange, and watercress salad and warm pita bread to complete the meal. See facing page for how to truss a bird.

The Couscous Stuffing:

1 tablespoon olive oil

1 medium-size onion, peeled and chopped

1 medium-size zucchini, ends trimmed, diced

3 tablespoons chopped fresh basil; or 2 teaspoons dried

Salt and freshly ground black pepper

1/2 cup slivered almonds

1/4 cup raisins

2 teaspoons ground cinnamon

1 1/2 cups cooked couscous, regular or whole wheat (see Note)

2 tablespoons lemon juice

Preheat the oven to 450 degrees.

Prepare the stuffing: In a large skillet, heat the oil over moderate heat. Add the onion and cook, stirring, until soft, about 2 minutes. Add the zucchini and cook, stirring, until lightly browned and tender, another 8 minutes. Add half of the basil and the salt, pepper, almonds, raisins, and cinnamon; cook, stirring, until warmed through, about 1 minute more. Stir the cooked vegetables into the couscous along with the lemon juice. Add the remaining basil and taste for seasoning. Let cool to room temperature.

Stuff the cavity of the chicken, pressing down the couscous mixture firmly, but do not overstuff because the stuffing swells during cooking. Truss the bird or sew up the cavity of the chicken with small wooden skewers or poultry lacers.

Place the stuffed chicken, breast-side up, in a medium-size or large roasting pan and surround with the zucchini. Pour the wine over the chicken and season the skin with salt and pepper. Drizzle the honey over the chicken, using a pastry brush to coat the entire surface.

Roast the chicken for 10 minutes, reduce the oven temperature to 325 degrees, and continue roasting until the juices run clear yellow and not pink when the inside of a thigh is pierced, about 1 hour longer. Baste the chicken frequently. If the chicken is not well glazed and browned, raise the oven temperature to 450 degrees for the last 10 minutes of roasting.

Remove the roasting pan from the oven. Place the chicken on a carving board and let sit, loosely covered with aluminum foil, for 10 to 15 minutes. Discard the trussing string or skewers from the chicken. Remove the couscous stuffing and spoon into a warm bowl; cover loosely with foil to keep warm.

Discard any excess fat from the roasting pan and bring the juices to a simmer over moderately low heat. Simmer for 5 minutes and season to taste. Carve the chicken into serving pieces and serve topped with warm pan juices. Pass the stuffing separately.

Makes 4 servings

The Chicken and Zucchini:

One 3- to 4-pound chicken

$^3/_4$ cup dry red wine

Salt and freshly ground black pepper

$^1/_3$ cup honey

3 large zucchini, ends trimmed, cut lengthwise into quarters

> Note: *To make $1^1/_2$ cups cooked couscous, bring $^3/_4$ cup water or chicken stock or broth to a boil over high heat. Reduce the heat to moderate and stir in $^1/_2$ cup couscous. Cook for 1 minute, cover the saucepan, and remove from the heat. Let sit until all the liquid has been absorbed, about 5 minutes. Use a fork to fluff the couscous and separate the grains.*

How to Truss a Bird

One of the simplest, most straightforward ways to truss a bird is simply to tie it up with kitchen string or twine.

1. Take a 5- to 6-foot piece of kitchen string and make a loop in the center.

2. Place the loop around the ends of both drumsticks and pull tightly so you have two pieces of string of equal length on either side of the bird.

3. Pull the strings alongside the bird in order to hold the wings closely against the body and make a knot at the opposite end of the bird.

Larisa's Indian Roast Chicken with Masala-Apple Stuffing

Larisa Yaskell, a close family friend, came up with the recipe for this delicious spice-infused chicken. A mixture of Indian spices—chaat masala—is rubbed into the chicken's cavity, all over the skin, and finally under the skin. The chicken is then stuffed with a pungent combination of rice, apples, raisins, onions, nuts, and spices and roasted until golden brown. Serve the chicken with an assortment of chutneys, Indian pickles, raita, and pappadum, a flat, crackerlike Indian bread.

The Chicken:

1 teaspoon vegetable oil

One 3- to 3½-pound chicken

2 teaspoons chaat masala (see Note)

1 large onion, peeled and cut into quarters

¼ to ½ cup dry white wine or water

Grease the bottom of a medium-size or large flameproof roasting pan with the 1 teaspoon oil. Place the chicken, breast-side up, in the pan and rub the chaat masala inside the cavity, all over the outside skin, and under the skin on the breast. Let the chicken "marinate" for at least an hour at room temperature, or cover and refrigerate for up to 6 hours.

Preheat the oven to 400 degrees.

Prepare the stuffing: In a large skillet, heat the oil over moderate heat. Add the onion and cook, stirring occasionally, until soft but not brown, about 8 minutes. Add the apples and spices and cook, stirring frequently, for another 3 minutes. Add the raisins, butter, and nuts and cook another 30 seconds. Remove the skillet from the heat and stir in the rice until well mixed, making sure it clumps up. Add salt and pepper to taste. The stuffing should have a very full flavor; add more chaat masala and garam masala if needed.

The Stuffing:

1 tablespoon vegetable oil

1 medium-size onion, peeled and chopped

2 tart apples, unpeeled, cored and chopped

About 1 teaspoon garam masala (see Note)

About 1 teaspoon chaat masala

$1/2$ cup raisins

1 tablespoon butter

1 cup chopped cashews or walnuts

1 cup cooked (about $1/3$ cup raw) rice

Salt and freshly ground black pepper

Tip the chicken up and stuff the cavity with the stuffing, pressing down to add as much as possible. Do not add so much stuffing that it begins to fall out. Tie the legs together with kitchen string. Add the onion to the pan and season the chicken with salt and pepper. Place the remaining stuffing in a lightly buttered casserole.

Roast the chicken for 30 minutes. Remove the roasting pan from the oven and baste the chicken with some of the wine or water. Continue roasting, basting occasionally with additional wine or water, until the chicken is golden brown and the juices run yellow and not pink, about an additional 30 minutes. Place the casserole with the extra stuffing in the oven about 10 minutes before the chicken is done.

Remove the roasting pan from the oven. Place the chicken on a carving board and let sit, loosely covered with aluminum foil, for 10 to 15 minutes.

Discard any excess fat from the roasting pan and bring the juices to a simmer over moderate heat. Simmer for 5 minutes and season to taste. Remove the casserole from the oven. Carve the chicken into serving pieces and serve topped with the warm pan juices. Pass the stuffing separately.

Makes 4 servings

Note: *Garam masala and chaat masala are mixtures of Indian spices available in many health or gourmet food stores. Chaat masala is a powdered spice combination made with mint, ginger, mango powder, asafetida, cumin, fennel seeds, and cayenne pepper. Garam masala, a traditional ground mixture from northern India, is a sweeter combination of cumin, coriander seeds, cardamom, black peppercorns, cloves, and cinnamon.*

Jamaican Roast Jerk Chicken and Breadfruit Salad

Jack Shapansky is an unlikely character in Jamaica. Maybe it's his mop of red hair or his whiter-than-white skin or his midwestern accent that makes him an unusual candidate to be one of the most creative chefs on the island. But there are few cooks who utilize the native fruits, vegetables, and traditions of this Caribbean island so well. Shapansky is the executive chef of the Cibboney resort in Ocho Rios, where he oversees three restaurants, all of which feature native ingredients.

Of all the foods I tasted in Jamaica, I was most intrigued with this breadfruit salad. According to Shapansky, breadfruit was brought to the island by Captain Bligh and was eaten in huge quantities aboard ships to "stay alive." This huge fruit resembling a coconut is related to the Asian durian. It is traditionally cooked in the hot coals of a fire made from pimiento wood, where it roasts until blackened on the outside and soft and tender inside. But it works equally well roasted in a regular kitchen oven.

Unless you live in a neighborhood that has a large Caribbean population, you'll probably have trouble finding breadfruit in your local market. Sweet potatoes make a fine substitute.

In this salad the roasted breadfruit or sweet potato is mixed with jerk chicken (perhaps Jamaica's most popular recipe) and a spicy mayonnaise.

One 3- to 4-pound chicken

About 6 tablespoons Jamaican jerk sauce (see Note)

1 cup water

1 large breadfruit; or 3 pounds sweet potatoes, unpeeled

1 cup trimmed and chopped scallions (white and green parts)

Place the chicken, breast-side up, in a medium-size or large roasting pan or large ovenproof skillet. Rub the skin of the chicken and inside the cavity with 2 to 6 tablespoons of the jerk sauce, depending on how spicy you want the dish to be. Pour the water on top and marinate for at least 2 hours, preferably overnight, turning the chicken over once or twice.

Preheat the oven to 400 degrees.

Roast the chicken, basting frequently, until the juices run clear yellow and not pink when an inner thigh is pierced, about 1 hour. Roast the breadfruit or sweet potatoes alongside the chicken until tender when pierced, about 1 hour. Remove the roasting pan from the oven and let everything cool.

1 tablespoon chopped fresh thyme;
   or 1 teaspoon dried

2 tablespoons chopped fresh parsley

$1/2$ cup cored and diced red bell pepper

Salt and freshly ground black pepper

About 1 cup mayonnaise, homemade or
   bottled

Prepare the salad: Remove and discard the skin from the cooled chicken. Pull the meat from the bone and cut into bite-size pieces. Reserve the jerk sauce in the roasting pan.

Prepare the breadfruit: Peel off the skin, core the fruit, and dice. The sweet potatoes should be peeled and diced.

In a large bowl, combine the chicken, breadfruit or sweet potatoes, and remaining ingredients, gently folding in about $1/2$ cup of the mayonnaise and adding more as needed to moisten the salad. Add 3 to 5 tablespoons of the defatted jerk sauce from the bottom of the roasting pan. Refrigerate until ready to serve; the salad tastes even better the next day.

Makes 4 to 6 servings

Note: *Jerk sauce is available in specialty food shops and Caribbean markets.*

Poultry Safety

With all the things you have to worry about in the world, the last thing you want to think about is salmonella and poultry bacteria. But there are a few basic safety tips to consider when dealing with raw poultry to avoid these hazards:

- Never leave raw poultry out of the refrigerator for long periods of time. To play it safe, never leave poultry unrefrigerated for more than 15 minutes.

- Always defrost frozen poultry *in the refrigerator* rather than letting it sit on the kitchen counter to thaw.

- When dealing with raw poultry, always wash your hands and your work surface and utensils with soapy hot water.

- Always wash a raw bird, inside and outside, and dry thoroughly before roasting.

- To prevent bacteria, never stuff a bird ahead of time. Stuff the bird *just before you're ready to roast*.

Buttermilk Chicken

My aim with this dish was to make fried chicken without frying. This is definitely not fried chicken, but whatever it is, it's damn good. The chicken is cut into pieces and marinated in buttermilk for 4 to 48 hours. Then it is coated in a homemade breadcrumb mixture and roasted until crisp and golden brown—very close to fried chicken but without any of the oil or heaviness.

The texture of the chicken will astonish you. The acidity of the buttermilk acts as a tenderizer for the chicken and produces outrageously tender meat. Serve the chicken hot, at room temperature, or cold, with lemon wedges, coleslaw, and warm biscuits or Spider Corn Cake (see recipe on page 247). This is ideal picnic food.

One 3^1/$_2$-pound chicken, cut into 8 pieces

1^1/$_2$ cups buttermilk

1 teaspoon vegetable oil

3 cups coarse fresh breadcrumbs (see Note), about ^{3}/$_4$ loaf dried-out baguette with crust

Salt and freshly ground black pepper

3 tablespoons chopped fresh rosemary; or 1 tablespoon dried

^{1}/$_2$ cup chopped fresh chives or parsley

1 lemon, cut into 4 to 8 wedges

Place the chicken in a large bowl. Pour the buttermilk on top and coat on all sides. Cover and refrigerate for 4 to 48 hours, turning the chicken over after a few hours.

Preheat the oven to 400 degrees. Grease the bottom of a large shallow roasting pan or ovenproof skillet with the oil.

On a large plate, mix the breadcrumbs, salt, pepper, rosemary, and chives together. Remove the chicken from the buttermilk, letting some of the milk cling to the skin. Discard the buttermilk. Dredge each piece of chicken in the breadcrumb mixture, patting the breadcrumbs on to make sure they adhere to all sides. Place the coated chicken in the prepared roasting pan.

Roast the chicken until it is tender and the juices run clear yellow and not pink when one of the pieces is pierced, about 45 minutes. If you want the chicken to have a firmer crust, place it under the broiler until golden brown, 3 to 5 minutes. Serve hot, at room temperature, or cold, surrounded by the lemon wedges.

Makes 4 servings

> Note: *Place dried-out bread in a food processor and process until broken down into large crumbs.*

Roast Chicken with Linguica Sausage and Tomato Sauce

Fans of chicken cacciatore will love the rich flavors of this sauce. The chicken is roasted with chunks of linguica (a slightly spicy Portuguese sausage), chopped garlic, and parsley and then smothered in a rich tomato sauce laced with black olives and capers. Serve the chicken with a bowl of cooked linguine tossed with a touch of olive oil, salt, and pepper. The pasta is excellent mixed into the tomato sauce from the chicken.

One 3- to 4-pound chicken

4 cloves garlic, peeled and chopped

1 cup finely chopped fresh parsley

$^1/_2$ pound linguica or Italian sausage, cut into thick slices

$^3/_4$ cup dry red or white wine

Freshly ground black pepper

Sweet Hungarian paprika

1 cup tomato sauce, homemade or canned

1 cup good-quality black olives, pitted (optional)

$1^1/_2$ tablespoons capers, drained (optional)

Preheat the oven to 400 degrees.

Place the chicken, breast-side up, in a large flameproof roasting pan. Place half of the garlic and half of the parsley in the cavity of the chicken. Surround the chicken with the sausage and the remaining garlic and parsley. Pour the wine around the chicken. Sprinkle with pepper and paprika.

Roast the chicken and sausage for 30 minutes. Reduce the oven temperature to 350 degrees. Pour the tomato sauce on top of the chicken and baste it well with the juices in the bottom of the pan. Roast another 30 minutes, basting every 10 minutes. Add the olives and capers and taste the sauce for seasoning. Continue roasting the chicken until the juices run clear yellow and not pink when an inner thigh is pierced, about 5 to 10 minutes longer.

Remove the roasting pan from the oven. Place the chicken on a carving board and let sit, loosely covered with aluminum foil, for 10 to 15 minutes. Place the sausage in a bowl and cover loosely to keep warm.

Discard any excess fat from the roasting pan and bring the juices to a simmer over moderate heat. Simmer for 5 minutes and season to taste. Carve the chicken into serving pieces and serve topped with the sausage and plenty of sauce.

Makes 4 servings

Is It a Sauce, *Jus*, or Gravy?

The words sauce, *jus*, and gravy seem to appear interchangeably in many cookbooks, which has caused a great deal of confusion over what the differences actually are. These cooking terms overlap somewhat, but they each have a distinct definition.

A sauce can be made from meat or poultry juices mixed with any number of other ingredients. There is usually stock or broth added as well. The main distinction between a sauce and a gravy is that sauces are frequently made in a separate pan, whereas gravies are generally made directly in the roasting pan.

According to *Cordon Bleu Basic Cookery Methods*, "The basis of gravy is, of course, the meat's sediments and juices left in the roasting tin." Others claim that a gravy is a type of sauce, usually flour-based, that is made directly in the roasting pan. Gravies are made by removing the roast from the pan, along with any excess fat. The pan juices are heated up on top of the stove, and often a sprinkling of flour is added. Water, wine, stock or broth, and herbs and seasonings are then added, and the gravy is simmered until thickened and flavorful.

According to *Larousse Gastronomique,* the French word *jus* "is roughly equivalent to 'juice,' but has more specific meanings in French cookery than the English word. It is used primarily for the gravy of a roast." The word *jus* brings to mind the wonderful brown juice left in the bottom of a roasting pan after you've removed the roast. It is the natural juices of a roast, the very essence of its flavor. *Au jus* generally refers to meat, most often roast beef, that is simply served with its natural, unadorned juices.

Roast Chicken, Sweet Potato, and Vegetable Stew

It was a cool October night, one of the first frosts of the season, and I wanted something warm and hearty. Because stews are generally full of butter or oil and flour, I decided to experiment with a flavorful fat-free version.

The beauty of "roasting" a stew—that is, roasting the solid ingredients rather than browning them in fat on the stove top—is that you get the same depth of flavor without adding any butter or oil.

This stew combines roast chicken, sweet potatoes, carrots, onions, celery, and peppers in a flavorful brown stock with absolutely no added fat. You can "roast" the stew using a whole or cut-up chicken. Serve it with Spider Corn Cake (page 247) or biscuits.

One 3- to 4-pound chicken, whole or cut into serving pieces

5 large carrots, peeled and cut into 3-inch pieces

5 large ribs celery, trimmed and cut into 3-inch pieces

5 medium-size onions, peeled and cut into quarters; or 10 small white boiling onions, peeled and left whole

4 cloves garlic, peeled and left whole

2 large sweet potatoes, cut into fairly large chunks

1 tablespoon chopped fresh thyme; or 1 teaspoon dried

Salt and freshly ground black pepper

1¼ cups water

2 cups homemade chicken stock or low-sodium canned chicken broth

2 tablespoons all-purpose flour (optional)

2 bay leaves

6 black peppercorns

1 large green bell pepper, cored and cut into strips

6 medium-size ripe tomatoes, cored and cut into quarters; or 1 cup canned whole tomatoes cut in half

½ cup chopped fresh parsley

Preheat the oven to 400 degrees.

In a large flameproof roasting pan, surround the chicken with the carrots, celery, onions, garlic, and sweet potatoes. Sprinkle everything with the thyme, salt, and pepper and pour ¼ cup of the water over the chicken. Roast the chicken and vegetables for 45 minutes.

Meanwhile, in a small saucepan, heat the remaining cup of water and the stock or broth over moderate heat until simmering.

Remove the roasting pan from the oven. Discard any excess fat from the pan. Stir the flour into any juices that may have accumulated in the pan. If there are no juices, simply stir the flour gently into the vegetables. (The flour will thicken the stew slightly but is not necessary for a delicious-tasting sauce.) Pour the hot stock or broth and water over the vegetables, scraping up any browned juices, and whisk to create a smooth sauce. Add the bay leaves, peppercorns, bell pepper, and tomatoes and season with salt and pepper.

Place the stew back in the oven and continue roasting until the juices run yellow and not pink when the inside of a thigh is pierced and the potatoes are tender, about 15 minutes. Sprinkle with the parsley and serve very hot.

Makes 4 servings

Tarragon Chicken and Potato Salad

Ideally, this salad is made with Tarragon Chicken with Roast Pears and Potatoes (page 84), but it can be made using any leftover roast chicken and potatoes. Serve with a loaf of French bread.

2 tablespoons Dijon mustard

1 clove garlic, finely chopped

Salt and freshly ground black pepper

3 tablespoons raspberry vinegar or another fruit vinegar

6 tablespoons fruity olive oil

1 tablespoon chopped fresh tarragon; or 1/2 teaspoon dried

2 cups mixed salad greens, thoroughly washed and dried

2 cups skinned and thinly sliced leftover roast chicken

1 cup peeled and chopped leftover roast potatoes

1 large carrot, peeled and cut into thin strips

Make the vinaigrette: In a small bowl, mix the mustard, garlic, salt, and pepper to make a paste. Slowly whisk in the vinegar and then the oil. Add half of the tarragon and taste for seasoning.

Arrange the greens on a large platter. Place the chicken in the center, the potatoes around it, and the carrot strips on the outside of the plate. Pour the vinaigrette on top and sprinkle with the remaining tarragon.

Makes 2 to 4 servings

Roast Chicken Salad with Blue Cheese and Roasted Jalapeño Vinaigrette

Leftover roast chicken makes frequent appearances in my refrigerator. This is an unusual salad, combining roast chicken with mixed salad greens and crumbled blue cheese and then tossing it all with a vinaigrette spiked with the smoky, spicy flavor of roasted jalapeño peppers.

The Salad:

2 cups mixed salad greens, thoroughly washed and dried

1 cup thinly sliced leftover roast chicken

$1/2$ cup crumbled Roquefort or other blue cheese

1 cup croutons, homemade (see Note) or packaged

The Vinaigrette:

About 1 teaspoon roasted jalapeño pepper puree (see page 154)

3 tablespoons red wine vinegar or balsamic vinegar

Salt

5 tablespoons good-quality olive oil

Place the greens on a large serving platter and arrange the chicken on top. Scatter the cheese over the greens and poultry and sprinkle the croutons over the salad.

In a small bowl, mix the roasted chile pepper puree with the vinegar and a touch of salt. Whisk in the oil and taste for seasoning. The vinaigrette should have a real punch; add more chile puree if necessary.

Drizzle the vinaigrette over the salad and serve at room temperature.

Makes 2 to 4 servings

> Note: *If you're making your own croutons, make them on the large size, about 1 inch by 1 inch.*

Roast Cornish Hens with a Hoisin-Ginger Glaze and Chinese-Style Rice Stuffing

Cornish hens are small, generally weighing between 1 and 2 pounds, ideal for a family meal or a special occasion. Although this recipe involves several steps, it's really quite simple to make and with some organization can be put together in very little time.

The birds are stuffed with a delicious crunchy stuffing—rice, scallions, water chestnuts, walnuts, and ginger—and the outside of the hen is brushed with a glaze made from hoisin sauce, fresh orange juice, and fresh ginger. The combination of Asian flavors works beautifully with the delicate taste of the hen. As an accompaniment, serve a steamed or stir-fried green vegetable (green beans are particularly good with this) and a big salad.

The Stuffing:

1 cup raw white rice

2 cups cold water

Salt

1 cup trimmed and thinly sliced scallions

1 cup chopped walnuts

1 cup thinly sliced water chestnuts, fresh (see Note) or canned

1½ tablespoons peeled and grated or finely chopped ginger

Preheat the oven to 400 degrees.

Prepare the stuffing: In a small saucepan, mix the rice with the water and a touch of salt and bring to a boil over high heat. Reduce the heat to low, cover, and let simmer until the rice has absorbed all the liquid, about 20 minutes. Remove the pan from the heat, let cool slightly, and place the cooked rice in a large bowl, breaking up any clumps. Mix with the remaining stuffing ingredients and taste for seasoning. You want the stuffing to be highly seasoned; the flavors will dissipate slightly when roasted inside the hens.

Prepare the glaze: In a small bowl, mix the hoisin, orange juice, soy sauce, ginger, and ½ tablespoon of the orange zest. (The recipe can be made several hours ahead up to this point. Cover the stuffing and the glaze and refrigerate until needed.)

2 tablespoons low-sodium soy sauce

2 tablespoons hoisin sauce (see Note)

2 tablespoons orange juice, fresh-squeezed or "old-fashioned" type with pulp

¼ cup raisins (optional)

½ cup cored and chopped red bell pepper

¼ teaspoon hot pepper sauce or Chinese chile paste (see Note), or to taste

The Glaze:

3 tablespoons hoisin sauce

3 tablespoons orange juice, fresh-squeezed or "old-fashioned" type with pulp

1 teaspoon low-sodium soy sauce

1½ teaspoons peeled and grated or finely chopped ginger

1½ tablespoons grated orange zest

The Hens:

Four 1½- to 1¾-pound Cornish hens, totally thawed if frozen

Salt and freshly ground black pepper

½ cup dry sherry, Madeira, rice wine (see Note), or dry white wine

Prepare the hens: Season the cavity of each hen with salt and pepper and a sprinkling of the remaining orange zest. Stuff the hens, using enough stuffing to fill the cavity without overflowing. (Place any remaining stuffing inside a lightly greased casserole and roast in the oven until heated through, 15 to 20 minutes.) Using kitchen string, truss the hens to prevent the stuffing from spilling out. Place the hens in a medium-size flameproof roasting pan; you can place them on a small roasting rack if you choose. Brush the entire skin of the hens with some of the glaze and pour ¼ cup of the sherry, Madeira, or rice wine around the hens.

Roast the hens for 30 minutes. Baste them with the remaining glaze and add the remaining ¼ cup of sherry. Continue roasting, adding ¼ cup water if the pan begins to dry out, until the hens are tender and the juices run clear yellow and not pink. The hens should be a dark mahogany color.

Remove the roasting pan from the oven. Place the hens on a carving board and let sit, loosely covered with aluminum foil, for 5 to 10 minutes.

Discard any excess fat from the roasting pan and bring the juices to a simmer over moderate heat. Simmer for 5 minutes and season to taste. Discard the kitchen string. Serve the hens split in half or whole. Spoon the pan juices on top.

Makes 4 servings

Note: *Fresh water chestnuts, rice wine, hoisin sauce, and Chinese chile paste are available in Asian markets and some gourmet food shops.*

Thanksgiving Turkey with Sun-Dried Cherry and Pecan Stuffing

As far as I'm concerned, it is not possible to have too much turkey. A fresh, naturally raised turkey is one of the finest roasting birds around. The recipe that follows is for a large turkey—about 18 to 25 pounds—and makes enough stuffing to amply fill the turkey, as well as fill a good-size casserole. An unbelievably rich gravy is made directly in the pan by simply diluting the turkey essence that forms while the bird is roasting with a homemade stock made from the turkey parts.

The accompaniments to a traditional holiday turkey are different for every family. In our house they usually include at least one type of cranberry sauce or relish, creamed spinach, sweet potatoes, mashed potatoes with gravy, Brussels sprouts or string beans with slivered almonds, and a watercress, red onion, and Mandarin orange salad. But you could serve this bird with just about anything and it would still be wonderful.

The Stuffing:
About 12 cups dried assorted bread chunks

1 tablespoon olive oil

8 tablespoons (1 stick) butter

6 medium-size onions, peeled and chopped

2 shallots, peeled and chopped

8 to 10 cloves garlic, peeled and chopped

2 tablespoons chopped fresh thyme;
 or ¹/₂ tablespoon dried

1 large bunch celery, trimmed and chopped

2 cups chopped pecans

Preheat the oven to 450 degrees.

Meanwhile, prepare the stuffing: Place the bread in a large bowl. In a large skillet, heat the oil and 1 tablespoon of the butter over moderate heat. Add the onions and shallots and cook, stirring constantly, until soft, about 5 minutes. Stir in the garlic, thyme, celery, and remaining butter and cook until the celery just begins to soften, 3 to 5 minutes. Remove the skillet from the heat and stir in the nuts, parsley, sun-dried cherries or cranberries, basil, and rosemary. Stir this mixture into the bread. Add the milk to the skillet and heat over moderate heat, scraping up any bits clinging to the bottom of the pan. Pour the warm milk over the stuffing in the bowl and stir well to moisten all the ingredients. Taste for seasoning and add salt and pepper as needed. The stuffing should be moist and very flavorful.

1 cup chopped fresh parsley

1 cup sun-dried cherries or cranberries
(see Note)

3 tablespoons chopped fresh basil;
or 2 teaspoons dried

3 tablespoons chopped fresh rosemary;
or 2 teaspoons dried

1 cup milk

Salt and freshly ground black pepper

The Turkey:
1 tablespoon vegetable oil

One 18- to 25-pound fresh turkey

3 tablespoons butter

10 cloves garlic, peeled and left whole

2 tablespoons chopped fresh thyme;
or $1/2$ tablespoon dried

Salt and freshly ground black pepper

Sweet Hungarian paprika

Grease the bottom of a large flameproof roasting pan with the oil. Loosely stuff both the body and neck cavities of the turkey with the stuffing and close both ends with trussing needles, poultry lacers, and/or kitchen string. Place the turkey, breast-side up, in the roasting pan. Place the remaining stuffing in a large well-greased ovenproof casserole with a cover.

In the large skillet in which you prepared the stuffing, melt the 3 tablespoons butter over moderate heat. Add the garlic cloves and season with the thyme, salt, and pepper. Pour the butter and garlic over the turkey, and sprinkle the top of the bird liberally with pepper and paprika.

Roast the turkey until golden brown, 20 to 30 minutes. Reduce the oven temperature to 325 degrees and place a very loose aluminum foil "tent" over the turkey. Roast about 12 to 20 minutes per pound, depending on how fresh the turkey is—the fresher the bird, the faster it will cook— basting the bird every 20 minutes or so. The turkey is done when the juices run clear and not pink when the inside of a thigh is pierced and the internal temperature reaches 180 degrees.

Place the remaining stuffing in the oven 30 minutes before the turkey will be done, adding a few tablespoons of pan juices from the roasting pan.

While the turkey is roasting, prepare a turkey stock for the gravy: Place the neck, heart, and gizzard from the turkey in a large saucepan. Cover with cold water and add the parsley, onions, 1 tablespoon of the thyme, the peppercorns, the celery, and a generous pinch of salt. Bring to a boil over high heat, then reduce the heat to low and let simmer, partially covered, until flavorful, about 2 hours. (The liver should be saved for another dish or for the pâté on page 118.)

Remove the roasting pan from the oven. Place the turkey on a carving board and cover loosely with aluminum foil. Let rest for about 15 to 20 minutes before carving. Spoon the stuffing and place in a bowl, loosely covered with foil to keep warm.

The Stock (see Note) and Gravy:

1 turkey neck

1 turkey heart

1 turkey gizzard

1/2 cup coarsely chopped fresh parsley

2 large onions, peeled and cut into quarters

3 tablespoons chopped fresh thyme; or 1 tablespoon dried

6 black peppercorns

2 large ribs celery, trimmed and chopped

Salt and freshly ground black pepper

2 to 3 tablespoons all-purpose flour

Meanwhile, finish the gravy: Strain the turkey stock and set aside. Discard the excess fat from the roasting pan. Place the pan over two burners. Bring to a simmer over moderate heat, scraping up any bits and pieces that are clinging to the bottom of the pan. Sprinkle in about 2 tablespoons of the flour and the remaining thyme and mix with the pan juices. Cook for about 1 minute. Slowly whisk in 1 cup of the strained turkey stock (or 1 cup homemade chicken stock or canned low-sodium chicken broth) and bring it to a boil. Slowly add another 1/2 cup of stock, whisking to create a smooth, slightly thick gravy. If the gravy is too thick, add more stock or water to thin it. Taste for seasoning.

Carve the turkey. Pour any juices released from the turkey into the gravy. Serve warm with hot gravy and stuffing.

Makes 10 to 12 servings with leftovers

> **Note:** *Sun-dried cherries and cranberries are available in gourmet food shops.*
> *If you don't want to bother with a homemade stock, you can simply substitute 1 cup low-sodium canned chicken broth.*

Apricot, Walnut, and Bread–Stuffed Roast Turkey with Whole Roasted Garlic and Potatoes

Don't wait until Thanksgiving to try this recipe. Make half or a quarter of the stuffing and try it in a large chicken, capon, or several Cornish hens. (A capon is a 10-week-old cock that was castrated when young. They are generally 7 to 10 pounds and quite tender.)

This recipe makes enough stuffing to generously fill the cavity and neck of a 16-pound turkey, as well as a small casserole dish.

The Stuffing:

2 large loaves bread (see Note), broken into small pieces, about 12 cups

3 tablespoons butter

3 tablespoons olive oil

3 large onions, peeled and chopped

1/2 head garlic, peeled and chopped

12 large ribs celery, trimmed and chopped

1 bunch scallions, trimmed and chopped

1/4 cup chopped fresh thyme; or 2 tablespoons dried

1 cup chopped fresh parsley

1 cup walnut halves, chopped

1 cup dried apricots, chopped

Salt and freshly ground black pepper

About 1/2 cup milk

The Turkey, Garlic, and Potatoes:

1 tablespoon mild vegetable or olive oil

One 16-pound turkey, totally thawed if frozen

5 tablespoons butter

12 cloves garlic, peeled and left whole

Salt and freshly ground black pepper

Sweet Hungarian paprika

1 cup chopped fresh chives (optional)

2 whole heads garlic, unpeeled

About 30 small new potatoes, scrubbed

Preheat the oven to 450 degrees.

Prepare the stuffing: Place the bread in a large bowl. In a large skillet, melt the butter and the oil over moderate heat. Add the onions and cook, stirring, until soft, about 5 minutes. Add the garlic, celery, scallions, thyme, and half of the parsley and cook until soft, about 5 minutes longer. Add the walnuts, apricots, and a hefty sprinkle of salt and pepper. The mixture should be cooked through but not soft and limp. Add this mixture to the bowl with the bread and mix well. Add the remaining parsley and additional salt and pepper. Pour 1/2 cup milk into the empty skillet and heat for 1 minute, scraping up any bits clinging to the bottom. Pour the warm milk over the stuffing and mix well. The stuffing should be somewhat moist; add more milk (or water) if needed. Do not make the stuffing more than 1 hour ahead of time and *never* stuff the turkey more than 30 minutes before roasting.

Grease the bottom of a large flameproof roasting pan with the oil. Using your hands, generously stuff the cavity of the turkey, pressing down firmly to get as much stuffing in as possible without letting it overflow. Stuff the neck cavity, being careful not to overstuff it. Sew the openings with a trussing needle and string or poultry lacers, or close with wooden skewers. Place the turkey in the roasting pan, breast-side up. Pack any remaining stuffing into a small or medium-size lightly greased casserole and set aside.

In the same skillet used to cook the stuffing, melt the butter over moderate heat. Add the cloves of garlic and cook, stirring, for 1 minute. Pour the melted butter and garlic over the turkey. Sprinkle the skin with salt, pepper, and a generous pinch of paprika. Sprinkle the chives over the turkey.

Roast the turkey for 15 minutes. Reduce the oven temperature to 325 degrees and baste the turkey. Cover the turkey very loosely with aluminum foil, creating a kind of tent. Continue roasting the turkey, basting it every 20 minutes or so, for 15 to 20 minutes per pound. (Farm-raised fresh turkeys roast much faster than grocery store brands, so generally a fresh turkey needs only 15 minutes per pound.) The turkey is done when the juices run clear and not pink when an inner thigh is pierced.

About 1 hour 15 minutes before the turkey is done, add the 2 heads of garlic and the potatoes to the pan and baste well.

During the last 20 to 30 minutes of roasting time, add the casserole of extra stuffing to the oven and bake until heated through.

While the turkey is roasting, prepare a turkey stock for the gravy: Place all the ingredients for the gravy except the flour and ground pepper in a medium-size saucepan and bring to a boil over high heat. Reduce the heat to low and simmer until the stock is flavorful, about 2 hours. Season to taste.

Remove the roasting pan from the oven and place the turkey on a carving board. Let sit, loosely covered with aluminum foil, for 15 to 20 minutes. Place the whole garlic, potatoes, and loose garlic cloves in a bowl, loosely covered with foil to keep warm.

Meanwhile, finish the gravy: Using a large spoon or a gravy or grease separator, discard all but a few tablespoons of the fat. Place the roasting pan over two burners. Bring to a simmer over moderate heat, scraping up any bits and pieces clinging to the bottom of the pan. Whisk in 2 tablespoons of flour. Cook for about 2 minutes and then slowly strain in about 4 cups of the turkey stock you've been cooking. Whisk to prevent lumps. Bring to a simmer and add salt and pepper to season.

Scoop the stuffing out of the turkey and place in a warm bowl. Carve the turkey and serve with the hot gravy, roasted garlic, and potatoes. Pass the additional stuffing separately.

Makes 10 servings

The Stock (see Note) and Gravy:

1 turkey neck

1 turkey gizzard

1 turkey heart

About 8 cups cold water

2 small onions, peeled and cut into quarters

2 large ribs celery, trimmed and chopped

1/4 cup chopped fresh parsley

1 bay leaf

5 black peppercorns

Salt

4 sprigs fresh thyme; or 1 teaspoon dried

About 2 tablespoons all-purpose flour

Freshly ground black pepper

Note: *You can use any type of bread you like for this stuffing or, even better, a mixture of several types of bread. Ideally, you will start collecting scraps of bread a few days before making the turkey and let them dry out in a large bowl. If you buy bread specifically for the stuffing, break it apart in small pieces and let it dry out overnight before proceeding.*

If you don't want to bother with a homemade stock, you can simply substitute 1 cup low-sodium canned chicken broth.

Roast Turkey Legs with Onions and Cinzano

Around Thanksgiving, when fresh-killed turkeys appear in just about every butcher shop in town, you might want to think about buying an extra bird and either freezing it whole or having the butcher cut it into small serving pieces and then freezing them so you can enjoy turkey throughout the year.

These turkey legs are superb roasted with small white boiling onions and a splash of Cinzano, or sweet vermouth. You can substitute red wine mixed with 2 tablespoons honey to duplicate the sweet, intense flavor of Cinzano. You can also use 1 pound of chicken legs, instead of the turkey.

2 turkey legs, totally thawed if frozen

10 small white boiling onions, peeled and left whole, or 4 medium-size onions, peeled and cut in half

8 cloves garlic, peeled and left whole

1 cup Cinzano

Salt and freshly ground black pepper

1 tablespoon chopped fresh thyme; or 1 teaspoon dried

Preheat the oven to 400 degrees.

Place the turkey legs in a medium-size roasting pan. Surround them with the onions and garlic and pour the Cinzano on top. Season well with salt, pepper, and thyme.

Roast the turkey and vegetables, basting occasionally and stirring the onions and garlic once so they brown evenly, until the drumsticks feel tender when pressed and the internal temperature reaches 165 degrees, about 1 hour.

Makes 2 to 4 servings

Sitting Makes a Juicy Roast

The reason so many recipes call for roasted meats and poultry to "sit" or "rest" once they have been removed from the oven is that this process allows the juices to redistribute themselves throughout the interior of the meat. If you carve a roast too soon, the juices will ooze out of the roast, causing the meat to dry out. This "sitting time" also makes the meat easier to carve. Always let meat and poultry stand for about 15 minutes, loosely covered with aluminum foil to keep it warm, before carving while you finish off the gravy or any other dishes.

How to Carve Poultry

These carving instructions are for right-handed carvers. Lefties should simply reverse the following instructions.

1. Place the bird on a carving board or platter to rest.
2. Place the bird with the legs facing toward you.
3. Place the fork in your left hand and insert it firmly into the thigh, between the leg and the body.
4. With the knife in your right hand, cut down to separate the thigh from the body, slicing through the joint.

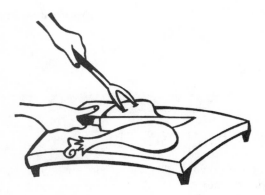

5. To separate the drumstick from the thigh, lay the drumstick and thigh flat on the carving board and, using some force, cut through the knee joint that connects them. Place on a serving platter. Repeat with the other leg. (For larger birds, such as turkey, you can then carve the meat from the thigh and the drumstick into thin slices.)

6. To remove the wings, turn the bird with the wings toward you. Insert the fork in the breast of the bird and cut off the wings where they join the body, cutting through the joint that connects them to the body.

7. To carve the breast, slice thinly, starting from the top of the bird and working your way down at a 45-degree angle.

Beach Plum Inn's Roasted Duck with Honey-Curry Sauce

Perched high on a bluff overlooking the fishing village of Menemsha on the island of Martha's Vineyard lies the Beach Plum Inn. There are few spots on earth quite so spectacular, where the flowers grow in abundance and the food comes from nearby waters, gardens, and farms. Owners Paul and Janie Darrow sent me this recipe for duck, and it's become an instant favorite.

Cubes of fresh lemon, lime, and orange are stuffed into the bird's cavity and permeate the flesh throughout. The duck is roasted with a soy sauce, vinegar, and honey glaze. Once the duck is golden brown, a simple sauce is made by retrieving the citrus juices from the duck's cavity and mixing them with white wine, honey, orange juice, and curry powder.

If you've been turned off in the past by duck's fattiness, here's is a technique you should know about. The duck is roasted at high heat and the skin is pricked throughout the cooking time to release as much fat as possible. You can easily cut this recipe in half if you want to roast only one duck, but it makes for some great leftovers.

Two 4-pound ducks, completely thawed if frozen

1/2 cup peeled and chopped onion

1/2 cup trimmed and chopped celery

2/3 cup low-sodium soy sauce

3 teaspoons sugar

1/3 cup dry sherry

1 orange, scrubbed and cut into small pieces

1 lemon, scrubbed and cut into small pieces

Preheat the oven to 475 degrees.

Using a small skewer or a trussing needle and thread, close up the opening at the duck's neck.

In a medium-size pan, combine the onion, celery, half of the soy sauce, the sugar, and sherry. Bring to a boil over high heat and continue cooking until somewhat thickened, about 3 minutes.

Stuff half of the pieces of orange, lemon, and lime into the cavity of each duck. Pour half of the soy mixture into each cavity and close the openings with wooden skewers or sew them with a trussing needle and kitchen string. Pat the outside of the ducks well with paper towels and then rub the skin with the salt. Place the ducks, breast-side up, on a rack in a large flameproof roasting pan.

Roast the ducks, pricking the skin from time to time with a fork, for 30 minutes. Remove the roasting pan from

1 lime, scrubbed and cut into small pieces

1 tablespoon salt

1$\frac{1}{3}$ cups orange-blossom honey

3 tablespoons red wine vinegar

1 cup dry white wine

1 cup orange juice, fresh-squeezed or
"old-fashioned" type with pulp

3 tablespoons curry powder

Parsley or watercress

the oven and discard the fat. Combine the remaining soy sauce with $\frac{1}{3}$ cup of the honey and the vinegar in a small bowl. Brush this honey mixture over the ducks and reserve the rest for later.

Reduce the oven temperature to 325 degrees and continue roasting the ducks, brushing them with the honey mixture every 30 minutes, until the juices run clear yellow and not pink when an inner thigh is pierced, about 15 minutes per pound or a total cooking time of about 2 hours.

Remove the roasting pan from the oven. Place the ducks on a carving board and let sit, loosely covered with aluminum foil, for about 10 minutes.

Discard all the fat and any burned particles from the roasting pan. Add the wine to the pan and bring to a boil, scraping up any browned juices. Using a large spoon, remove the filling and any juices from the cavities of the ducks and add them to the pan.

Prepare the honey-curry sauce: Strain the juices in the roasting pan into a medium-size saucepan. Add the remaining 1 cup of honey, the orange juice, and curry powder and simmer over moderate heat until thickened and flavorful, 5 to 8 minutes. Strain sauce through cheesecloth into a small bowl or a sauceboat; it should be the consistency of maple syrup.

Cut the ducks into serving pieces and arrange them on a warm platter. Serve the duck with the warm honey-curry sauce and garnish with parsley or watercress.

Makes 6 servings

Roast Duck with Ginger-Mango Sauce

This dish combines some of my favorite flavors—pungent ginger, soy sauce, fresh mango, and the rich, meaty essence of duck. I was inspired to mix mango and duck when our good friends Bob and Becky Schultze brought me a basket of fresh mangoes from their own orchard in south Florida. I had never tasted mangoes so sweet and juicy. They seemed the perfect foil for the rich flavor of duck.

You could make this recipe without the mangoes, substituting apples, pears, cherries, or oranges. But if you have a market—or a friend—who can provide you with fresh mangoes, by all means go out of your way to find them.

One 5- to 6-pound duck, totally thawed if frozen

Salt and freshly ground black pepper

4 thin slivers ginger, peeled

¹/₄ cup fresh thyme sprigs; or 2 tablespoons dried

1 cup low-sodium soy sauce

3 tablespoons chopped ginger

Preheat the oven to 400 degrees.

Using a sharp knife, prick the duck skin in several places. (This will allow the fat to be released during roasting.) Place the duck, breast-side up, on a roasting rack set in a large roasting pan. Add about 1 cup water to the bottom of the pan to keep the fat from burning. Season the inside of the cavity with salt, pepper, the slivers of ginger, and half of the thyme.

Mix the soy sauce and chopped ginger in a small bowl. Using a pastry brush, brush some of the soy-ginger mixture all over the surface of the duck. Sprinkle with pepper and the remaining thyme.

Roast the duck for 15 minutes. Reduce the oven temperature to 325 degrees. Turn the duck over (breast-side down), baste it with the soy-ginger mixture, and continue roasting another 45 minutes. Turn the duck breast-side up again, baste, and continue roasting another 35 minutes.

At this point the duck will have roasted for 1 hour 35 minutes. Remove the roasting pan from the oven and place the duck on a carving board.

Remove the roasting rack and set aside. Discard any excess fat from the roasting pan. Place the duck back into the roasting pan (without the rack) and pour the sherry and any remaining soy-ginger mixture on top. Arrange the mangoes on and around the duck and roast until the juices run clear yellow and not pink when the inner thigh is pierced, 15 to 20 more minutes.

3 tablespoons dry sherry

4 ripe mangoes, seeded, peeled, and thinly sliced or chopped (be careful to save all the juices while chopping)

Remove the roasting pan from the oven. Tip the duck over the pan to catch any juices from the cavity and place the duck on a carving board. Let sit, loosely covered with aluminum foil, for 10 to 15 minutes.

Discard any excess fat from the roasting pan. Scrape up the juices in the pan and pour them and the mangoes into a small serving bowl or gravy boat. Carve the duck into serving pieces and top with the warm pan juices and mango.

Makes 4 servings

High Heat–Low Heat: The Searing Question

Many of the roasting recipes found throughout this book begin with a blast of high heat to seal in the ingredients' natural juices and provide a brown or golden "crust." The temperature is then reduced to prevent burning and provide a perfectly cooked roast.

I have found that everything from roast beef, chicken, and duck to roast pork and fish benefits from this high-temperature searing technique. The reason I enjoy this technique so much may be that, in general, I prefer roasted foods that have a golden, crisp skin on the outside and meat that is relatively rare inside. I have also found that when you roast poultry at high heat, the bird's skin creates a natural seal that results in a juicier bird. I experimented by roasting chicken at a low, even temperature (300 degrees for well over an hour), and the bird was far less flavorful. But there is some controversy over high-temperature searing.

Harold McGee, author of *The Curious Cook*, says that searing meat to seal in the juices is nothing more than a cooking "myth." He claims that "juices seep and evaporate from the meat throughout cooking . . . the juiciness of meat is determined by the doneness to which the meat is cooked: the rarer the juicier." Even though McGee doesn't believe that searing seals in juices, he claims it is a "useful" technique. "A very hot pan will begin cooking the meat right away and will intensify the meat's flavor by browning the juices that flow from it," he writes. "Because juiciness is determined almost entirely by the meat's doneness, there's no point in worrying about it. Just cook meat to your taste. The juices will take care of themselves."

Ultimately, I don't think you can go wrong following this technique. Who can argue against the golden-brown crisp skin of a turkey, or a roast pork or duck with a crackling-crisp crust and succulent, juicy pieces of meat within?

Roast Duck with Honey-Tangerine Sauce

It was one of the coldest days of the year—minus five without the wind-chill factor—and our local butcher had just received a shipment of fresh ducks. I went home, lit a fire, and marinated the duck in honey, grated ginger, balsamic vinegar, and a touch of orange juice, and then roasted it until crisp. I then simmered the marinade down with some stock until intensely flavored and mixed in tiny sections of winter tangerines. A bottle of Beaujolais Nouveau and some roast potatoes sure made that evening feel a whole lot warmer.

The Marinade:

1 cup flower-scented honey

One 2-inch piece ginger, peeled and grated (2 tablespoons)

2 tablespoons balsamic vinegar

1 tablespoon low-sodium soy sauce

1½ tablespoons orange juice, fresh-squeezed or "old-fashioned" type with pulp

1½ tablespoons chopped fresh thyme; or 1 teaspoon dried

Freshly ground black pepper

The Duck:

One 4- to 6-pound duck, totally thawed if frozen

1 cup water

3 small tangerines, peeled and separated into sections

In a medium-size bowl, whisk together all the marinade ingredients.

Using a fork, prick the duck in several places all over the breast and thighs. Place the duck in a medium-size roasting pan and pour the marinade on top of the bird and inside the cavity. Let marinate in the refrigerator, basting every few hours, at least 1 hour or up to 24 hours.

Preheat the oven to 400 degrees.

Make the stock: Place the duck neck and heart in a medium-size saucepan. Add the carrot, celery, onion, bay leaf, peppercorns, and salt and cover with water. Bring to a boil over high heat, reduce the heat to low, and simmer until the broth is well flavored, 1 to 2 hours.

Drain the duck from the marinade, reserving the marinade, and place the duck, breast-side up, on a rack in a large flameproof roasting pan. Pour the water into the bottom of the pan to prevent the fat from spattering during roasting. Baste the duck with some of the marinade.

Roast the duck for 15 minutes. Reduce the oven temperature to 325 degrees, turn the duck over, and roast with the breast-side down for 45 minutes, basting every 15 minutes or so. Turn the duck over again, baste, and continue roasting until the juices run clear yellow and not pink when an inner thigh is pierced, about an additional 30 minutes. The duck should be cooked after a total of about 1½ hours of roasting.

The Stock (see Note):

Neck and heart from the duck (reserve liver for another recipe)

$\frac{1}{2}$ large carrot, peeled and cut into thin slices

1 rib celery, trimmed and cut into thin slices

1 small onion, peeled and cut in half

1 bay leaf

6 black peppercorns

Pinch salt

Remove the roasting pan from the oven and pour any juices from the duck's cavity into the remaining marinade. Place the duck on a carving board and let sit, loosely covered with aluminum foil, for about 5 to 10 minutes.

Discard all the fat and any blackened bits in the bottom of the roasting pan. Add the remaining marinade and 1 cup of the stock and bring to a boil over high heat, scraping up any browned juices. Boil for about 5 minutes, reduce the heat to low, and add the tangerine sections. Let simmer while carving the duck, about 5 minutes. Taste the sauce for seasoning and serve alongside the duck.

Makes 4 servings

Note: *If you don't want to bother with a homemade stock, you can simply substitute 1 cup low-sodium canned chicken broth.*

Roasted Duck Pâté with Cognac, Raisins, and Sun-Dried Tomatoes

Most people think making pâté is a fancy, complex procedure, but as this recipe demonstrates, it's really quite simple.

½ cup fresh duck livers, washed and thoroughly dried

1 teaspoon olive oil or melted butter

Salt and freshly ground black pepper

1 tablespoon Cognac

12 tablespoons (1½ sticks) unsalted butter, at room temperature

1 clove garlic, peeled and chopped

Pinch ground allspice

2 tablespoons chopped raisins or currants (optional)

2 tablespoons chopped marinated sun-dried tomatoes (optional)

Toast or crackers

Preheat the oven to 350 degrees.

Place the livers in small roasting pan and toss with the oil or butter. Season well with salt and pepper. Roast for 12 minutes.

Remove the roasting pan from the oven and stir in the Cognac, scraping up any browned juices. Transfer the livers and pan juices to a food processor and process until smooth. Add the butter, garlic, allspice, and salt and pepper to taste. Transfer this mixture to small ramekins or a small serving bowl and stir in the raisins and sun-dried tomatoes if using. Smooth the top, cover, and chill for at least 3 hours before serving. Remove from the refrigerator 30 minutes before serving and accompany with the toast or crackers.

Makes about 1 cup

Roast Quail with Soy-Honey Glaze

Small, delicate quail are stuffed with lemon and chives and marinated in a simple glaze made from soy sauce, balsamic vinegar, chives, sesame oil, and honey. Then they are wrapped in a strip of bacon before roasting. The bacon keeps the delicate breast meat moist and tender and lends a smoky taste to the meat, while the soy-honey glaze creates a light, sticky coating that complements the flavor of the birds. With the quail, serve rice or crisp-fried noodles and a simple stir-fried vegetable combination.

3 tablespoons low-sodium soy sauce

1 tablespoon honey

1 teaspoon toasted sesame oil

2 teaspoons balsamic vinegar

1 tablespoon finely chopped fresh chives

4 quail, whole or boned with legs intact

4 strips bacon

1 lemon, cut into quarters

¼ cup fresh chives cut into small pieces

Freshly ground black pepper

1½ teaspoons vegetable oil

In a large bowl, mix the soy sauce, honey, sesame oil, vinegar, and chopped chives and add the quail. Marinate for 30 minutes or cover and marinate in the refrigerator for up to 6 hours.

Preheat the oven to 400 degrees.

Bring a small saucepan of water to a boil over high heat. Reduce the heat to moderate and simmer the bacon for about 8 minutes. Drain and dry thoroughly and set aside.

Drain the quail from the marinade, reserving the marinade, and pat the skin dry with paper towels. Place a lemon quarter inside each quail along with a tablespoon of chive pieces and a generous sprinkling of pepper. Wrap the boiled bacon around the quail and tie in place with kitchen string.

In a medium-size roasting pan or ovenproof skillet, heat the vegetable oil over moderately high heat. Brown the quail on all sides, about 5 minutes. Remove from the heat, place the quail breast-side down, and pour the marinade on top.

Roast the quail, basting occasionally, for 7 minutes. Turn the bird over, baste, and roast another 7 minutes.

Remove the roasting pan from the oven and place the quail on a carving board, loosely covered with aluminum foil, for about 5 minutes.

Discard any excess fat from the roasting pan and heat the pan juices over low heat. Discard the kitchen string from the quail and serve them with or without the bacon, drizzled with the pan juices.

Makes 2 servings

Roast Stuffed Quail with Cognac-Grape Sauce

The stuffing for these quail is totally straightforward—coarse breadcrumbs, chopped fresh parsley, garlic, and olive oil—but it's perfect for the delicate flavor of the birds. The quail are roasted until tender and then topped with a simple sauce made with chicken stock, Cognac, and red and green grapes.

4 strips bacon

2 tablespoons olive oil

2 tablespoons peeled and finely chopped garlic

1 cup coarse fresh breadcrumbs

$^1/_2$ cup finely chopped fresh parsley

2 tablespoons milk

Salt and freshly ground black pepper

4 quail, boned (see Note)

2 teaspoons butter

$^1/_3$ cup dry white wine

1 cup homemade chicken stock or low-sodium canned chicken broth

Preheat the oven to 400 degrees.

Bring a small saucepan of water to a boil over high heat. Add the bacon, reduce the heat to moderate, and simmer for about 8 minutes. Drain and dry thoroughly. Set aside.

In a small skillet, heat $^1/_2$ tablespoon oil over moderate heat. Add the garlic and cook, stirring, until it just begins to turn golden brown and softens, about 30 seconds. Do not let the garlic burn.

In a medium-size bowl, mix the breadcrumbs, the garlic, 1 tablespoon of the oil, the parsley, milk, salt, and a generous grinding of pepper.

Press the stuffing into the cavities of the quails, dividing the mixture equally. Wrap a slice of boiled bacon around each quail, tying it in place with a small piece of kitchen string.

In a medium-size roasting pan or skillet, heat the remaining $^1/_2$ tablespoon of oil and the butter over moderately high heat. Brown the quail on all sides, about 5 minutes. Remove from the heat and place the quail breast-side down, and pour the wine on top. Sprinkle the quail with pepper.

Roast the quail for 7 minutes, basting occasionally. Turn the quail over and baste again. Continue roasting another 7 minutes. Remove the roasting pan from the oven. Discard the kitchen string and the bacon. Place the quail on a warm platter, loosely covered with aluminum foil, for about 5 minutes.

2 tablespoons Cognac

½ cup seedless red and/or green grapes,
     cut in half

Discard any fat from the roasting pan and place over two burners. Add the stock or broth and bring to a boil over high heat, scraping up any browned juices. Add the Cognac and let simmer until the juices are somewhat thickened, about 5 minutes. Add the grapes and salt and pepper to taste and spoon the sauce on top of the quail.

Makes 2 servings

Note: *Have the butcher bone the quail for you, leaving the legs intact.*

Pheasant Roasted with Wild Mushrooms

Unless you're a hunter or live in the country, chances are good you've never encountered the marvelous flavor of fresh pheasant. When plucked, the bird looks something like a small chicken, but it has a distinct gamy flavor. It is a very rich bird and a little bit goes a long way—a 2-pound pheasant can easily feed four.

Because small game birds tend to be dry, the pheasant is covered with a thin layer of prosciutto ham or bacon. I also season it with fresh thyme sprigs and then roast it with earthy fresh shiitake mushrooms, basting the pheasant with a good dry sherry. The bird is seared with high heat and then roasted at a lower temperature, which results in a golden crust and juicy, highly seasoned meat. Serve the pheasant with polenta or risotto and stir-fried greens.

1 teaspoon mild vegetable or light olive oil

One 2- to 4-pound fresh pheasant

6 sprigs fresh thyme; or 1 tablespoon dried

$1/3$ cup chopped fresh chives

Freshly ground black pepper

3 thin (but not paper-thin) slices prosciutto; or 2 strips bacon

1 cup dry sherry

6 ounces fresh shiitake mushrooms, stems
removed, or other fresh wild mushrooms, trimmed and cut in half if
large

Preheat the oven to 400 degrees.

Grease the bottom of a medium-size roasting pan or ovenproof skillet with the oil. Place the pheasant, breast-side up, in the pan. Tuck half of the thyme and half of the chives into the cavity of the bird and sprinkle liberally with pepper. Tie the legs together with kitchen string. Lay one piece of the prosciutto or bacon over the breast of the bird, tucking the sides into the cavity. Tie the prosciutto or bacon on with kitchen string. Sprinkle the top of the bird with more pepper and the remaining thyme and chives.

Roast the pheasant 15 minutes, then remove the roasting pan from the oven and run a wide metal spatula under the bird to keep it from sticking to the pan. Reduce the oven temperature to 325 degrees and pour $1/4$ cup of the sherry over the bird and surround it with the mushrooms. Baste the bird every 15 minutes and add another $1/4$ cup sherry every 15 minutes. Roast the pheasant until the juices run slightly pink when pricked in the thickest part of the leg, a total of about 50 minutes.

Remove the roasting pan from the oven and place the pheasant on a carving board. Let sit, loosely covered with aluminum foil, for 10 minutes before discarding the string, and the prosciutto or bacon, if desired. Place the mushrooms in a small bowl, loosely covered with foil to keep warm.

Discard any excess fat from the roasting pan. Scrape up any bits stuck to the bottom of the pan. Carve the bird and serve with the roasted mushrooms, topped with the pan juices.

Makes 4 servings

A Shield for Meat

Many cooks strive to find the leanest, most fat-free piece of meat, poultry, or game they can find. While this provides a "healthier" cut of meat, it can also translate to a *dry* roast. Some roasted foods need a layer of fat to protect the meat from drying out.

"Barding" is the term used for wrapping bacon or a thin layer of fat around unusually lean cuts of meat, game, poultry, or even fish. The fat is usually tied on with kitchen string and placed on the outside of the roast. "Larding" is a similar process in which thin strips (*lardons*) of fat (usually pork) or bacon are actually threaded into a cut of meat with something called a larding needle. It is rare that I have called for adding fat to any of the roasts in this book, but there are a few examples. Strips of bacon are wrapped around the Stuffed Roasted Whole Bluefish (page 136) in order to keep it moist, and bacon is used in both of the roast quail recipes (see pages 119 and 120). Pheasant Roasted with Wild Mushrooms is topped with a slice of prosciutto to keep it from drying out while roasting.

Roast Goose with Wild Rice, Nut, Pear, and Fig Stuffing

This is an adaptation of Roast Goose with New Year's Eve Stuffing, a recipe from my book *Leftovers*. Goose is an extremely fatty bird that requires a rather unusual roasting technique. The skin of the goose is pricked (to allow excess fat to escape) and the bird is doused with boiling water every 15 minutes throughout the roasting time to remove additional fat. This may sound like a lot of fuss, but believe me it's well worth the effort.

This stuffing is rich and full of interesting flavors and textures—a combination of wild rice, nuts, dried cranberries, figs, and raisins. This is an ideal dish for a holiday meal or a special dinner.

The Stuffing:

2½ cups water

1 cup wild rice

2 tablespoons butter

1 large onion, peeled and chopped

1½ tablespoons chopped fresh thyme; or 1½ teaspoons dried

⅓ cup raisins

1 cup coarsely chopped pecans, almonds, or walnuts

1 cup peeled, cored, and chopped ripe (or almost ripe) pear

¾ cup chopped fresh or dried figs

½ cup sun-dried cranberries or cherries (optional)

½ cup chopped fresh parsley

Salt and freshly ground black pepper

Prepare the stuffing: In a medium-size saucepan, bring the water to a boil over high heat. Add the rice and stir well. Reduce the heat to low, cover, and let cook until tender, 30 to 40 minutes. Drain thoroughly and transfer to a large bowl.

In a small to medium-size skillet, melt the butter over moderate heat. Add the onion and cook, stirring occasionally, until soft but not brown, about 8 minutes. Sprinkle in the thyme and add this mixture to the rice.

Place the raisins in a small bowl, cover with boiling water, and let sit about 10 minutes. (This process plumps the raisins.) Drain. Add the drained raisins, chopped nuts, pear, figs, cranberries or cherries if using, parsley, salt, and pepper. (The stuffing can be made several hours ahead of time and covered and refrigerated. Never stuff the goose until you're ready to roast it.)

Preheat the oven to 425 degrees.

Prepare the goose and goose stock: Remove the gizzard, heart, and neck from the goose. Put them in a medium-size saucepan along with the onion, parsley, peppercorns, and a touch of salt. Cover with cold water. Bring to a boil over high heat, reduce the heat to moderately low, and let simmer, partially covered, while the goose roasts, until you have a flavorful stock.

The Goose:

One 9-pound goose, with gizzard, hearts, and neck, totally thawed if frozen

1 medium-size onion, peeled and cut into quarters

3 sprigs fresh parsley

6 black peppercorns

Salt

The Gravy:

¼ cup dry sherry or port

Salt and freshly ground black pepper

Lightly salt the cavity of the goose and add the stuffing. Sew or skewer the cavity closed. Prick the skin with a fork in several spots. Dry the goose thoroughly with paper towels. Place it, breast-side up, on a rack set inside a large flameproof roasting pan.

Bring a large saucepan or teakettle of water to a boil.

Roast the goose until brown, about 15 minutes. Reduce the oven temperature to 350 degrees. Turn the goose on its side, pour 3 tablespoons of the boiling water over the goose, and continue roasting. Pour another 3 tablespoons of boiling water over the goose about every 15 minutes. Using a bulb baster, remove any fat in the roasting pan. After about 40 minutes, turn the goose on its other side and roast for another 40 minutes. Continue pouring boiling water over the goose. Turn the goose breast-side down and continue roasting for 15 minutes. Turn the goose over, breast-side up, and continue roasting until the juices run pale yellow and not pink when an inner thigh is pierced. The goose should cook for a total of 2 to 2½ hours, depending on how fresh it is.

Remove the roasting pan from the oven. Place the goose on a carving board and take off the string or skewer. Let the goose sit, loosely covered with aluminum foil, while you make the gravy.

Prepare the gravy: Discard any excess fat from the pan. Place the roasting pan over two burners and bring the pan juices to a simmer over moderately high heat. Strain the simmering stock into the pan and bring to a boil, scraping up any bits and pieces clinging to the bottom of the pan. Add the sherry, salt, and a grinding of pepper and let simmer until slightly reduced and flavorful, 5 to 10 minutes.

Carve the goose and serve. Pass the gravy and stuffing separately.

Makes 6 servings

Seafood

Summer Salmon Roast

This is a wonderful light dish brimming with the flavors of summer—fresh herbs, ripe cherry tomatoes, and lemon juice. The fish is finished off with a crunchy nut topping. With the salmon, serve couscous, rice salad, or French bread.

½ tablespoon olive oil or flavored olive oil (pages 198 and 236)

½ cup chopped fresh chives, parsley, or other fresh herb

One 1-pound salmon fillet, skin on

2 tablespoons chopped fresh basil

Juice of 1 lemon

14 cherry tomatoes; or 2 medium-size ripe tomatoes, cut into cubes

1 tablespoon chopped fresh dill

1½ tablespoons butter

½ cup chopped walnuts, almonds, or pine nuts

Salt and freshly ground black pepper

Preheat oven to 400 degrees.

Grease the bottom of a medium-size roasting pan or ovenproof skillet with the oil. Place the chives in the pan and top with the fish. Sprinkle with the basil and lemon juice. Surround the fish with the tomatoes and dill.

In a small skillet, heat 1 tablespoon of the butter over moderate heat. Add the nuts and cook, stirring, until golden brown, 3 to 4 minutes. Season with salt and pepper. Sprinkle the nuts over the fish. Top the nuts with the remaining ½ tablespoon butter, cut into small cubes.

Roast the fish until opaque in the center, 10 to 12 minutes, depending on the thickness of the fish.

Makes 2 servings

The Right Fish for Roasting

There is a wide variety of seafood that works well when roasted. In this chapter I have given recipes for roasting everything from scallops, shrimp, and shellfish, to flounder, bluefish, swordfish, and salmon. But there are many others types of seafood that you can substitute and experiment with successfully. In general, there are a few general tips to consider when choosing fish for roasting:

- Try to pick large, thicker pieces of seafood rather than thin fillets, which can easily dry out.

- You want to choose firmer varieties of fish that have some natural oil, which will act as a natural baster.

- Many roasted seafood recipes leave the skin on the fish, which provides a protection from the oven's dry, high heat and keeps the fish's flesh moist.

- Almost all the recipes for roasting fish start with a high temperature to sear the exterior of the seafood and seal in the juices.

- Other varieties of seafood that take well to roasting include cod, monkfish, halibut, red snapper, shad, mahi-mahi, hake, pike, pompano, grouper, striped bass, catfish, haddock, tuna, squid, and lobster.

How Much Per Person: Seafood

For a whole, bone-in fish: about $3/4$ to 1 pound per person.

For fillets: about 6 to 8 ounces per person.

For shrimp: about $1/4$ to $1/2$ pound per person, depending on the size of the shrimp.

For clams and mussels: about $1/2$ to 1 pound, or 9 to 12 clams/mussels, per person, depending on the size.

J.R.'s Roasted Salmon with Avocado

Avocado may seem like an unlikely roasting ingredient, but the results are surprisingly good. When you roast an avocado, it takes on a silky, buttery flavor and texture. This recipe works well with any type of oily fish fillet. Serve this dish with a ripe tomato and sweet onion salad and hot orzo mixed with garlic and chopped fresh parsley.

1 tablespoon olive oil

1/4 cup plus 2 tablespoons coarsely chopped fresh basil or dill

One 1 1/2-pound salmon fillet, skin on

1 clove garlic, peeled and chopped

1/2 ripe avocado, pitted, peeled, and cut lengthwise into 4 slices

Salt and freshly ground black pepper

1/2 cup dry white wine

1 lemon, cut into 4 wedges

Preheat the oven to 400 degrees.

Grease the bottom of a medium-size roasting pan with 1/2 tablespoon of the oil. Sprinkle 1/4 cup basil or dill over the bottom of the pan and set the salmon on top. Rub the garlic into the salmon's flesh and scatter the remaining 2 tablespoons of basil on top. Place the avocado slices on top of the salmon, season with salt and pepper, and drizzle the remaining 1/2 tablespoon oil over the top.

Roast the salmon for 10 minutes. Remove the pan from the oven and pour the white wine around the salmon. Continue roasting until the salmon is opaque in the center, another 3 to 8 minutes, depending on the thickness of the fish. Serve with the lemon wedges.

Makes 4 servings

Arrows' Plank-Roasted Salmon

Down a winding, narrow country road in Ogunquit, Maine, is Arrows restaurant. It is one of those hidden gems, a culinary secret you only want to share with good friends. But everyone deserves to know about this country restaurant in an 18th-century farmhouse, with its manicured herb, vegetable, and flower gardens. Chefs/owners Mark Gaier and Clark Fraser love to experiment with a wide variety of ingredients; their eclectic menu combines foods from East and West. In this recipe, fresh salmon is roasted on a pine board (which provides a wonderful woody flavor) and then served with a simple tarragon vinaigrette.

Plank roasting is a traditional method from the northwestern United States, and plank-roasted fish was once standard fare at Native American potlatch parties. The trick is to find an untreated piece of wood to roast on—just about any soft- or hardwood will do. If you want to add an herb flavor to the fish, place a bed of fresh thyme or tarragon on the wooden plank and place the fish on top. The herb and the wood flavors infuse the fish. You can also substitute halibut, sea bass, sturgeon, or another dense white fish.

Chefs Gaier and Fraser suggest serving the salmon with roasted or mashed potatoes or french fries or yam fries and wilted spinach or a warm asparagus dish.

Four 7-ounce salmon fillets; or one 2-pound salmon fillet, skin on

1 cup plus 2 tablespoons olive oil

Kosher salt and freshly ground black pepper

1 *untreated* pine or other wood plank, large enough to hold all the fish and have about an extra inch of border on all sides

¼ cup fresh tarragon leaves

¼ cup fresh parsley leaves

1 shallot, peeled and chopped

8 black peppercorns

1 teaspoon Dijon mustard

2 tablespoons red wine vinegar

Preheat the oven to 450 degrees.

Rub the salmon fillets with the 2 tablespoons oil, salt, and pepper. Place the salmon, skin side down, on the plank. Set the plank on a baking sheet to keep the juices from spilling. If you can't find a wood plank, simply place the fish directly on a baking sheet.

Roast the salmon until opaque in the center, about 12 minutes.

Place the 1 cup olive oil, the tarragon, parsley, shallot, peppercorns, mustard, vinegar, and salt in a blender or food processor and puree. Taste for seasoning and serve with the hot salmon.

Makes 4 servings

Roast Swordfish with Pancetta, Garlic, and Parsley Sauce

Pancetta, an Italian-style bacon, creates a richly flavored sauce for a swordfish steak. The pancetta is cut into thin slivers and mixed with garlic, parsley, lemon juice, and pepper and then roasted on top of the fish. Just before the swordfish is done, a touch of heavy cream and capers are added to the sauce, and the whole dish is placed under the broiler until it is golden brown and bubbling. This dish takes only minutes to put together and works well for a family dinner or as part of an elegant party. With the swordfish, serve a simple pasta dish or risotto, and broiled tomatoes or sautéed zucchini.

5 tablespoons pancetta (see Note) or prosciutto

3 cloves garlic, peeled and chopped

1/2 cup chopped fresh parsley

2 tablespoons lemon juice

Freshly ground black pepper

1 teaspoon olive oil

One 1-pound swordfish steak, about 1/2 to 3/4 inch thick

Preheat the oven to 350 degrees.

In a small skillet, cook the pancetta over moderate heat, stirring occasionally, until it begins to turn crisp, about 5 minutes. If using prosciutto, cook for only 2 minutes. Add the garlic and cook, stirring, for 1 minute. Remove the skillet from the heat and add the parsley, lemon juice, and a generous grinding of pepper.

Grease a medium-size roasting pan or ovenproof skillet with half of the oil. Place the fish in the pan. Rub the remaining oil all over the fish. Spoon the pancetta mixture on top.

Roast the fish until just about opaque in the center, about 15 minutes.

2 tablespoons capers, drained

2 tablespoons heavy cream

1 small lemon, cut into 4 wedges

Remove the roasting pan from the oven and pour the cream and capers around (not on top of) the fish. Preheat the broiler and broil the fish until golden brown and bubbling, about 5 minutes. Serve the fish with the pan juices and lemon wedges.

Makes 2 servings

Note: *Pancetta is the same cut of pork as bacon, but it is cured in salt and spiced rather than smoked. It is available at gourmet food shops and Italian groceries.*

Roasted Swordfish with Olive Puree

This dish presents a memorable combination of flavors and colors. The white swordfish is "painted" with a black olive puree and surrounded with bright red cherry tomatoes. A few tablespoons of cream tenderize the fish and create a simple, creamy sauce mingled with the natural fish juices. Fresh salmon works equally well in this recipe.

With the swordfish, serve roasted eggplant and steamed or roasted baby new potatoes.

One 1¹/₂-pound swordfish steak or salmon steak or fillet, about ¹/₂ to ³/₄ inch thick

2¹/₂ tablespoons heavy cream or milk

3 tablespoons olive puree (see Note)

Freshly ground black pepper

2 teaspoons lemon juice

1 teaspoon olive oil

12 cherry tomatoes

Sea salt

1 lemon, cut into 4 wedges

Preheat the oven to 350 degrees.

Place the swordfish in a medium-size roasting pan or shallow ovenproof skillet and pour the cream or milk on top. Let "marinate," covered and refrigerated, for 15 minutes to several hours.

In a small bowl, mix the olive puree, a few grindings of black pepper, the lemon juice, and oil. Using a spoon or a pastry brush, "paint" the puree on the top of the fish in stripes or in whatever design you choose, making sure to leave some of the fish white and unadorned. Place the tomatoes around the fish and season them with salt and pepper.

Roast the fish for about 15 minutes. Remove the roasting pan from the oven and baste the fish with the creamy juices. Continue roasting until the fish is opaque in the center, 3 to 5 minutes. If you want to "firm up" the olive topping, preheat the broiler and broil the fish for about 2 minutes. Serve the fish with the lemon wedges.

Makes 3 to 4 servings

Note: *Olive puree and tapenade are available in gourmet food shops.*

Roasted Swordfish with Red Pepper, Anchovies, and Capers

Roasted red peppers and anchovies is one of my favorite flavor combinations. Add capers and I love it even more. Add the meaty taste of fresh swordfish and you've got a winning dish. All you need is a bowl of linguine tossed in a fruity olive oil, a mixed green salad, and a good bottle of crisp, dry white wine to complete the meal.

The colors and textures in this dish are as appealing as its flavor. The swordfish steak is marinated in milk, which turns into a creamy custard when roasted. The fish is topped with bright red strips of bell pepper, thin brown anchovies, tiny green capers, and green chives. And it's surrounded with long, thin strips of green zucchini and pale yellow summer squash.

One $1^1/_2$-pound swordfish steak, about $^1/_2$ to $^3/_4$ inch thick

$^3/_4$ cup milk

$^1/_2$ large red bell pepper, cored and cut into very thin strips

About 6 cured anchovy fillets, with some of their oil

3 teaspoons tiny capers, drained

1 small zucchini, cut lengthwise into thin strips

1 small summer squash, cut lengthwise into thin strips

2 teaspoons chopped fresh chives or parsley

Salt and freshly ground black pepper

1 lemon, cut into 4 wedges

Place the swordfish in a medium-size to large roasting pan or ovenproof skillet and pour the milk on top. Let marinate, covered, in the refrigerator for at least 1 hour or overnight.

Preheat the oven to 400 degrees.

Arrange the strips of red pepper on the swordfish and place the anchovy fillets on top, making an "X" design. Sprinkle the capers over the whole fish. Scatter the zucchini and squash around the fish. Sprinkle the chives, salt, and pepper over all. Roast the swordfish until opaque in the center, about 15 minutes.

Remove the roasting pan from the oven. Preheat the broiler and broil the swordfish until golden brown and bubbling. Serve the swordfish surrounded by the lemon wedges.

Makes 4 servings

Stuffed Roasted Whole Bluefish

What a smile my husband wore as he walked into the house holding a 6-pound bluefish, just caught off the coast of Martha's Vineyard. His look was the one every successful fisherman shares—the look of total triumph.

Bluefish is a particularly oily fish (you can also substitute a whole snapper or salmon) and holds up well when roasted. Here it is gutted and cleaned and then stuffed with a rich combination of tomatoes, onions, garlic, herbs, and pieces of crisp bacon. The outside of the fish is then covered with strips of bacon, which not only baste the fish during the roasting time but also keep the flesh moist and savory. The crisp, golden-brown bacon is a fabulous garnish. If you don't eat pork, the bacon can easily be omitted.

The Fish and Vegetables:

1 teaspoon vegetable oil

One 5- to 6-pound whole bluefish, snapper, or salmon, scaled and gutted, head on

1 clove garlic, peeled and chopped

Salt and freshly ground black pepper

1 teaspoon chopped fresh thyme; or ½ teaspoon dried

4 strips bacon (optional)

3 medium-size summer squash, cut lengthwise into thin strips

3 medium-size zucchini, cut lengthwise into thin strips

1 medium-size ripe tomato, cubed; or 10 cherry tomatoes, cut in half

1 cup dry white wine

1 lemon, cut into 6 wedges

Grease the bottom of a large roasting pan with the oil and place the fish in the pan. Make a slit in the cavity of the fish to hold the stuffing. Rub half the garlic, salt, pepper, and thyme into the cavity and rub the remaining half all over the skin.

Prepare the stuffing: In a large skillet, cook the pieces of bacon over moderate heat until almost crisp. Remove the bacon and all but 1 teaspoon of the bacon fat. (If you're making the dish without the bacon, simply heat 1 teaspoon olive oil.) Add the onions and garlic and cook over moderate heat, stirring occasionally, until the onions are soft but not brown, about 5 minutes. Add the salt, pepper, thyme, tomato, and cooked bacon and cook, stirring, another minute. Remove the skillet from the heat and stir in the breadcrumbs. Season to taste.

Press the stuffing into the cavity of the fish. If it doesn't all fit, don't overstuff, or it will overflow during roasting. Skewer or sew the fish together. Place the bacon strips over the top of the fish. Surround the fish with the summer squash, zucchini, and tomato. Season the vegetables with salt and pepper. Pour the wine on top of the fish. (The dish can be made up to this point 1 or 2 hours ahead of time and refrigerated, covered.)

The Stuffing:

4 strips bacon, cut into small pieces
    (optional)

2 medium-size onions, peeled and chopped

2 cloves garlic, peeled and chopped

Salt and freshly ground black pepper

4 teaspoons chopped fresh thyme;
    or 2 teaspoons dried

1 medium-size ripe tomato, chopped

³/₄ cup plain dry breadcrumbs, preferably
    homemade, or croutons, slightly
    crumbled

Preheat the oven to 400 degrees.

Roast the fish until opaque in the center, about 50 minutes. Serve some of the stuffing and a lemon wedge with each portion of fish.

Makes 6 servings

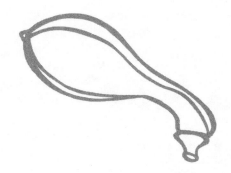

Roasted Bluefish with Vermouth, Tomatoes, Basil, and Black Olives

This simple summer dish can be made with any firm-fleshed fish, such as snapper, halibut, or striped bass. Fresh basil and tomatoes make all the difference.

1 tablespoon olive oil

One 2-pound bluefish fillet or another firm fish, skin on

2 cloves garlic, peeled and thinly sliced

¼ cup thinly sliced fresh basil

1 medium-size onion, peeled and very thinly sliced

2 medium-size ripe tomatoes, thinly sliced

3 tablespoons dry breadcrumbs

Salt and freshly ground black pepper

About ⅓ cup dry vermouth or dry white wine

1 cup pitted black olives, preferably oil-cured

1 lemon, cut into 4 wedges

Preheat the oven to 400 degrees.

Grease the bottom of a medium-size roasting pan or a large ovenproof skillet with half of the oil. Add the fish, skin side down, to the pan. Press the garlic into the flesh and top with half of the basil. Arrange the onion in a thin layer on top. Repeat with the tomatoes. Sprinkle the breadcrumbs, remaining basil, salt, and pepper over all. Drizzle the remaining oil on top. Pour half of the vermouth around the fish. (The recipe can be made up to this point and refrigerated, covered, for up to 3 hours.)

Roast the fish for 10 minutes. Remove the roasting pan from the oven and add the remaining vermouth. Arrange the olives in a layer on top of the fish. Continue roasting until opaque in the center, 5 to 10 minutes, depending on the thickness of the fish.

Preheat the broiler and broil the fish until golden brown, 3 to 5 minutes. Serve with lemon wedges.

Makes 4 servings

Roasted Chinese-Style Flounder

A whole flounder is surrounded with thin strips of fresh ginger, scallions, garlic, chives, and cilantro and then splashed with soy sauce, sesame oil, and rice wine. Next the fish roasts until tender and moist. The Chinese ingredients permeate the fish's flesh and produce an incredibly flavorful dish. Serve with steamed white rice.

1 teaspoon vegetable oil

One 1½-pound whole flounder, scaled and gutted, head removed (see Note)

2 tablespoons very thin matchstick strips peeled fresh ginger

2 scallions, cut into 3-inch strips

2 tablespoons chopped fresh cilantro (see Note)

2 tablespoons chopped fresh chives

1 clove garlic, peeled and thinly sliced

1 tablespoon lemon juice

2 tablespoons rice wine, sake, or dry sherry

1½ tablespoons low-sodium soy sauce

1 teaspoon toasted sesame oil

The Garnishes:

1 lemon, cut into 4 wedges

⅓ cup chopped fresh cilantro

Preheat the oven to 400 degrees.

Grease the bottom of a medium-size shallow roasting pan, ovenproof skillet, or gratin dish with the vegetable oil. Place the fish in the pan. Scatter the ginger, scallions, cilantro, chives, and garlic over the fish. Pour the lemon juice, rice wine, soy sauce, and sesame oil on top. (The fish can marinate in these ingredients, covered and refrigerated, for about 2 hours.)

Roast the fish, basting it once or twice with the juices from the bottom of the pan, until opaque in the center, 10 to 12 minutes.

To serve, cut down the backbone of the fish to separate the two fillets on top. Gently lift them from the bones with a spatula. Discard the bones and serve the remaining fillets, with any pan juices poured on top. With the fish, serve the lemon wedges and cilantro if desired.

Makes 2 servings

Note: *Have your local fishmonger prepare the fish for you. If you don't like the taste of fresh cilantro, substitute parsley.*

Littleneck Clam Stew with Linguine

This Mediterranean-style stew combines some of my favorite flavors—garlic, tomatoes, fresh thyme, olive oil, capers, and olives—with whole littleneck clams. The stew is served over linguine and sprinkled with chopped parsley. You can also serve the stew over warm mashed potatoes. It's a feast for the eyes as well as the palate.

2 pounds littleneck clams, scrubbed

2 cloves garlic, peeled and thinly sliced

$^1/_4$ cup chopped fresh parsley

$1^1/_2$ cups chopped tomatoes, canned or fresh

1 tablespoon chopped fresh thyme; or 1 teaspoon dried

Pinch cayenne pepper or dash hot pepper sauce

1 bay leaf

$^1/_2$ pound linguine

$1^1/_2$ tablespoons good-quality olive oil

Salt and freshly ground black pepper

1 tablespoon capers, drained

1 cup oil-cured black olives, pitted

Preheat the oven to 425 degrees.

Place the clams in a medium-size shallow roasting pan or a large ovenproof skillet. Add the garlic, parsley, tomatoes, thyme, cayenne or hot pepper sauce, and bay leaf and stir well to coat the clams with all the ingredients.

Roast the clams for 8 minutes. Turn them over and roast until the shells open, 6 to 8 minutes.

While the clams are roasting, bring a large pot of water to a boil. Add the linguine and cook until al dente, about 10 to 12 minutes. Drain the linguine and place it on a large warm platter. Add the olive oil, salt, and pepper and toss to mix.

Remove the roasting pan from the oven and gently stir in the capers and olives. Spoon the stew on top of the linguine, sprinkle with the remaining parsley, and serve immediately.

*Makes 2 servings as a main course
or 4 servings as an appetizer*

Roasted Littleneck Clams with Garlic and Scallions

I love linguine with clam sauce, but I can't stand the thought of losing any of the precious clam juice, which often happens when clams are opened before they are cooked. Why not roast the clams in their shells, I thought, and create a sauce directly in the roasting pan?

The clams are placed in a single layer in an attractive ovenproof pan, doused with white wine, garlic, scallions, parsley, and a touch of red chile pepper, and then roasted at high heat for about 10 minutes. The result is flavorful clams in a rich, garlic-laced sauce that can be spooned directly over linguine, or eaten straight out of the pan accompanied by a chunk of crusty bread for soaking up all the scrumptious sauce.

1 tablespoon good-quality olive oil

3 pounds littleneck clams, scrubbed

3 cloves garlic, peeled and chopped

3 scallions, thinly sliced

1 cup dry white wine

1/2 cup chopped fresh parsley

1/2 to 1 dried red chile pepper, crumbled with seeds

Freshly ground black pepper

3/4 to 1 pound linguine, cooked and kept warm (optional)

Preheat the oven to 500 degrees.

Grease the bottom of a large shallow ovenproof casserole or ovenproof skillet with the oil. Place the clams on top in a single layer. Top with the remaining ingredients and stir to coat the clams thoroughly.

Roast the clams for 5 minutes. Turn them over and roast until the shells open, 4 to 5 minutes. Serve the clams hot from the oven or, if desired, spoon them over the linguine.

Makes 4 servings

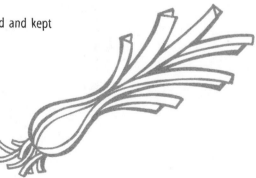

Open Wide: Roasting Clams and Mussels

I first tasted roasted clams at Al Forno restaurant in Providence, Rhode Island. Chefs Johanne Killeen and George Germon serve Rhode Island littleneck clams roasted with spicy sausage, chile peppers, and onions in a garlicky broth. This clam dish is such an outrageously successful combination that I'd recommend a trip to Providence from just about anywhere.

Clams and mussels should be roasted until their shells open. Once the shells open, however, the shellfish are done and the dish should be removed from the oven *immediately*, or you risk serving overcooked, rubbery shellfish. Remember that some clams open faster than others. If a clam or mussel is still somewhat closed after roasting, it doesn't necessarily indicate that it's bad. Simply pry open the clam or mussel with your fingers, or use a clam or paring knife. If the shellfish still doesn't open, you should throw it away.

Portuguese Roasted Clams with Chorizo

Based on an old Portuguese recipe, these clams are roasted in a very hot oven with slices of onion, spicy chorizo sausage, tomato chunks, garlic, and white wine. Serve them as a first course or as a main dish, accompanied by a loaf of warm, crusty bread for mopping up the juices, a salad of mixed greens, and a cold bottle of crisp, white wine, such as a Portuguese Vinho Verde. This dish is also excellent served over mashed potatoes.

1 tablespoon olive oil

1/2 pound chorizo, linguica, or fairly spicy Italian sausage, sliced about 1 inch thick

1 large onion, peeled, cut in half, and thinly sliced

Pinch cayenne pepper or dash hot pepper sauce

16 cherrystone clams (see Note), scrubbed

1 large ripe tomato; or 1 1/2 cups canned whole tomatoes, chopped

4 cloves garlic, peeled and chopped

1 cup dry white wine

Preheat the oven to 450 degrees.

In a large ovenproof skillet, heat the oil over moderate heat. Add the sausage slices and onion and cook, stirring, until the onion is soft but not brown, about 5 minutes. Add the cayenne or hot pepper sauce.

Remove the skillet from the heat and arrange the clams on top of the sausage and onion. Scatter the tomato and garlic on top of the clams and pour the wine over everything.

Roast the clams for 5 minutes. Turn them over and roast until the shells open, 5 to 7 minutes.

***Makes 2 servings as a main course or
4 servings as an appetizer***

Note: *If the cherrystones are unusually large, use about 24 littlenecks.*

Roasted Mussels with Tomatoes, Basil, and White Wine

This is a variation on Roasted Littleneck Clams with Garlic and Scallions (page 141). In this recipe, mussels are roasted with fresh tomatoes, basil, garlic, and splash of dry white wine. Serve them on a bed of linguine (about a pound) or accompanied by a loaf of crusty French bread.

1 tablespoon olive oil

1 large onion, peeled and thinly sliced

4 cloves garlic, peeled and finely chopped

2 tablespoons chopped fresh basil

2 tablespoons chopped fresh chives

¼ cup finely chopped fresh parsley

3 dozen mussels, scrubbed and debearded

2 cups coarsely chopped fresh or canned
    tomatoes

Freshly ground black pepper

½ cup dry white wine

Heat the oil in a large ovenproof skillet over moderate heat. Add the onion and cook, stirring occasionally, for 5 minutes. Add half of the garlic, basil, chives, and parsley and cook, stirring, until the onion is soft, 2 or 3 minutes. Remove the skillet from the heat and let cool.

Place the mussels (preferably in a single layer) on the onion and top with the tomatoes and the remaining garlic, basil, and chives. Add a grinding of pepper and pour the wine over all. (The dish can be made to this point and refrigerated, covered, for up to 2 hours.)

Preheat the oven to 500 degrees.

Roast the mussels for 5 minutes. Turn them over and roast until the shells open, 5 to 7 minutes, depending on the size of the mussels. Sprinkle with the remaining parsley and serve immediately.

Makes 4 servings

Roasted Mussels in Tomato-Cream Sauce

This is a beautiful luncheon dish served with crusty bread for sopping up the juices, a mixed green salad, and a good dry white wine (preferably the wine you use to cook the mussels with). The mussels are also delicious served over risotto, couscous, or polenta.

1 tablespoon olive oil

2 pounds mussels, scrubbed and debearded

2 cloves garlic, peeled and chopped

1 small onion, peeled and very thinly sliced

1 cup chopped fresh or canned tomatoes

2 tablespoons chopped fresh chives

1 tablespoon chopped fresh thyme

$^1\!/_2$ cup dry white wine

2 tablespoons heavy cream

Freshly ground black pepper

Preheat the oven to 500 degrees.

Grease the bottom of a heavy, shallow casserole or roasting pan with the oil. Place the mussels in the casserole. Sprinkle with the garlic, onion, tomatoes, chives, and thyme. Pour the wine and cream on top and grind black pepper over the whole dish.

Roast the mussels for 5 minutes. Turn them over and roast until the shells open, 5 to 7 minutes, depending on the size of the mussels. Serve hot.

Makes 4 servings

Roasted Soft-Shell Crabs with Lemon-Caper Sauce

Kevin Graham, the former executive chef at the impeccable Grill Room at the Windsor Court Hotel in New Orleans and author of *Simply Elegant,* had never tasted a soft-shell crab until he arrived in Louisiana in 1980 from his native England. "I immediately became hooked," he says, "and in the years since have experimented with many soft-shell crab recipes."

What interests me most about Graham's recipes is his method of cooking the crabs: first he sautés them over high heat and then roasts them in the oven. The result is remarkably juicy crabs. Here I present his method with a simple lemon-caper sauce. But this cooking method will work with any of your favorite soft-shell crab sauces.

As an accompaniment, serve steamed asparagus and boiled baby potatoes.

4 large soft-shell crabs, cleaned and trimmed

All-purpose flour for dusting

Salt and freshly ground black pepper

2 tablespoons light vegetable oil

1 tablespoon olive oil

1½ tablespoons butter

¼ cup tiny capers, drained

Juice of 1 large lemon

1 lemon, cut into 4 wedges

Preheat the oven to 400 degrees.

Wash and dry the crabs thoroughly. Place the flour on a plate and season it lightly with salt and pepper. Lightly dredge the crabs in the seasoned flour, patting off any excess flour.

Heat the vegetable oil in a large skillet over moderately high heat until shimmering. Place the crabs in the hot oil and cook for 2 minutes. Turn the crabs over and cook on the other side for 2 minutes.

Transfer the crabs to a medium-size roasting pan, ovenproof plate, or skillet. Roast them until they are firm, about 5 minutes.

While the crabs are roasting, heat the olive oil and butter in a small saucepan over moderate heat until they begin to sizzle. Add the capers and lemon juice and remove the skillet from the heat.

Remove the pan from the oven and place 1 or 2 crab(s) on each dinner plate. Spoon the lemon-caper sauce on top and serve with a wedge of lemon on the side.

Makes 2 to 4 servings

Roasted Sea Scallops with Breadcrumb-Garlic Topping

I always used to prepare scallops by broiling them with a simple splash of lemon juice or pan-frying them with garlic and parsley. I was afraid that roasting might produce dry scallops. I have now discovered that roasting produces incredibly moist scallops that require a minimum amount of effort to prepare. If you like your scallops golden brown, simply place them under a hot broiler for a minute or two just before serving.

You want to find really fresh, medium-size scallops for this dish. If the scallops are particularly large, cut them in half horizontally so that each large scallop yields two round halves.

1 tablespoon olive oil

1 pound medium-size fresh sea scallops

2 tablespoons lemon juice

2 cloves garlic, peeled and chopped

Freshly ground black pepper

Pinch sweet Hungarian paprika

1 teaspoon chopped fresh thyme;
    or ¼ teaspoon dried

3 tablespoons dry breadcrumbs

1 lemon, cut into 4 wedges

Preheat the oven to 400 degrees.

Grease a small roasting pan with the oil. Add the scallops to the pan and pour the lemon juice on top. Toss to coat thoroughly. Sprinkle the garlic, pepper, paprika, and thyme on the scallops, and top with the breadcrumbs.

Roast the scallops until opaque in the center, 12 to 15 minutes, depending on the size. The scallops should still be soft when pressed with your finger. You want to avoid a hard, rubbery texture. Remove the roasting pan from the oven. Preheat the broiler and broil the scallops until golden brown, about 2 minutes. Serve the scallops with the lemon wedges.

Makes 4 servings

Salt-Encrusted Roasted Shrimp

In this recipe whole shrimp in their shells are literally smothered in coarse kosher salt and then roasted. The salt forms a kind of crust that seals in the shrimp's juices, resulting in unbelievably moist shrimp without a trace of saltiness. (The salt is simply brushed off before serving.)

The shrimp can be served hot, warm, or even cold with a variety of dipping sauces. I particularly recommend Green Sauce (page 227) or Aioli Sauce (page 231). Serve this dish as an appetizer or as an entree with a rice dish, roasted red peppers, and a green vegetable.

1 pound medium-size shrimp in their shells (see Note)

About 4 cups kosher salt

1 lemon and/or lime, cut into wedges

Green Sauce (page 227) (optional)

Aioli Sauce (page 231) (optional)

Preheat the oven to 350 degrees.

Rinse and thoroughly dry the shrimp. Place the shrimp in a medium-size roasting pan or shallow casserole and pour the salt on top. (The salt should totally cover the shrimp.)

Roast the shrimp for 15 minutes. Remove the pan from the oven and dig the shrimp out from under the salt. Using a pastry brush or a paper towel, brush off any remaining salt clinging to the shells. Serve the shrimp in their shells and let everyone peel their own. Pass the lemon and lime wedges separately. Serve with Green Sauce or Aioli Sauce, if desired.

Makes 4 servings

> **Note:** *You can use larger shrimp as well and increase the cooking time by a few minutes.*

Vegetables

Salad of Three Roasted Peppers

This is a fresh, very colorful summer salad that goes well with just about any main dish. If you like your food spicy, you can easily make this a four-pepper dish by roasting a jalapeño (or the chile pepper of your choice) alongside the sweet peppers. Yellow, orange, and red bell peppers (most of which are imported from Holland) can be costly, but if you can find them for a reasonable price, they are well worth it. In addition to the flavors, the combination of colors creates a beautiful presentation.

Serve this salad with a loaf of crusty bread and a bottle of crisp, cold white wine. You can pair any roast with roasted red peppers, particularly poultry and seafood.

1 large red bell pepper

1 large yellow bell pepper

1 large orange or green bell pepper

1 to 2 chile peppers (optional)

1 tablespoon chopped fresh basil

1 tablespoon chopped fresh chives
    (optional)

1 scallion, trimmed and finely chopped

Salt and freshly ground black pepper

1/2 cup good-quality olive oil

3 1/2 tablespoons balsamic or red or white
    wine vinegar

1/3 cup tiny black Niçoise olives

1/3 cup tiny green olives

Preheat the oven to 450 degrees.

Place all the peppers on a baking sheet lined with a piece of aluminum foil. Roast the peppers on the top shelf of the oven, turning them until soft and slightly blackened all over, 15 to 20 minutes.

Remove the baking sheet from the oven and wrap the peppers tightly in the aluminum foil for about 3 minutes. Using a small sharp knife, core, seed, and peel them, and then cut into thick slices.

While the peppers are roasting, prepare a vinaigrette: In a small bowl, mix the basil, chives, scallion, salt, and pepper. Whisk in the oil and vinegar and taste for seasoning.

Arrange the peeled peppers, alternating colors, on a platter. Pour the vinaigrette on top and scatter the olives over the peppers. Serve warm or at room temperature.

Makes 4 servings

Roasted Red Peppers with Olive Vinaigrette

Olive vinaigrette, made with olive puree, chopped fresh basil, and scallions, adds a dramatic black color to the bright red strips of roasted pepper. It also goes well with roasted leeks or onions, any salad of mixed greens, or roasted vegetables.

Serve this dish with swordfish or another firm-fleshed fish, roast chicken or beef, or as part of an antipasto platter.

1 large red bell pepper

1 tablespoon chopped fresh basil

1 tablespoon olive puree or tapenade (see Note)

2 trimmed and thinly sliced scallions

Salt and freshly ground black pepper

2 1/2 tablespoons red wine vinegar

5 tablespoons olive oil

4 to 6 thin slices lightly toasted French or Italian bread

Preheat the oven to 450 degrees.

Place the bell pepper on a piece of aluminum foil and roast on the top shelf of the oven, turning it until soft and slightly blackened all over, 15 to 20 minutes.

Remove the pepper from the oven and wrap it tightly in the foil for about 5 minutes. Using a small sharp knife, core, seed, cut the pepper in half, and peel off the skin. Cut the pepper into thin strips.

Meanwhile, prepare the vinaigrette: In a small bowl, mix the basil, olive puree, scallions, salt, and pepper. Whisk in the vinegar and then the oil and taste for seasoning. (The vinaigrette can be made one day ahead of time, then covered and refrigerated.)

Arrange the pepper strips in a pinwheel design on a small serving plate. Pour the vinaigrette in a circle through the middle of the peppers and serve at room temperature with the bread.

Makes 2 servings as a lunch dish
or 4 servings as a side dish

> Note: *Olive puree and tapenade are available in gourmet food shops.*

Roasted Red Peppers with Anchovies and Capers

This classic Italian combination—roasted red peppers, tart capers, and anchovy fillets topped with a garlicky vinaigrette—makes a great first course. It can also be served as part of an antipasto platter.

The Salad:

2 large red bell peppers

6 cured anchovy fillets

2 tablespoons small capers, drained

The Vinaigrette:

1 clove garlic, peeled and chopped

1 cured anchovy fillet

Freshly ground black pepper

1 tablespoon oil from the anchovies

5 tablespoons olive oil

3 tablespoons red or white wine vinegar

Preheat the oven to 450 degrees.

Place the peppers on a piece of aluminum foil and roast on the top shelf of the oven, turning them until soft and almost blackened all over, 15 to 20 minutes.

Remove the peppers from the oven and wrap them tightly in the foil for about 5 minutes. Unwrap the peppers, peel the skin off, and remove the seeds and core. Cut the peppers into thin strips.

Meanwhile, make the vinaigrette: In a small bowl, use the back of a spoon to mash the garlic with the anchovy fillet. Add a generous grinding of pepper and whisk in the oils and the vinegar.

Place the roasted pepper strips in a single layer on a medium-size platter. Lay the anchovy fillets diagonally across the peppers and sprinkle with the capers. Pour the vinaigrette on top and serve at room temperature.

Makes 4 servings

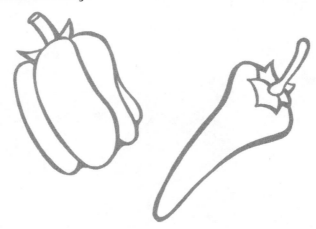

Warm Avocado Soup
with Roasted Jalapeño Peppers

This striking green soup comes from Lindsay Knapp, a private chef and caterer in southern Maine. Smooth and creamy, the soup is spiked with roasted jalapeño peppers, which add quite a "pow" to the mild soup and should be added cautiously. As Knapp explains, "The jalapeño puree delivers a kick that goes largely unnoticed when you first taste the soup. Wait for it!"

Knapp serves the soup warm, topped with a dollop of sour cream and homemade croutons. It's also lovely chilled.

4 jalapeño peppers, roasted, peeled, and seeded (see Box, page 154)

2 ripe or overripe avocados, halved, pitted, and peeled

About 1½ cups homemade chicken stock or low-sodium canned chicken broth

1 cup heavy cream

Salt and freshly ground black pepper

Sour cream

Croutons

Place the roasted peppers in a food processor or blender and puree. Take care not to breathe in the spicy fumes while pureeing. Transfer the puree to a small serving bowl and set aside.

Place the avocados in a food processor or blender and whirl a few times until mashed. Add 1 cup of the stock or broth and the cream and puree until smooth. Season to taste with salt and pepper; remember, the flavor will develop later with the addition of the jalapeño pepper puree.

To serve the soup warm, transfer it to a medium-size saucepan and bring to a gentle simmer over moderate heat. Place in soup bowls and swirl in a tiny bit of the pepper puree, a dollop of sour cream, and a few croutons.

To serve the soup chilled, transfer it to a serving bowl, cover, and refrigerate for about 4 hours. Place in soup bowls and swirl in the pepper puree and top with the sour cream and croutons.

Makes 4 to 6 servings

Roasted Fire: How to Roast Chile Peppers

Aaah (or ouch), chile peppers. Those tiny, innocent-looking red and green peppers can add so much flavor to a dish. But raw they can be harsh and overwhelming, particularly when mixed with other raw fresh foods. Roasting chiles subdues the heat and produces a musty, smoky flavor. What follows is a master recipe for roasting all types of chile peppers—from fresh jalapeños and serranos to habaneros and poblanos.

Always use chiles that are firm, smooth, and without wrinkles. Preheat the oven to 500 degrees. Place the chile peppers on a baking sheet lined with aluminum foil. Make a tiny slit in the side of each pepper to prevent it from bursting. Place the baking sheet on the top shelf of the oven and roast the peppers, shaking the baking sheet every few minutes to make sure they blacken on all sides, for 8 to 10 minutes, depending on the thickness and variety of the pepper. Wrap the peppers in the aluminum foil to "sweat"— which makes the skin easy to remove—for 5 to 10 minutes.

Put on rubber gloves before removing the skin and seeds from the peppers. You need to be very careful when handling chile peppers; the seeds are extraordinarily hot and can be dangerous if they accidentally get into your eyes. If you don't wear gloves, be sure to wash your hands after touching chiles. In either case, wash the cutting surface with soap and warm water at the end of the process.

The peppers are now ready to use. They can be cut into thin slices, chopped, or pureed in a blender or food processor. Keep in mind that a tiny bit adds an incredibly powerful, intensely spicy flavor.

Here are some ideas for using roasted chile peppers:

- Swirl a teaspoon of roasted pepper puree into soups, stews, or sauces, such as Warm Avocado Soup (page 153).

- Add a teaspoon of roasted pepper puree to a basic vinaigrette and wake up a salad. Try it in Chicken Salad with Blue Cheese and Roasted Jalapeño Pepper Vinaigrette (page 101).

- Make roasted chile pepper–flavored vinegar: Roast 6 chile peppers following the master recipe above. Thinly slice the peppers and push them into a long, thin bottle. Cover with white wine vinegar and let steep for about 2 weeks before using. Store in a cool, dark spot. Use in marinades, barbecue sauces, salads, etc.

- Add chopped roasted chile peppers to wake up coleslaw or carrot salad.

- Mix a teaspoon of roasted pepper puree into a homemade mayonnaise and add to potato salads and sandwiches.

- Mix chopped roasted peppers into homemade tartar sauce and serve with fried clams.

- Stuff whole roasted peppers with goat cheese and top with a mild tomato sauce. Bake until the cheese is melted.

Roasted Maple Carrots

A spoonful of maple syrup enhances the naturally sweet flavor of carrots and gives them a rich-tasting glaze that both adults and kids love. These carrots go particularly well with roast chicken, beef, or pork.

1 teaspoon mild vegetable oil or butter

4 large carrots, peeled and cut into matchstick strips

Salt and freshly ground black pepper

1 to 1½ tablespoons pure maple syrup

Preheat the oven to 400 degrees.

Grease the bottom of a small roasting pan or a medium-size ovenproof skillet with the oil or butter. Add the carrots, salt, and pepper and toss well to coat with the oil.

Roast the carrots for 10 minutes. Remove the roasting pan from the oven and drizzle the maple syrup on the carrots. Continue roasting the carrots until they are tender but not falling apart, 3 to 6 minutes.

Makes 4 servings

Roasted Sesame Snow Peas and Carrots

When I was a kid, we often ate peas and carrots, the frozen kind with carrots cut into uniform little cubes and soft little peas. I always loved the flavor but hated the mushy texture. In this updated version, thin slices of carrots are lightly coated with sesame oil and soy sauce and roasted until their natural sweetness is brought out. They are then mixed with snow peas and roasted until just tender. This is really like a roasted stir-fry—the dish uses almost no oil and comes together with very little effort. With the roasted peas and carrots, serve steamed white rice.

½ teaspoon peanut or vegetable oil

4 medium-size carrots, peeled and cut into 3-inch-long thin slices

1 teaspoon toasted sesame oil

1 tablespoon low-sodium soy sauce

1 tablespoon peeled and chopped fresh ginger, or 1 teaspoon ground ginger

1 cup fresh snow peas, ends trimmed

Preheat the oven to 400 degrees.

Grease the bottom of a small roasting pan or medium-size ovenproof skillet with the peanut or vegetable oil. Add the carrots, sesame oil, soy sauce, and ginger and stir to coat.

Roast the carrots for 10 minutes. Remove the roasting pan from the oven and add the snow peas, stirring well to coat them with the sauce. Roast until the vegetables are crisp-tender, 10 to 12 minutes.

Makes 4 servings

Roasted Chinese-Style Green Beans

Roasting green beans produces an extremely juicy vegetable with just a slightly crunchy "skin." These beans are tossed with sesame oil, soy sauce, and butter and then roasted until tender. You can substitute Chinese chile oil for the sesame oil for a spicy dish. Serve the green beans with poultry, beef, or fish and steamed rice.

³/₄ pound green beans, ends trimmed

1 tablespoon low-sodium soy sauce

1 teaspoon toasted sesame oil or Chinese chile oil

1 tablespoon butter, cut into small pieces

Preheat the oven to 350 degrees.

In a small roasting pan, shallow casserole, or ovenproof skillet, toss the beans with the soy sauce and oil until well coated. Dot with the butter.

Roast the beans about 5 minutes. Remove the pan from the oven and stir the beans well. Continue roasting until the beans are just tender but still a bit crunchy, 3 to 10 minutes, depending on the size of the beans.

Makes 4 servings

Roasted Beets with Ginger Butter

You can roast the beets ahead of time and toss them with the ginger butter just before serving. This dish goes particularly well with roast chicken.

1¹/₂ pounds small to medium-size beets, ends trimmed

2 tablespoons butter

1 tablespoon peeled and finely chopped ginger

Salt and freshly ground pepper

¹/₂ cup watercress, trimmed, thoroughly washed, and dried (optional)

¹/₂ cup arugula, thoroughly washed and dried (optional)

Preheat the oven to 350 degrees.

Wrap the beets tightly in aluminum foil.

Roast the beets until they are tender when pierced, 30 minutes to 1¹/₂ hours. (Timing varies wildly, depending on the size of the beets.) Let the beets cool slightly. Using a small sharp knife, peel the beets and cut them into quarters.

In a large skillet, heat the butter over moderate heat. Add the ginger and the beets, season with salt and freshly ground pepper, and cook, stirring constantly, until the beets are heated through, 4 to 5 minutes. Serve the beets on a bed of mixed watercress and arugula if desired.

Makes 4 servings

Roasted Beet Salad

A delicious salad for summer or fall, full of the bright colors of the garden, this can be served as a main course with crusty bread for a light lunch or as an accompaniment to any roasted fish or poultry dish. The beets can be roasted several hours ahead of time.

The Beets:

3 large red or yellow beets, ends trimmed

The Salad:

1 small head butter, red leaf, or another lettuce, thoroughly washed and dried

1 large ripe tomato, cut into small cubes; or 6 cherry tomatoes, cut into quarters

1 scallion, trimmed and finely chopped

3 tablespoons finely chopped fresh parsley

1 teaspoon Dijon mustard

5 tablespoons olive oil

$2^1/_2$ tablespoons balsamic or wine vinegar

Salt and freshly ground black pepper

Preheat the oven to 350 degrees.

Wrap the beets tightly in a large sheet of aluminum foil and roast until tender, 30 minutes to $1^1/_2$ hours. (Timing varies wildly, depending on the size of the beets.) Remove from the oven and let cool slightly.

Place the lettuce on a large serving plate.

In a medium-size bowl, mix the tomato, scallion, parsley, mustard, oil, vinegar, salt, and pepper. Taste for seasoning and adjust if needed.

Using a small sharp knife, peel the beets and cut them into cubes slightly larger than the tomato cubes. Toss the cubed beets into the tomato mixture. Arrange the beet and tomato mixture over the greens and serve cold or at room temperature.

Makes 4 to 6 servings

Roasted Beets with Goat Cheese Topping

Look for golden-colored beets at specialty food shops or farmers' markets or grow them yourself. Not only do they add a subtle color to salads, but they lend an especially sweet, buttery flavor.

12 small mixed red and yellow or all red beets; or 6 medium-size ones

1 tablespoon Dijon mustard

Salt and freshly ground black pepper

1 tablespoon chopped fresh chives or parsley

3 tablespoons balsamic vinegar

6 tablespoons olive oil

About 1 cup crumbled goat cheese (chèvre) (see Note)

Preheat the oven to 350 degrees.

Wrap the beets in aluminum foil and roast until tender when pierced, 30 minutes to 1¹/₂ hours. (Timing varies wildly, depending on the size of the beets.) Let the beets cool slightly, about 5 minutes. Using a small sharp knife, peel the beets and cut them in half if small or into quarters if medium-size.

In a medium-size bowl, mix the mustard, salt, pepper, and chives. Whisk in the vinegar and then the oil. Add the warm beets and toss until coated with the dressing. Place the beets on a platter and top with the goat cheese.

Makes 4 servings

> **Note:** *Goat cheese is available in specialty food shops and some supermarkets.*

Roasted Borscht Salad

This is a wonderfully colorful salad with the flavors of the classic Russian beet soup, borscht. Here fresh beets are roasted and then tossed, while still warm, in a light vinaigrette. The beets are then placed on a bed of endive spears and surrounded with a dilled sour cream sauce.

Serve this salad as a main course with crusty bread or as a side dish with a brisket of beef.

6 medium-size beets, ends trimmed (see Note)

5 tablespoons olive oil

3 tablespoons balsamic vinegar

3 tablespoons chopped fresh dill

Salt and freshly ground black pepper

1/3 cup sour cream or plain low-fat yogurt

1 head endive, spears separated; or about 2 cups assorted salad greens, thoroughly washed and dried

2 scallions, trimmed and chopped

Preheat the oven to 350 degrees.

Wrap the beets tightly in aluminum foil and roast until they are tender when pierced, 30 minutes to 1½ hours. (Timing varies wildly, depending on the size of the beets.)

Remove the foil-wrapped package from the oven and let the beets cool slightly. Using a small sharp knife, peel the beets and cut them into 1½-inch cubes or wedges.

In a medium-size bowl, whisk together the oil, vinegar, half of the dill, and the salt and pepper. Add the cut-up beets and mix well.

In a small bowl, mix the sour cream with the remaining dill and salt and pepper. Taste for seasoning.

Line the edge of a large platter with the endive spears or greens and spoon the beet salad into the center. Spoon the sour cream sauce into a circle around the edge of the beets. Sprinkle the scallions over the salad and serve at room temperature or chilled. The salad can be refrigerated, covered, for 2 to 3 hours before serving.

Makes 4 servings

Note: *If you can find a mixture of red and yellow beets, use 3 of each. If you can only find large beets, use 4 and cut them in half before roasting.*

Roasted Dilled Beet Chips

The bright pink color and the tangy flavor of these chips appeal to both children and adults. Try them with Yogurt Dill Sauce (page 228), as an appetizer, or serve as an accompaniment to roast chicken, pork, or beef.

Olive oil

1 large beet, peeled and cut into ¼-inch slices

2 tablespoons chopped fresh dill

Salt and freshly ground black pepper

Preheat the oven to 350 degrees.

Lightly grease a baking sheet with the oil and place the beet slices on top, spacing them well apart. Lightly brush the tops of the beets with the oil and sprinkle with half of the dill and the salt and pepper.

Roast the beets for 10 minutes. Turn the beets over, lightly brush the other side with the oil, and sprinkle with the remaining dill and salt and pepper. Roast the beets until they are tender in the middle and crisp along the edges. Drain on paper towels and serve hot or at room temperature.

Makes 2 to 3 servings

Roasted Asparagus

When you roast asparagus instead of steaming or boiling them, they retain all their vitamins, color, and flavor; nothing is lost in the cooking process. Roasted asparagus also have an intriguing smoky flavor that complements seafood dishes, especially salmon.

Serve these asparagus with lemon wedges or accompany them with a hollandaise sauce, Green Sauce (page 227), or Roasted Pepper Aioli (page 231). They make a spectacular cold salad served with 1 cup of Chinese Sesame-Chile-Lemon Dipping Sauce (page 226).

1 pound asparagus, tough ends trimmed

1 to 2 teaspoons olive oil or butter

Preheat the oven to 350 degrees.

Wrap the asparagus tightly in aluminum foil and top with the oil or butter. (You can also grease a large, shallow roasting pan, add the asparagus, and cover with aluminum foil.)

Roast the asparagus until they are tender but not falling apart, 12 to 25 minutes, depending on the thickness of the asparagus. Remember that the asparagus will continue to cook for a few minutes after they have been removed from the oven. Discard the foil before serving.

Makes 4 servings

Roasted Corn

Why would anyone want to roast corn when it tastes so good simply cooked in a pot of boiling water? I wasn't sure either, but when I tasted my first ear of roasted peak-of-the-season corn, I was amazed. It was sweet and flavorful, as any good ear of just-picked corn is in August. But it was also positively juicy, as in "dripping down your chin" kind of juicy!

This recipe is quite easy: Soak unhusked ears of corn in cold water for about 1 hour. The husks, fully moistened from soaking, protect the delicate kernels and keep them from overcooking or drying out. Drain the corn and place in a preheated 400-degree oven, turning them once, for 10 minutes. If you're roasting particularly young corn, you may want to reduce the roasting time to about 7 minutes. Let the corn cool slightly (until you're able to handle it without scorching your hands) and pull off the husks and silks. Serve hot, with or without butter, with or without salt. If the corn is super fresh, you won't need a thing except a napkin. Figure on at least 1 or 2 ears of corn per person.

You can also partially husk the corn (after soaking) and slip a teaspoon or so of Roasted Garlic and Herb Butter (page 197) between the husk and the kernels before roasting as described above.

Roasted Corn and Red Pepper Relish

There are three roasted ingredients in this luscious relish—corn, red bell pepper, and garlic cloves. The relish is both sweet and savory, a perfect match for everything from grilled steaks and burgers to fish and chicken. The relish also makes a great topping for bruschetta (grilled garlic bread), or it can be served as part of an antipasto platter.

6 ears very fresh corn, unhusked

8 cloves garlic, unpeeled and left whole

5 tablespoons plus 1 teaspoon olive oil

1 large red bell pepper

¹/₄ to 1 teaspoon seeded and chopped jalapeño pepper

2¹/₂ tablespoons white wine vinegar

¹/₄ cup chopped fresh parsley

1 scallion, trimmed and thinly sliced

Salt and freshly ground black pepper

Soak the corn in a pot of cold water for about 1 hour.

Preheat the oven to 400 degrees.

Place the garlic in a piece of aluminum foil, drizzle with 1 teaspoon of the oil, and wrap tightly. Place the bell pepper on another piece of aluminum foil. Do not wrap.

Place the drained corn directly on the oven rack and roast along with the garlic and bell pepper. Remove the corn and garlic after 10 minutes and let cool slightly. Squeeze the garlic cloves out of their skins and chop. Husk the corn and, using a sharp knife, cut the kernels off the cobs into a medium-size bowl.

Roast the bell pepper, turning it every few minutes, until almost charred on all sides, for a total of about 15 minutes. Wrap the pepper in the foil and let cool slightly, about 5 minutes. Peel the skin off the pepper, remove the seeds and core, and chop it.

Mix the corn with the chopped garlic and bell pepper and add the remaining ingredients. Taste for seasoning, adding more jalapeños if desired.

Makes about 2 cups

Newcastle Inn's Corn Polenta with Roasted Wild Mushrooms

Ted and Chris Sprague run one of the most charming inns in Maine. The Newcastle Inn is tucked away on a quiet street overlooking the Damariscotta River in the small town of Newcastle. Each evening as guests watch the sunset and sip cocktails on an outdoor porch, Chris Sprague works away in her kitchen, turning out five-course dinners that make her guests come back year after year.

One of Chris's favorite foods, polenta, is a traditional Italian dish made of cornmeal; Chris refers to it as the "ultimate comfort food, right up there with mashed potatoes and pasta." In this version the cornmeal is mixed into simmering chicken stock along with fresh corn kernels and grated Parmesan cheese; the polenta is then topped with wild mushrooms that have been roasted with garlic, rosemary, and olive oil. This makes a great main course, or it can be served as an elegant first course followed by any of the roast beef, pork, poultry, or seafood dishes in this book. Best of all, the whole dish can be put together in less than 30 minutes.

The Mushroom Topping:

3 tablespoons plus 1 teaspoon olive oil

6 cloves garlic, peeled and thinly sliced

1 tablespoon red wine vinegar

1 tablespoon chopped fresh rosemary; or 1 teaspoon dried

1½ pounds assorted wild or full-flavored mushrooms, such as shiitake, oyster, portobello, cèpes, or cremini, trimmed (see Note)

Salt and freshly ground black pepper

Preheat the oven to 425 degrees.

Prepare the mushroom topping: Lightly grease a baking sheet or very shallow roasting pan with 1 teaspoon of the oil. Combine the garlic, remaining 3 tablespoons oil, the vinegar, rosemary, and mushrooms in a small bowl, making sure to coat the mushrooms thoroughly. Place the mushrooms on the baking sheet and sprinkle with salt and pepper. Roast the mushrooms until they are tender, about 25 minutes.

The Polenta:

3 cups homemade chicken stock or low-sodium canned chicken broth

1 cup regular yellow cornmeal or quick-cooking polenta

1 cup fresh or frozen, thawed corn kernels

1/2 cup grated Parmesan cheese

3 tablespoons butter

Salt and freshly ground black pepper

Meanwhile, prepare the polenta: In a medium-size saucepan, bring the stock to a boil over high heat. Reduce the heat to moderately low and gradually whisk in the cornmeal in a steady stream. Stir the polenta with a wooden spoon until it begins to pull away from the sides and bottom of the pan in a solid mass, 15 to 20 minutes for regular cornmeal or 5 minutes for quick-cooking. Remove from the heat and stir in the corn, cheese, butter, salt, and pepper. Serve immediately, topped with the roasted mushrooms.

Makes 4 to 6 servings

Note: *If the mushrooms are small, leave them whole; cut larger varieties in half or into quarters, depending on their size.*

Polenta Topping Ideas

You can use just about any roasted food found in this book to create a delicious topping for polenta. Here are just a few ideas—many of which incorporate roasted foods—to inspire you.

- Roasted asparagus, shallots, and black olives
- Grated Parmesan cheese, chopped smoked ham, and rosemary
- Roast chicken slices, goat cheese, and sun-dried tomatoes
- Black and green olives and parsley
- Pesto and roasted shrimp
- Slivers of roasted pork, mushrooms, and scallions
- Roasted tomatoes and basil
- Roasted garlic, mixed herbs, and grated Romano cheese
- Roasted eggplant and roasted red pepper strips
- Roast duck slivers and pesto
- Roasted clams and Green Sauce (page 227)
- Roasted red peppers and crumbled blue cheese

Roasted Polenta Triangles with Red Pepper, Garlic, and Prosciutto Topping

Polenta is a great way to use up roasted leftovers—everything from vegetables to poultry and garlic. Cornmeal is whisked into simmering stock and then the thickened mixture is placed in a cake pan to cool. Once the polenta is cool and firm, it is cut into triangles, topped with leftovers, and roasted at a high temperature. The topping I use here is a colorful combination of roasted peppers, garlic, and slivers of prosciutto. But like a good pizza dough, you can use polenta to create any appealing combination; see the list of possible ideas on page 167.

The polenta needs at least 2 hours to chill before it can be cut into triangles, so plan your time accordingly. You can make the polenta and the topping a day ahead of time and assemble the dish at the last minute. These triangles make a great first course or hors d'oeuvre. I also like to serve them with roast chicken.

The Polenta:

3 cups water, homemade chicken stock, or
    low-sodium canned chicken broth

Pinch salt

1 cup regular cornmeal or quick-cooking
    polenta

1 tablespoon chopped fresh rosemary;
    or 1 teaspoon dried

Freshly ground black pepper

Prepare the polenta: In a medium-size saucepan, bring the water, stock, or broth to a boil over high heat. Add the salt if using water. Reduce the heat to moderately low and gradually whisk in the cornmeal in a steady stream. Stir the polenta with a wooden spoon until it begins to pull away from the sides and bottom of the pan in a solid mass, 15 to 20 minutes for the cornmeal or 5 minutes for the polenta. Stir in the rosemary and pepper.

Line a 9×12-inch cake pan with a sheet of plastic wrap. Pour the hot polenta into the pan, smooth the top with a spatula, and let it cool slightly. Cover the pan with another sheet of plastic wrap and refrigerate for at least 2 hours or overnight.

Prepare the topping: In a skillet, heat the oil over moderately low heat. Add the garlic and cook, stirring, until it begins to soften and turn golden, about 1 minute. Do not let the garlic burn. Add the rosemary and prosciutto and cook, stirring, another minute. Remove the skillet from the heat and reserve.

The Topping:

2 tablespoons olive oil

5 cloves garlic, peeled and chopped

1 tablespoon chopped fresh rosemary;
    or 1 teaspoon dried

About ½ pound thinly sliced prosciutto, cut
    into thin strips (¾ cup)

2 roasted red bell peppers (see page 150),
    cored, seeded, peeled, and cut into
    thin strips

About 1 cup grated Parmesan cheese

Freshly ground black pepper

Make the polenta triangles: Preheat the oven to 450 degrees. Remove the polenta from the pan and plastic wrap and place on a clean cutting board. Cut the polenta into 12 triangles about 4 inches long. Very lightly grease a baking sheet with oil and place the triangles on the sheet. Do not crowd the baking sheet; the polenta triangles should not touch.

Roast the polenta for 5 minutes. Turn the polenta over with a wide spatula and spread the topping on each triangle. Place several strips of red pepper on each triangle and sprinkle with the cheese and black pepper. Continue roasting until the cheese melts and bubbles, about 5 minutes. Serve hot or at room temperature.

Makes 6 servings as an appetizer
or 12 servings as a side dish

Roasted Tomatoes

In early September, when the garden is at its peak, I am blessed with rows of plump and juicy red tomatoes. After we have eaten our fill (can you ever really get your fill of fresh vine-ripened tomatoes?), I make a huge batch of sauce to can for the winter. But I save the biggest, most promising-looking tomatoes to roast.

Roasting is a wonderful way to bring out the essence of tomatoes. The tomatoes are sliced in half and sprinkled with good olive oil, sea salt, a grinding of black pepper, and some fresh basil and rosemary from the garden. Let them roast until your whole kitchen is bursting with their rich, seductive smell, and have a crusty loaf of bread ready.

Roasted tomatoes are also a great base for pasta sauce or can be cut into small chunks and served on top of rice, chicken, or fish dishes.

6 large ripe but not overripe tomatoes, cut
   crosswise in half

5 tablespoons good-quality olive oil

Sea salt and freshly ground black pepper

1 tablespoon chopped fresh basil;
   or 1 teaspoon dried

1 tablespoon chopped fresh rosemary;
   or 1 teaspoon dried

Preheat the oven to 425 degrees.

Place the tomatoes in a medium-size roasting pan or ovenproof skillet and sprinkle with the oil, salt, pepper, and herbs.

Roast the tomatoes for 10 minutes. Reduce the oven temperature to 300 degrees and continue roasting until the tomatoes are soft but not falling apart, 20 to 30 minutes longer. Serve hot or at room temperature.

Makes 6 servings

Roasted Tomato Cream

This rich sauce comes from Peter Abrahamson, executive chef of the Sundial Beach resort on Sanibel Island, Florida. Summer tomatoes are roasted with garlic, fresh rosemary, pink peppercorns, and olive oil and then pureed with cream. The sauce goes particularly well with grilled swordfish, scallops, and steamed mussels. It's also delicious spooned over linguine or roast chicken.

To create a less rich (not to mention, less caloric) sauce, simply omit the cream and thin the puree with fish stock, clam juice, or chicken stock or broth.

You can also simplify this recipe by roasting the tomatoes with the herbs and garlic without pureeing them. Try this result on top of pasta or mashed potatoes.

1 pound ripe plum tomatoes, cut into quarters

$1/3$ cup good-quality olive oil

3 tablespoons chopped fresh rosemary

2 tablespoons pink peppercorns (see Note)

2 cloves peeled and chopped garlic

$1/2$ to 1 cup heavy cream (optional)

$1/2$ to 1 cup fish stock, homemade chicken stock, low-sodium canned chicken broth, or bottled clam juice (optional)

Preheat the oven to 300 degrees.

Place the tomatoes in a large roasting pan. Sprinkle the oil and then the rosemary, peppercorns, and garlic over the tomatoes.

Roast the tomatoes for 1 to $1^{1}/_{2}$ hours.

Finish the sauce: Place the tomatoes while still warm in a food processor or blender and puree. Add the cream if using, and puree until smooth. Or omit the cream and add $^{1}/_{2}$ to 1 cup stock, broth, or clam juice until the sauce is thinned to the desired consistency.

Transfer the sauce to a medium-size saucepan and bring to a simmer over low heat.

Makes 2 cups

Note: *Pink peppercorns are available at gourmet food shops.*

Provençal Eggplant Terrine with Fresh Tomato Sauce

All over the south of France, chefs transform shiny purple eggplant into luscious, savory terrines. This recipe was inspired by many dishes I tasted there—from coarse eggplant purees seasoned with garlic and onions to sophisticated terrines surrounded by juicy tomatoes, olives, and anchovies.

The eggplant puree, which is the first step in this recipe, can be served on its own as a spread with crackers, pita bread triangles, or slices of crusty bread. But by all means try the terrine. It's surprisingly quick and simple to put together, and the fresh flavors of the eggplant, tomatoes, garlic, anchovies, and olive oil make a wonderful appetizer or luncheon dish served with a mixed greens and tomato salad and a loaf of French bread. Don't be turned off by the anchovies; when cooked, they produce a very subtle flavor.

The Terrine:

3 small eggplant, ends trimmed

2 small white boiling onions, peeled and left whole

2 cloves garlic, peeled and left whole

2 cured anchovy fillets, cut into small pieces

2 tablespoons olive oil

Freshly ground black pepper

About ¼ cup dry breadcrumbs

1 cup tiny black Niçoise olives, pitted

Preheat the oven to 400 degrees.

Wrap the eggplant, onions, and garlic together in a large piece of aluminum foil and seal tightly.

Roast the vegetables until the eggplant are soft when touched with your finger, about 45 minutes.

Remove the foil-wrapped package from the oven and let the vegetables cool slightly. Peel off the eggplant skin and discard.

Place the peeled eggplant, onions, garlic, anchovies, and oil in a food processor or blender and puree until coarse, not smooth. This is best done by pureeing with the on-off or pulse switch 1 second at a time instead of just letting the machine run. Season to taste. (Chances are, you won't need a grain of salt because of the anchovies.) You can serve this eggplant puree as is or proceed with the terrine.

Prepare the tomato sauce: Place all the ingredients in a food processor or blender and process until chunky, not smooth. Taste for seasoning.

The Tomato Sauce:

8 medium-size ripe tomatoes, cut into chunks

1 clove garlic, peeled and left whole

2 cured anchovy fillets, cut into small pieces

1 tablespoon oil from the anchovies

Freshly ground black pepper

Prepare the terrine: Gently stir the $1/4$ cup of breadcrumbs into the eggplant puree. (You may need an additional tablespoon or two of breadcrumbs in order to make the puree thick enough to handle.) Using your hands, form the eggplant mixture into an oval shape. Place the eggplant mixture in the center of a medium-size roasting pan or ovenproof skillet and surround with the tomato sauce.

Roast the terrine until the sauce is thickened and bubbling hot, about 12 minutes. Remove the roasting pan from the oven, surround the terrine with the olives, and serve hot.

Makes 2 servings as a main course
or 4 servings as an appetizer

Roasted Eggplant Salad

This combination of roasted eggplant, sweet green and red peppers, spicy jalapeño peppers, scallions, and garlic, all tossed with lemon juice and olive oil, makes a light and refreshing salad. It has a silky texture and slightly smoky flavor from the roasted eggplant.

You can serve this salad in any number of ways. It's delicious spooned over lightly buttered toast or a bagel, as a topping for bruschetta (grilled garlic bread), or as a dip for pita bread, cooked shrimp, or raw vegetables. If you finely chop the vegetables and eggplant, you can also serve this dish as a relish with roasted meats, fish, or poultry. The salad can be refrigerated, covered, for several hours before serving.

2 small eggplant

1/3 cup cored chopped red bell pepper

1/3 cup cored chopped green bell pepper

2 cloves garlic, peeled and chopped

2 tablespoons chopped fresh chives

1/4 cup peeled and chopped onion or scallions

About 1 tablespoon seeded and chopped jalapeño pepper

Salt and freshly ground black pepper

Juice of 1 large lemon

4 1/2 tablespoons good-quality olive oil

Preheat the oven to 400 degrees.

Prick the eggplant in one or two spots with a small sharp knife and place on a sheet of aluminum foil or on a baking sheet. Roast the eggplant until they are tender and the skins are charred, 20 to 40 minutes, depending on the size of the eggplant.

Remove from the oven and let the eggplant cool slightly. While the eggplant are still warm, peel off their skins, using your fingers or a small sharp knife. Cut the eggplant flesh into small chunks, or if you are going to serve the salad as a relish, chop the eggplant finely.

In a medium-size serving bowl, mix the bell peppers, garlic, chives, onion or scallions, jalapeño, salt, and pepper. Add the warm eggplant and toss. Sprinkle with the lemon juice and olive oil and taste for seasoning.

Makes 4 servings; makes about 2 cups

Roasted Eggplant and Shallot Dip

This dip, made from roasted eggplant and shallots pureed with lemon juice, yogurt, and a little olive oil, is a low-fat version of the popular Middle Eastern dish baba ganoush. The earthy flavor of the roasted eggplant mixes well with the sweetness of roasted shallots.

With the dip, serve wedges of warm pita bread, raw vegetables, and a marinated cucumber and mint salad.

1 large eggplant, ends trimmed and cut into quarters

3 large shallots, peeled and left whole

2 tablespoons good-quality olive oil

4 tablespoons plain low-fat yogurt

Juice of $1/2$ lemon

$1/3$ cup chopped fresh chives or trimmed and chopped scallions

Salt and freshly ground black pepper

Sweet Hungarian paprika (optional)

1 lemon, cut into 8 wedges

4 rounds of pita bread, cut into eighths

Preheat the oven to 400 degrees.

Wrap the eggplant tightly in an aluminum foil pouch. Roast the eggplant for 30 minutes, then remove the pouch from the oven and add the shallots. Roast the vegetables until the eggplant is tender, another 20 to 30 minutes.

Remove the pouch from the oven and let the vegetables cool slightly before opening it. While the eggplant is still just a bit warm, use your fingers or a small sharp knife to peel off the skin.

Place the peeled eggplant and the shallots, oil, yogurt, and lemon juice in a food processor and blend until almost smooth. Add the chives, salt, and pepper and process until the chives are just blended in, 1 or 2 seconds.

Transfer the dip to a medium-size serving bowl and taste for seasoning. Sprinkle with paprika if desired, and surround the dish with lemon wedges and pita bread. Serve cold or at room temperature.

Makes about 2 cups

Gratin of Roasted Whole Baby Zucchini with Red Pepper and Herbs

Look for farm-fresh baby zucchini with the blossoms still attached. Come August, when zucchini threatens to take over the garden, just about anyone who grows them will be more than willing to give a few away. With the gratin, serve a grilled steak, chicken, or shrimp.

1½ tablespoons olive oil

4 baby zucchini with blossoms, cut lengthwise into quarters; or 2 large zucchini, ends trimmed, cut crosswise in half and then lengthwise into quarters (see Note)

1 red bell pepper, cored and cut lengthwise into 8 strips

6 cloves garlic, peeled and left whole

1 tablespoon chopped fresh thyme; or 1 teaspoon dried

1 tablespoon chopped fresh basil; or 1 teaspoon dried

Salt and freshly ground black pepper

3 tablespoons coarse dry breadcrumbs

3 tablespoons grated Parmesan cheese

Preheat the oven to 400 degrees.

Grease the bottom of a medium-size gratin dish or shallow casserole with 1 tablespoon of the oil. Alternate the zucchini and pepper strips in the bottom of the dish, and scatter the garlic and herbs around the edges. Sprinkle generously with salt and pepper. Drizzle the remaining ½ tablespoon oil over the top.

Roast the vegetables until they are almost tender when pierced, 15 to 20 minutes.

Mix the breadcrumbs and cheese in a small bowl. Remove the dish from the oven and top the vegetables with the breadcrumb-cheese topping. Continue roasting until the cheese is golden brown and bubbling, 3 to 5 minutes. Serve hot or at room temperature.

***Makes 2 servings as a main course
or 4 servings as a side dish***

Note: *When cutting the zucchini, be careful not to cut through the blossom.*

Pureed Roasted Zucchini and Leek Soup

This is a simple, absolutely delicious way to make soup without a lot of fat or hassle. A variety of vegetables is roasted in a hot oven with fresh herbs and garlic. The pan is then deglazed with chicken stock or broth and all the ingredients are thrown into a food processor or blender and pureed. A small amount of cream smoothes out the flavor. You can try this method with just about any combination of vegetables and herbs.

This soup tastes wonderful hot or cold with garlic bread and a roasted asparagus salad for a light lunch or dinner.

1 1/2 teaspoons olive or vegetable oil

4 medium-size zucchini, ends trimmed, cut into 1/2-inch pieces

1 large leek, trimmed, cut lengthwise in half and then crosswise into 1-inch pieces

2 scallions, trimmed and chopped

2 tablespoons chopped fresh basil; or 1 teaspoon dried

Salt and freshly ground black pepper

4 to 6 cloves garlic, peeled and left whole (see Note)

1/4 cup dry white wine

3 1/2 cups homemade chicken stock or low-sodium canned chicken broth

1/4 to 1/3 cup heavy cream

2 tablespoons chopped fresh chives; or 2 scallions, trimmed and chopped

Preheat the oven to 400 degrees.

Grease the bottom of a large roasting pan with the oil. Add the zucchini, leek, scallions, basil, salt, and pepper and stir well to coat the vegetables and herbs with the oil.

Roast the vegetables for 15 minutes and then add the garlic. Roast another 10 minutes.

Remove the roasting pan from the oven and immediately pour the wine and stock or broth into the vegetables, scraping up any browned bits. Transfer the vegetable mixture to a food processor or blender and puree. Add 1/4 cup of the cream and puree again until smooth. Taste for seasoning, adding the remaining cream if desired. Swirl in the chives or scallions just before serving.

Makes 4 to 6 servings

> Note: *If you want the soup to have a really garlicky flavor, add all 6 cloves.*

Roasted Leek and Tomato Soup

Farmers' markets are always inspiring places to shop for vegetables. On one late-autumn Saturday at an outdoor market in Millbrook, New York, tomatoes and gorgeous-looking leeks called out to me. I promptly went back to my father-in-law's house and roasted the tomatoes and leeks with a little olive oil and then pureed them with white wine and chicken stock. A creamy, soothing, autumnal vegetable soup was served less than an hour later, topped with fresh chives and croutons. We ate the soup with Herb-Crusted Goat Cheese (page 210) and a loaf of black bread.

1½ teaspoons olive oil

2 medium-size leeks, trimmed, cut lengthwise in half, and then crosswise into thin slices

4 medium-size ripe tomatoes, cut into cubes

Salt and freshly ground black pepper

¼ cup dry white wine

2½ cups homemade chicken stock, low-sodium canned chicken broth, or vegetable broth

¼ cup heavy cream

3 tablespoons of chopped fresh chives or parsley

The Garnishes:

1 tablespoon chopped fresh chives or parsley

1 cup croutons

1 small ripe tomato, finely diced

Preheat the oven to 350 degrees.

Grease the bottom of a medium-size roasting pan or ovenproof skillet with the oil. Add the leeks and tomatoes and stir lightly to coat the vegetables with the oil. Season with salt and pepper.

Roast the vegetables, stirring occasionally, for 30 minutes.

Remove the roasting pan from the oven and immediately pour the wine and then the stock into the vegetables, scraping up any browned juices. Working in batches, puree this mixture in a food processor or blender until smooth.

Transfer the soup to a medium-size saucepan and season to taste. Add the cream and chives or parsley and simmer over low heat until slightly thickened, 10 to 15 minutes. Serve hot, topping each bowl with a sprinkling of chives, a few croutons, and a spoonful of fresh tomato.

Makes 4 to 6 servings

Roasted Leek, Pancetta, and Sun-Dried Tomato Sauce

This is a very quick, simple sauce that can be used in a number of ways. Toss it with ¹/₂ pound cooked linguine, adding a sprinkling of grated Parmesan cheese; spoon it onto lightly toasted French bread slices; or use it as a topping for grilled chicken breasts, fish fillets, mashed or baked potatoes, polenta, or risotto.

1 teaspoon olive oil

¹/₂ cup chopped pancetta, prosciutto, or bacon

1 large leek, trimmed, cut lengthwise in half and then crosswise into thin slices

2 shallots, peeled and chopped

3 tablespoons thinly shredded fresh basil or sage

Salt and freshly ground black pepper

¹/₄ cup sun-dried tomatoes, chopped

2 tablespoons dry white wine

Preheat the oven to 350 degrees.

In a medium-size ovenproof skillet, heat the oil over moderate heat. Add the pancetta or prosciutto and cook, stirring, until it begins to get crisp, about 4 minutes. If using bacon, cook until crisp and then discard the excess fat from the pan, leaving about 1 teaspoon. Remove the skillet from the heat, add the leek, shallots, 2 tablespoons of the basil, and the salt and pepper and stir well.

Roast the leek mixture for 10 minutes. Remove the skillet from the oven and stir in the sun-dried tomatoes and wine. Roast the leeks, stirring after 5 minutes, until tender and golden brown and the pancetta is nearly crisp, about another 10 minutes.

Remove the skillet from the oven, stir in the remaining tablespoon of basil, and taste for seasoning.

Makes 2 to 4 servings

Roasted Leeks with Blue Cheese Vinaigrette

In this recipe, leeks are roasted with a small amount of olive oil and heavy cream, tossed with a simple vinaigrette, and topped with crumbled blue cheese. This salad is a great dish to bring to a summer picnic or to serve with grilled foods. The entire dish can be put together ahead of time.

The leeks can also be served hot from the oven, sprinkled with the cheese, without the vinaigrette. However you choose to serve them, make sure you have a good crusty loaf of bread on hand.

5½ tablespoons olive oil

2 large leeks, trimmed, cut lengthwise in half and then crosswise into 3-inch pieces

Salt and freshly ground black pepper

3 tablespoons heavy cream

2½ tablespoons balsamic or wine vinegar

⅓ cup crumbled blue cheese or goat cheese (chèvre)

2 tablespoons chopped fresh chives or parsley

Preheat the oven to 350 degrees.

Spread the bottom of a medium-size gratin dish or ovenproof skillet with ½ tablespoon of the oil. Add the leeks and top with another ½ tablespoon olive oil, the salt, and a generous grinding of pepper. Top with the cream. Cover with aluminum foil.

Roast the leeks for 10 minutes. Remove the foil, toss the leeks gently, and continue roasting until the leeks are tender and lightly browned, another 5 to 10 minutes.

To serve the leeks with the vinaigrette, in a small bowl, mix the vinegar with the remaining 4½ tablespoons of olive oil. Season to taste. Spoon the vinaigrette over the warm leeks and then top with the cheese and chives or parsley.

To serve the leeks warm, without the vinaigrette, sprinkle with the cheese and place under the broiler until the cheese is bubbling and golden, about 1 minute. Sprinkle with the chives or parsley and serve.

Makes 4 to 6 servings

Three-Onion Roast

Small white boiling onions, shallots, and garlic are roasted together in a slightly sweet, vinegary glaze. These onions are totally irresistible and can be eaten hot from the oven, at room temperature, or chilled. They will keep in a sealed jar in the refrigerator for up to two months. Use them in salads, antipasto platters, or serve them with cold meats and cheese.

3 cups small white boiling onions, peeled and left whole (18 to 20 onions)

12 shallots, peeled and left whole

12 cloves garlic, peeled and left whole

About ¼ cup olive oil

About ½ cup balsamic vinegar

2 tablespoons water

2 tablespoons sugar

2 tablespoons chopped fresh thyme; or 1½ teaspoons dried

2 tablespoons chopped fresh rosemary; or 1½ teaspoons dried

Salt and freshly ground black pepper

Preheat the oven to 400 degrees.

In a medium-size roasting pan or shallow casserole, mix all the ingredients, making sure the onions, shallots, and garlic are thoroughly coated.

Cover the pan with aluminum foil and roast the onions, stirring them once or twice, for about 1 hour. Check the onions after 40 minutes to make sure they are not drying out and add more oil and vinegar if needed.

Remove the roasting pan from the oven and serve the onions, or spoon them into a glass jar and cover with the marinade from the pan. If there is not enough marinade to cover the onions, add additional oil and vinegar.

Makes 6 to 8 servings

Roasted Onions in Cinzano

The sweet flavor of Cinzano (sweet vermouth) provides a thick glaze for whole roasted onions. Serve these hot from the oven or slice them thinly and toss with angel hair pasta and a spoonful of olive oil or use them as a topping for pork, lamb, or veal chops. These onions are an ideal accompaniment to any roast.

10 small white boiling onions, peeled and left whole; or 5 large onions, peeled and cut in half

6 cloves garlic, peeled and left whole (optional)

About 1 cup Cinzano (sweet vermouth)

Salt and freshly ground black pepper

Preheat the oven to 325 degrees.

Place the onions in a small roasting pan and surround with the garlic if desired. Pour 1 cup of the Cinzano on top and season liberally with salt and pepper.

Roast for 45 minutes, stirring the onions in the Cinzano every 15 minutes or so. If the Cinzano starts to dry out, add another $1/4$ to $1/3$ cup.

Preheat the broiler and broil the onions until they have a nice dark glaze, about 5 minutes.

Makes 4 servings

Roasted Three-Onion and Potato Soup

This soup is a rich, multidimensional version of vichyssoise—the classic cold leek and potato soup—filled with the flavor of roasted potatoes, leeks, onions, and scallions. It is equally delicious hot or cold. For an extra flourish, swirl a teaspoon of heavy cream or crème fraîche through the soup just before serving. The soup is hearty enough to be served as a main course, accompanied by a roasted pepper salad and crusty bread.

1¹/₂ tablespoons olive oil

4 medium-size baking potatoes, peeled and cut into chunks

2 medium-size leeks, trimmed, cut lengthwise in half and then crosswise into chunks

4 scallions, trimmed and cut into chunks

2 medium-size onions, peeled and cut into quarters

3 tablespoons fresh thyme; or 2 teaspoons dried

Salt and freshly ground black pepper

6 to 8 cups homemade chicken stock, low-sodium canned chicken broth, or vegetable stock

About ¹/₂ cup heavy cream or crème fraîche (optional)

Preheat the oven to 400 degrees.

Grease the bottom of a large roasting pan with ¹/₂ tablespoon of the oil. Add the potatoes, leeks, scallions, and onions and top with the thyme, salt, and pepper. Drizzle the remaining oil over the top, and stir to make sure the vegetables are thoroughly coated.

Roast the vegetables, stirring frequently, for 1 hour. Remove the roasting pan from the oven and pour 6 cups of the stock or broth into the vegetables, scraping up any browned bits. Working in batches, puree the mixture in a food processor or blender until smooth.

Transfer the soup to a medium-size saucepan. If the soup seems too thick, add another ¹/₂ cup to 2 cups of stock or broth, depending on how thick you like your soup. Season to taste and heat over moderately low heat until simmering. Just before serving, swirl the cream or crème fraîche into each bowl if desired.

Makes 6 to 8 servings

Roasted Fennel Parmigiana

Like so many vegetables, this anise-flavored bulb takes particularly well to roasting. Here it is simply roasted with a drizzle of olive oil, sea salt, and freshly ground pepper and then topped with a dusting of Parmesan cheese. Serve the fennel on its own or use as an accompaniment to fish, poultry, or meat.

1 large bulb fennel

1 tablespoon good-quality olive oil

Sea salt and freshly ground black pepper

¼ cup grated Parmesan cheese

Preheat the oven to 350 degrees.

Trim the tops and the feathery, dill-like fronds from the fennel bulb and discard. Cut the fennel bulb into thick slices through the base. Lightly grease the bottom of a small roasting pan or ovenproof skillet with half of the oil. Arrange the fennel in a single layer in the pan with the curved side up, and season with the salt and pepper. Drizzle the remaining oil over the fennel.

Roast the fennel for 20 minutes. Turn the fennel over and season the other side. Sprinkle the cheese on top and roast until the fennel is tender when pierced and the cheese is bubbling, 10 to 15 minutes more. Serve hot.

Makes 4 servings

Cream of Roasted Fennel Soup

For this soup, fennel, with its slightly sweet, anise flavor is first roasted and then pureed to a thick, creamy texture. The flavors are clean and fresh tasting. Serve this soup on a cold winter's day, topped with a dollop of crème fraîche and crunchy chopped fennel tops.

2 large bulbs fennel

1 large onion, peeled and cut into quarters

1 tablespoon olive oil

Salt and freshly ground black pepper

3 cups homemade chicken stock, low-sodium canned chicken broth, or vegetable broth

1 cup water

$^1/_2$ cup crème fraîche or heavy cream, plus about $^1/_4$ cup for spooning into the finished soup

Preheat the oven to 400 degrees.

Cut the tops and feathery fronds off the fennel. Discard the fronds; reserve the tops. Cut the bulb into small chunks and place in a medium-size roasting pan or oven-proof skillet. Add the onion and drizzle the oil on top. Stir the vegetables to coat them with the oil and season with the salt and pepper.

Roast the vegetables, stirring once or twice, until the fennel is somewhat brown and tender when pierced, 35 to 45 minutes.

While the fennel is roasting, finely chop the reserved fennel tops to make about 1 cup and set aside.

Remove the roasting pan from the oven. Add the broth and water to the vegetables, scraping up any browned bits. Working in small batches puree the mixture in a food processor or blender until smooth. Add $^1/_2$ cup of the crème fraîche to the last batch and blend until smooth.

Transfer the soup to a medium-size saucepan and season to taste. Bring to a gentle simmer over low heat. Serve hot, with a sprinkling of the reserved fennel tops and the additional crème fraîche or heavy cream if desired.

Makes 6 servings

Pureed Roasted Portobello Mushroom Soup

Portobellos are a large, earthy-flavored variety of mushroom that can be transformed into an outrageous, surprisingly rich soup. When they are roasted along with a few onions and cloves of garlic, your kitchen will fill with an irresistible meaty scent. You'll swear there's beef roasting in your oven.

If you can't find fresh portobello mushrooms, substitute fresh shiitakes or cèpes. You can also use regular white mushrooms, but in that case I'd suggest substituting beef broth for the vegetable or chicken stock.

This soup also makes a great first course for a roast beef or pork dinner. Serve it with warm black bread and a hearty red wine. It would also make a great addition to an elegant Thanksgiving dinner.

2 teaspoons olive oil

3 medium-size onions, peeled and cut into quarters

3 cloves garlic, peeled and left whole

1 pound fresh portobello mushrooms, trimmed and cut into small chunks

Salt and freshly ground black pepper

1 teaspoon chopped fresh thyme; or ¹/₄ teaspoon dried

2 tablespoons dry sherry

5 cups homemade chicken stock, low-sodium chicken broth, or vegetable stock

¹/₄ cup heavy cream

¹/₄ cup chopped fresh parsley

About 8 slices toast or crusty French bread

Preheat the oven to 400 degrees.

Grease the bottom of a medium-size roasting pan or ovenproof skillet with 1 teaspoon of the oil. Add the onions and garlic and top with the mushrooms. Drizzle the remaining teaspoon of oil on top and season with salt, pepper, and thyme.

Roast the mushrooms, stirring once or twice, for 20 minutes. Remove the roasting pan from the oven and pour the sherry into the mushrooms, scraping up any brown bits. Add the stock to the pan. Working in batches, puree the mushroom mixture in a food processor or blender until smooth.

Transfer the soup to a medium-size saucepan and season to taste. Add the cream and simmer over low heat until hot throughout, about 5 minutes. Sprinkle the soup with the parsley and serve hot with the toast or French bread.

Makes 4 servings

Roasted Acorn Squash
with Parsnips and Apple Cider

Ideal for a cool fall night, this is a main-course dish that needs to be served with only a bottle of cider or dry white wine, a good loaf of bread, and some tossed salad greens.

3 tablespoons butter, cut into small pieces

2 medium-size acorn squash, cut in half and seeded

2 parsnips, peeled and cut into thin slices

Salt and freshly ground black pepper

1 tablespoon chopped fresh thyme; or 1 teaspoon dried

³/₄ cup apple cider without preservatives

¹/₂ cup dry white wine

¹/₄ cup pure maple syrup

Preheat the oven to 350 degrees.

Grease the bottom of a medium-size roasting pan with 1 tablespoon of the butter. Place the squash halves in the pan and scatter the parsnips around them. Sprinkle the insides of the squash with salt, pepper, and thyme. Pour the cider and wine around (not on top of) the squash. Pour the maple syrup inside the squash cavities. Dot the top of the squash with the remaining 2 tablespoons of butter.

Roast the squash, basting every 15 minutes, until tender when pierced, about 1 hour.

Makes 2 servings as a main course
or 4 servings as a side dish

Roasted Parsnip, Mushroom, and Parmesan Salad with Red Onion–Mustard Vinaigrette

This composed salad combines a variety of flavors and textures—the sweetness of roasted parsnips, the mild butteriness of raw mushrooms, the crunch and anise taste of raw fennel, the pungency of Parmesan cheese shavings—all tossed with a red onion and mustard vinaigrette. This salad could easily be served as a main course or alongside any main dish.

The Salad:

1 tablespoon olive oil

2 large parsnips, peeled and cut into slices about 1-inch thick

Salt and freshly ground black pepper

1 cup trimmed and thinly sliced white mushrooms

1 cup thinly sliced fennel tops (the long thin ribs on top of the fennel bulb)

About ¹/₂ cup or 10 shavings of Parmigiano-Reggiano cheese from a ¹/₂-pound piece (see Note)

The Vinaigrette:

2 tablespoons peeled and finely chopped red onion

1 ¹/₂ teaspoons Dijon mustard

Salt and freshly ground black pepper

1 ¹/₂ tablespoons red wine vinegar

3 tablespoons olive oil

Preheat the oven to 400 degrees.

Grease a medium-size roasting pan or skillet with ¹/₂ tablespoon of the oil. Arrange the parsnips in a single layer in the pan. Drizzle the remaining oil on top and season with salt and pepper.

Roast the parsnips, turning them over after 5 minutes, until golden brown on both sides, about 15 minutes total.

Remove the roasting pan from the oven and drain off any excess oil. Place the roasted parsnips in a small salad bowl or on a medium-size serving plate. Place the mushrooms on top of or around the parsnips, then add the fennel and top with the cheese shavings.

Prepare the vinaigrette: In a small bowl, mix the onion and mustard with the salt and pepper. Whisk in the vinegar and oil and taste for seasoning.

Pour the vinaigrette over the salad and serve at room temperature.

Makes 2 servings as a main course or 4 servings as a side dish

Note: *Use a vegetable peeler to shave off thin slices from the cheese. If you can't find real Parmigiano-Reggiano cheese, don't substitute an imitation Parmesan; instead, use a sharp Cheddar or other hard, well-flavored cheese.*

Roasted Vegetable Platter

The combination of flavors, colors, and textures in this dish creates a spectacular centerpiece. But this assortment of roasted vegetables can also be served as an accompaniment to poultry, beef, lamb, or fish dishes. It's delicious served hot out of the oven or at room temperature, accompanied by a garlicky vinaigrette and a loaf of crusty bread.

2 medium-size eggplant, ends trimmed, cut lengthwise into quarters

Salt

3 tablespoons Garlic-Fennel-Chile Oil (page 236) or good-quality fruity olive oil

8 small to medium-size new potatoes, scrubbed and cut in half

4 large carrots, peeled, cut lengthwise in half and then crosswise into 2-inch pieces

2 small zucchini, ends trimmed, cut lengthwise into quarters

2 small summer squash, ends trimmed, cut lengthwise into quarters

2 red, green, or yellow bell peppers, cored and cut lengthwise into quarters

4 large, ripe tomatoes, cut into quarters (see Note)

8 cloves garlic, peeled and left whole

$1/4$ cup chopped fresh parsley

$1/4$ cup chopped fresh basil; or 1 teaspoon dried

2 tablespoons chopped fresh thyme; or $1^{1}/_{2}$ teaspoons dried

Freshly ground black pepper

Place the eggplant in a colander and sprinkle the cut sides with $1^{1}/_{2}$ tablespoons salt. Let sit about 20 minutes. Rinse under cold water to remove the salt and dry thoroughly.

Preheat the oven to 400 degrees.

Grease the bottom of a large roasting pan or heavy ovenproof skillet with half of the oil. Arrange the eggplant, potatoes, carrots, zucchini, squash, peppers, tomatoes, and garlic in a single layer in the pan. Sprinkle with the parsley, basil, thyme, salt, and pepper. Drizzle the vegetables with the remaining oil.

Roast the vegetables for 10 minutes. Reduce the oven temperature to 325 degrees and roast, gently stirring after about 20 minutes, until the potatoes are tender when pierced with a knife, an additional 50 minutes.

Makes 4 servings as a main course or 6 servings as a side dish

> Note: *If you can't find really ripe fresh tomatoes, simply omit them from the recipe.*

Stew of Roasted Vegetables

A "roasted" stew offers all the flavors and textures of roasted foods but there is absolutely no fat added, and the entire stew is made in the oven in one pan.

2 large onions, peeled and cut into quarters

4 large ribs celery, cut into 2-inch pieces

4 large carrots, peeled and cut into 2-inch pieces

2 medium-size leeks, trimmed, cut lengthwise in half, and then crosswise into 2-inch pieces

1 large acorn squash, cut in half, seeded, and cut into large chunks

8 cloves garlic, peeled and left whole

3 large potatoes, scrubbed and cut into chunks

2 scallions, trimmed and thinly sliced

Salt and freshly ground black pepper

1 tablespoon chopped fresh thyme; or 1 teaspoon dried

1½ tablespoons chopped fresh basil; or 1½ teaspoons dried

¼ cup Cinzano or dry red wine

6 medium-size ripe tomatoes, cut into quarters; or 2 cups canned whole tomatoes, chopped

2 tablespoons all-purpose flour

4 cups homemade chicken stock, low-sodium canned chicken broth, or vegetable stock

Preheat the oven to 400 degrees.

In a large flameproof roasting pan, place the onions, celery, carrots, leeks, acorn squash, garlic, potatoes, and scallions. Stir to distribute the vegetables and add the salt, pepper, thyme, basil, and Cinzano or wine.

Roast the vegetables, stirring once or twice, for 30 minutes. Remove the roasting pan from the oven and gently stir in the tomatoes. Reduce the oven temperature to 350 degrees and roast an additional 15 minutes.

Remove the pan from the oven and place over two burners. Bring to a simmer over moderately high heat. Thoroughly blend the flour into any juices that have accumulated on the bottom of the pan and coat the vegetables. Cook for 1 minute, stirring constantly. Gradually add the stock or broth and bring to a boil. Remove from the heat, season to taste, and place back in the oven. Continue roasting until the sauce is thickened and all the vegetables are thoroughly cooked, about 15 minutes. Adjust the seasoning and serve hot.

Makes 4 servings

Note: *You can make an even heartier stew by adding a 3-pound chicken cut into serving pieces or a few Italian sausages cut into chunks; roast the meat or poultry along with the vegetables.*

J.R.'s Winter Root Vegetable Stew

This is a particularly hearty stew that uses a variety of roasted root vegetables, potatoes, leeks, and onions. What distinguishes this stew from the others in this book is that it calls for no stock; instead, a touch of water or wine supplements the natural juices of the vegetables. Even though potatoes are a main feature here, the stew is delicious served over a bed of whole-wheat couscous. Serve as a main course with a variety of hot sauces on the side.

2 tablespoons olive oil

2 large baking potatoes or sweet potatoes, peeled and cut into quarters

4 medium-size parsnips, peeled and cut into 2-inch pieces

4 medium-size carrots, peeled and cut into 2-inch pieces

2 large ribs celery, trimmed and cut into 2-inch pieces

2 large onions, peeled and cut into quarters

1 medium-size leek, trimmed, cut lengthwise in half and then crosswise into 2-inch pieces

8 small beets, trimmed and peeled

Salt and freshly ground black pepper

1 bay leaf

About $^1/_2$ cup water

About 1 cup dry red or white wine

$^1/_2$ cup chopped fresh parsley

Preheat the oven to 425 degrees.

Grease the bottom of a large roasting pan or shallow ovenproof casserole with 1 tablespoon of the oil. Add the potatoes, parsnips, carrots, celery, onions, leek, beets, salt, and pepper. Add the bay leaf and pour $^1/_2$ cup water and 1 cup wine over the vegetables. Sprinkle with the parsley and remaining oil.

Cover the pan and roast for 20 minutes. Gently stir the vegetables and check the liquid in the pan, adding more water and/or wine if needed. Roast, stirring every 20 minutes and checking to make sure the stew remains juicy, until the vegetables are tender when pierced, a total of about 1 hour.

Makes 4 servings

Roasted Antipasto Platter

Most antipasto platters contain several types of meats, but this one—composed of an assortment of roasted vegetables, including potatoes—offers such a variety of colors, textures, and flavors that you won't miss the meat.

There are a number of other vegetable recipes in this chapter that would make good additions to this platter, particularly Roasted Asparagus (page 163), any of the roasted red pepper recipes, or Roasted Garlic (page 196). And if you do want to add meat to this dish, thin slices of prosciutto or a peppery salami would be ideal.

Although there are several steps involved with this antipasto, all the vegetables are roasted at the same temperature so that they can be cooked together. And all the roasting can be done a day ahead of time, which means the antipasto can be assembled at the last minute. Serve with cocktails, as a first course, or as dinner with a good crusty bread.

The Beets:

4 medium-size beets, ends trimmed

1 tablespoon chopped fresh dill

Salt and freshly ground black pepper

The Potatoes:

6 small to medium-size new potatoes, preferably a red variety, scrubbed

1 teaspoon olive oil

Sea salt

Freshly ground black pepper

1 tablespoon chopped fresh rosemary

Preheat the oven to 350 degrees.

Prepare the beets: Place the beets on a sheet of aluminum foil and wrap tightly. Roast until they are tender when pierced, 30 minutes to $1^1/_2$ hours. (Timing varies wildly, depending on the size of the beets.) Let the beets cool slightly in the foil, about 5 minutes. Using a small sharp knife, peel the beets and cut them into wedges. Reserve all the juices that have accumulated in the foil. Place the beet wedges in a small bowl and toss with the reserved juices, the dill, salt, and pepper. Cover and refrigerate.

Prepare the potatoes: Place the potatoes in a small roasting pan, and toss with the oil, salt, pepper, and rosemary. Roast, stirring occasionally, until tender when pierced, 45 minutes to 1 hour. Remove the potatoes from the oven and cut into wedges. Place in a small bowl, along with the salt and rosemary. Cover and refrigerate.

Prepare the leeks: Place the leeks in a small roasting pan, drizzle the oil on top, and sprinkle with the herbs, salt, and pepper. Roast, stirring once or twice, until tender when pierced, about 20 minutes. Remove from the oven, let cool, cover, and refrigerate.

The Leeks:

1 large leek or 2 small leeks, trimmed, sliced lengthwise in half and then crosswise into 2-inch pieces

1 tablespoon flavored oil (pages 198 and 236) or olive oil

1 teaspoon *fines herbes* (see Note)

Salt and freshly ground black pepper

The Shallots:

8 large shallots, peeled and cut in half

1 tablespoon olive oil

1 tablespoon balsamic vinegar;
 or 1 tablespoon red wine vinegar with 1 teaspoon of sugar added

Salt and freshly ground black pepper

The Salad and Roasted Pine Nut Vinaigrette:

1/3 cup pine nuts

1 tablespoon chopped fresh parsley

1 1/2 tablespoons chopped fresh chives

1 teaspoon Dijon mustard

Salt and freshly ground black pepper

1/4 cup balsamic vinegar or red wine vinegar

6 tablespoons olive oil

About 4 cups mixed salad greens, thoroughly washed and dried

About 1/2 cup or 10 shavings of Parmigiano-Reggiano cheese from a 1/2-pound piece (see Note)

Prepare the shallots: Place the shallots in a small roasting pan or ovenproof skillet and toss with the oil, vinegar, salt, and pepper. Roast until tender when pierced, 20 to 25 minutes. Place in a small bowl along with pan juices, cover, and refrigerate.

Prepare the salad and vinaigrette: Place the pine nuts in a small ovenproof skillet and roast until they just begin to brown and smell fragrant, about 5 minutes. Place the nuts in a small bowl while they are still warm and mix with the parsley, chives, mustard, salt, and pepper. Whisk in the vinegar and oil and taste for seasoning. Cover and refrigerate.

Assemble the platter: Remove everything from the refrigerator at least 1 hour before serving to bring to room temperature. Mound the greens in the center of a very large platter. Place small piles of each roasted vegetable around the greens. Spoon half of the vinaigrette over the vegetables and greens and pass the rest separately. Top with the cheese shavings and a generous grinding of black pepper.

Makes 6 servings

> Note: Fines herbes *is a blend or fresh chives, chervil, and* tarragon; herbes de Provence *is a mixture of dried thyme, rosemary, marjoram, sage, and basil; any one or any combination of these herbs can be substituted.*
>
> *Shave the Parmesan cheese slices using a vegetable peeler.*

Garlic

Roasted Garlic

Thanksgiving Day is the best-smelling day of the year in my kitchen. For quite some time I was under the impression that it was the roasting turkey that was the source of that glorious scent. But one winter's evening I decided to roast a few heads of garlic with olive oil and herbs sprinkled over the top. Within minutes my kitchen, actually my entire house, was filled with the heady aroma of Thanksgiving.

Roasted garlic can be used in any number of ways—aside from making your house smell like heaven. It can be squeezed out of its papery skin and spread on thinly sliced toast, pizza, or bruschetta; placed on top of fish, beef, or poultry dishes; mixed into pasta sauces or dips; or served as a side dish to just about any meal. If you're very comfortable with the people you're eating with, encourage them to take a few cloves of the garlic and pop them into their mouths. The idea is to suck the roasted garlic essence directly from the skin.

If you're in a rush, you can cut about $1/2$ inch off the top of the garlic head, exposing the cloves directly to the heat. The garlic will roast in 25 to 30 minutes.

2 large heads garlic, unpeeled and left whole

$1^1/_2$ tablespoons olive oil

1 tablespoon chopped fresh thyme; or 1 teaspoon dried

1 tablespoon chopped fresh rosemary; or 1 teaspoon dried

Salt and freshly ground black pepper

Preheat the oven to 350 degrees.

Place the garlic in a small roasting pan or ovenproof skillet and drizzle the oil on top. Sprinkle with the herbs, a pinch of salt, and a generous grinding of pepper.

Roast the garlic until soft, 45 minutes to 1 hour. Remove from the oven and serve.

Makes enough for 2 garlic lovers or 4 regular eaters

Roasted Garlic and Herb Butter

This is an extravagantly flavored butter, rich with the essence of roasted garlic and herbs. Spread it on toasted or grilled sliced French bread, toast, or spoon a tiny bit on a baked potato—regular or sweet—pasta, rice, grilled chicken, fish, corn on the cob, whatever. It's also outrageously good tossed with steamed vegetables. The point is that it goes well with just about everything. You can make the butter, roll it into a fat cigar shape, wrap it in plastic wrap, and freeze it for several months.

8 tablespoons (1 stick) butter, softened

2 heads of Roasted Garlic (facing page), still in the roasting pan and warm

Salt and freshly ground black pepper

Mash the butter in a small bowl and squeeze the garlic from its skin directly into the bowl. Mix in the herbs and olive oil from the garlic roasting pan and season to taste. (Take care not to add much salt if using salted butter.) Serve in a small ramekin or attractive bowl or freeze.

Makes $^1/_2$ cup

It's Time to Roast the Garlic

You don't need an excuse to roast garlic; it's good with just about any meal. Of course, the best time to roast garlic is when you already have the oven going to roast something else. So the next time you roast chicken, pork, fish, or eggplant . . . don't forget the garlic.

Roasted Garlic and Shallot-Flavored Oil

Infused with the mellow flavors of roasted garlic and shallots, this oil is wonderful drizzled over salads, roasts, potatoes, pasta dishes, and fish. It's also very good as a base for dips, aioli (a garlicky mayonnaise), or a vinaigrette.

I like to fill tall, lightly colored glass bottles with this oil and give it to friends for the holidays. Place a label on the bottle suggesting various uses.

6 cloves garlic, peeled and left whole

6 shallots, peeled and left whole

3 cups plus 1 tablespoon good-quality olive oil

Freshly ground black pepper

3 sprigs fresh rosemary; or 1 teaspoon dried

3 sprigs fresh thyme; or 1 teaspoon dried

6 black peppercorns

1 bay leaf

Preheat the oven to 350 degrees.

Place the garlic and shallots in a small roasting pan and drizzle 1 tablespoon of the oil on top. Sprinkle liberally with the pepper.

Roast the garlic and shallots, checking the garlic occasionally so it does not burn, until tender when pierced, about 15 minutes.

Place the garlic and shallots in a clean wine bottle or other glass jar. Add the remaining olive oil, rosemary, thyme, peppercorns, and bay leaf and seal tightly. Place in a dark, cool spot for 1 week before using. Store in the refrigerator or a very cool, dark spot. The oil should last for about 2 months. Discard the oil at the first sign of mold.

Makes 3 cups

Roasted Garlic, Herb, and Cheese Custards

These savory custards, silky and creamy, are laced with the distinctive flavors of roasted garlic, a variety of herbs, and Parmesan cheese. Serve them as a fancy lunch dish or as a first course, served on a small plate, surrounded by mixed greens that have been tossed with sparing amounts of oil and vinegar. Try them with just about any roasted poultry, meat, fish, or vegetable dish.

They can be made ahead of time and kept in the refrigerator. To reheat, wrap the custards in aluminum foil and place in a 350-degree oven for about 5 minutes.

1 tablespoon olive oil, plus additional for greasing

$^1/_2$ head garlic

2 large eggs

1 large egg yolk

$^1/_2$ teaspoon chopped fresh thyme; or $^1/_4$ teaspoon dried

$^1/_2$ teaspoon chopped fresh savory; or $^1/_4$ teaspoon dried (optional)

1 tablespoon chopped fresh rosemary; or $^1/_2$ teaspoon dried

Salt and freshly ground black pepper

$^1/_2$ cup heavy cream

$^3/_4$ cup low-fat milk

$^1/_4$ cup grated Parmesan cheese

Preheat the oven to 350 degrees.

Lightly grease a 6-cup muffin tin with olive oil and set inside a larger roasting pan.

Place the garlic in a small roasting pan and surround with 1 tablespoon olive oil.

Roast the garlic for 20 minutes. Remove the roasting pan from the oven and let the garlic cool slightly. Peel the garlic or squeeze it out of its skin.

Place the roasted garlic in a food processor along with the eggs, egg yolk, herbs, salt, and pepper and process until well blended. Keeping the machine on, slowly add the cream and milk until smooth. Add the cheese and process for another 30 seconds.

Pour the custard into the muffin tin. Pour enough boiling water in the large roasting pan to come halfway up the sides of the muffin tin. Loosely cover the tin with aluminum foil.

Roast the custards until the centers feel firm to the touch, about 20 minutes. Remove the muffin tin from the oven and let the custards cool for about 2 minutes. Run a small knife around the custards to loosen them from the tin. Place a large plate over the tin and carefully invert to release the custards. Serve warm or at room temperature.

Makes 6 servings

Roasted Pepper Aioli

Garlic lovers, rejoice! This sauce combines the mellowness of roasted garlic and the sharp bite of raw garlic with roasted red pepper, good olive oil, egg, and lemon juice. My friend Graham Smith created this beautifully colored sauce, which goes well with any type of fish dish, young new potatoes, or as a pungent replacement for mayonnaise in turkey or chicken sandwiches.

The sauce will keep, covered and refrigerated, for five days. The flavors tend to intensify with time, so it's best to make the sauce a day before serving.

7 cloves garlic, peeled and left whole

1¼ cups good-quality olive oil, at room temperature

½ large red bell pepper, cored

Salt and freshly ground black pepper

1 large egg, at room temperature

1 large egg yolk, at room temperature

3 tablespoons lemon juice

1 tablespoon Dijon mustard

Preheat the oven to 400 degrees.

Place 6 of the garlic cloves in a small ovenproof skillet (preferably cast iron) and drizzle 2 tablespoons of the oil over them. Place the bell pepper, skin side up, over the garlic cloves and drizzle with another 2 tablespoons of the oil. Add a pinch of salt and a grinding of pepper on top.

Roast the garlic and red pepper until the skin of the pepper blackens, about 45 minutes. Remove the skillet from the oven. Let the garlic cool. Place the red pepper in a plastic bag or aluminum foil, close tightly, and let steam for about 5 minutes. Using a small sharp knife or your fingers, peel the pepper.

Pour the oil from the skillet into the measuring cup with the remaining 1 cup oil and set aside. Puree the roasted garlic along with the remaining clove of raw garlic in a food processor or blender. Add the egg, egg yolk, lemon juice, mustard, and a grinding of pepper and process for about 20 seconds. Scrape down the sides of the container. With the motor running, slowly add the oil in a very thin stream. The sauce will thicken as the oil emulsifies. Stop the processor 5 seconds after the last drop of oil has been incorporated. Cover and refrigerate until ready to serve. Bring the aioli to room temperature before serving.

Makes about 1½ cups

Potatoes and Cheese

Roasted Potatoes

I love potatoes—mashed, fried, steamed, in salads and pancakes, or simply baked. But as far as I'm concerned, roasted potatoes are among the most satisfying foods. This is one of the most classic, straightforward recipes in this book and one of my favorites.

What could be better than fresh potatoes rubbed with olive oil, sprinkled with salt and pepper, and roasted until golden brown? The olive oil provides flavor and gives the potato skin a crispy coating. These potatoes taste so rich you'll swear they're coated in butter. Be sure to choose a roasting pan large enough to hold the potatoes in a single layer, so that they roast properly and do not steam.

Although these potatoes are roasted with sprigs of fresh rosemary (the herb I feel best plays up their buttery flavor), feel free to experiment with a variety of herbs and spices. There really isn't any flavor that doesn't work with them: curry powder, cumin, cayenne pepper, coriander, thyme, sage, caraway seeds, oregano, etc. And there isn't any roast that would not be complemented by these potatoes.

12 medium-size new potatoes, scrubbed

1 tablespoon light olive oil (see Note)

6 sprigs fresh rosemary; or 1 tablespoon dried (see Note)

Sea salt

Freshly ground black pepper

Preheat the oven to 350 degrees.

Place the potatoes in a medium-size roasting pan or a large cast-iron skillet, pour the oil on top, and sprinkle with the rosemary. Shake the pan so that the potatoes become coated on all sides with the oil and rosemary. Let "marinate" for at least 15 minutes or up to 3 hours. Sprinkle with the salt and pepper.

Roast the potatoes, shaking the pan every 15 minutes or so to brown the potatoes evenly on all sides, until they are tender, 45 minutes to 1 hour, depending on the size. Serve piping hot, with the oil from the pan poured on top.

Makes 6 servings

Note: *Use a light olive oil for this dish, or the flavor of the oil will overpower the potatoes.*

You can use the whole sprig of rosemary and let the leaves and the stem lend their flavor to the potatoes. Or simply strip the leaves off the stem and use only the leaves.

Bay Leaf–Infused Roasted Potatoes

Sometimes the best way to describe a dish is by its smell rather than the way it tastes. This aromatic dish combines the pungent, savory scent of fresh bay leaves with the earthy, inviting smell of roasted potatoes. The number of bay leaves may seem excessive, considering how much they cost, but the result is worth it.

¼ to ½ cup fresh bay leaves

6 medium-size baking potatoes, peeled and cut into quarters

Salt and freshly ground black pepper

2½ tablespoons fruity olive oil

5 tablespoons homemade chicken stock or low-sodium chicken broth (optional)

Preheat the oven to 400 degrees.

Scatter the bay leaves on the bottom of a medium-size roasting pan, shallow ovenproof casserole, or ovenproof skillet. Place the potatoes on top, season with salt and pepper, and drizzle with the oil.

Roast the potatoes, turning them once or twice to brown evenly on all sides and expose the whole potato to the bay leaves, for 1 hour. Add the stock or broth and roast another 5 minutes. Serve hot.

Makes 4 to 6 servings

Which Potato Is Best? A Roasting Guide

Lydie Marshall, the author of *A Passion for Potatoes* and an authority on potatoes, says: "To roast potatoes, choose an all-purpose variety: the red potato (Nordland and Pontiac), the California White Rose (sometimes called Long White), or the yellow-flesh potato (Yukon Gold, Yellow Finnish, and Bintje)." Although many of these varieties are fairly uncommon, it's worth seeking out a good roasting potato. Of course, you won't go wrong using a "normal" supermarket variety like Russet.

Even more important than which variety you use is finding really fresh potatoes. That means potatoes that do not have "eyes" forming on their flesh or any soft brown spots. If you use organically grown, fresh-dug potatoes, you'll find that a great dish becomes even more memorable.

Roasted Potatoes Buried in Sea Salt

Try using red new potatoes or small yellow potatoes in this dish, burying them completely in the coarse sea salt or kosher salt. The result is a perfectly roasted potato—crisp skin and soft, buttery insides—with just the right amount of saltiness. The salt acts as a kind of "crust" without overwhelming the potatoes. Brush the hot salt off the potatoes using a pastry brush or your hands well wrapped in a pot holder.

With the potatoes, serve any roast, or try these potatoes as an unusual first course accompanied by Roasted Pepper Aioli (page 200) or Green Sauce (page 227).

12 medium-size new potatoes

About 2 cups coarse sea salt or kosher salt

Preheat the oven to 350 degrees.

Place the potatoes in a medium-size roasting pan or ovenproof skillet; do not crowd the pan. Pour the salt over the potatoes; there should be enough salt so that only the very tops of the potatoes peek through.

Roast the potatoes until tender, about 45 minutes. Brush the salt off the potatoes before serving. Serve hot.

Makes 4 to 6 servings

Emma Potatoes

As unlikely as it may sound, the inspiration for this dish came from my four-year-old daughter, Emma. We were turning potatoes in the roasting pan so they would brown nicely on all sides when she accidentally dumped about half a jar of capers into the pan. (The capers were meant to go on top of the fish we were also cooking that evening.) "Oh well," Emma announced with a devilish grin. "Those little green things will taste good with the potatoes." And because I am an adventurous cook and, I like to believe, a fairly patient mother, I agreed. The tartness of the capers turned out to be an excellent foil for the potatoes, and this dish is dedicated to Emma Lu Gunst Rudolph.

6 medium-size potatoes, scrubbed and cut in half; or 3 large potatoes, cut into quarters

1 tablespoon olive oil

2 tablespoons chopped fresh chives or trimmed and chopped scallions

1 tablespoon chopped fresh rosemary; or 1 teaspoon dried

1 tablespoon chopped fresh thyme; or 1 teaspoon dried

Salt and freshly ground black pepper

3 tablespoons capers, drained

Preheat the oven to 375 degrees.

Place the potatoes in a medium-size roasting pan, shallow ovenproof casserole, or ovenproof skillet. Pour the oil on top and shake the potatoes to coat them on all sides with the oil. Sprinkle the chives, rosemary, thyme, salt, and pepper over the potatoes.

Roast the potatoes for about 30 minutes. Remove the pan from the oven and turn the potatoes over so they will brown on both sides. Continue roasting until the potatoes are almost tender when pierced, about 25 minutes longer. Add the capers and roast until the potatoes are tender and nicely browned, another 5 to 10 minutes. Serve hot.

Makes 4 to 6 servings

Roasted Sweet Potato Chips

These orange chips are sweet, "meaty," and positively addictive. Sprinkle with cayenne pepper to make the chips spicy. Serve them alongside roast chicken, beef, or pork or with hamburgers and hot dogs. You can also pass these chips at a cocktail party with a homemade (or bottled) salsa and cold beer.

Vegetable oil

1 large sweet potato, peeled and thinly sliced

Salt and freshly ground black pepper

Cayenne pepper (optional)

Preheat the oven to 350 degrees.

Lightly grease a baking sheet or sheets with oil. Place the potatoes slices on the sheet(s), spacing them well apart. Lightly brush the tops of the potato slices with oil and sprinkle with salt and pepper.

Roast the potatoes 8 minutes. Turn the potatoes over, lightly brush the other side with oil, and season with salt, pepper, and if desired, cayenne. Continue roasting the potatoes until they are tender in the middle and crisp along the edges. (Be careful not to let them burn.) Drain the potatoes on paper towels to remove any excess oil and serve hot or at room temperature.

Makes 2 to 4 servings

Roast Potatoes and Red Pepper Salad with Artichoke Hearts and Horseradish Vinaigrette

The traditional method for making potato salad—peel the potatoes, boil them until soft, and then toss with mayonnaise—is not necessarily the best. I decided to experiment with roasting the potatoes, which form a crisp "crust," and then tossing them with a simple vinaigrette spiked with horseradish. The result? No more mushy, bland potato salad.

10 medium-size potatoes, scrubbed and dried (see Box, page 203)

7 tablespoons good-quality olive oil

Salt and freshly ground black pepper

1 large red bell pepper

2 tablespoons chopped fresh parsley

1 teaspoon Dijon mustard

1 tablespoon horseradish, or to taste

3 tablespoons red wine vinegar

1 large cooked artichoke heart, cut into cubes; or 4 small bottled artichoke hearts, drained and cut into quarters

Preheat the oven to 450 degrees.

Place the potatoes in a medium-size roasting pan, ovenproof skillet, or shallow ovenproof casserole, top with 1 tablespoon of the olive oil, and sprinkle with salt and pepper. Shake the pan to coat the potatoes with the oil and seasonings.

Roast the potatoes until tender when pierced, 45 minutes to 1 hour. Let cool slightly and cut the potatoes into chunks, either large or small, depending on how you like them.

Place the bell pepper on a sheet of aluminum foil and roast, turning as needed, until almost blackened on all sides, about 20 minutes. Remove from the oven, wrap in the foil, and let sit for 5 minutes. When cool enough to handle, scrape off the peel using a small sharp knife. Core and seed the pepper, then cut into small or large chunks, depending on how you like it.

In a large bowl, mix the parsley, mustard, horseradish, salt, and pepper. Add the vinegar and whisk in the remaining 6 tablespoons olive oil. Taste for seasoning, adding more horseradish if needed. Add the warm potatoes, pepper chunks, and artichoke hearts to the vinaigrette and toss. Serve at room temperature or cold.

Makes 4 to 6 servings

Roasted New Potato and Green Bean Salad

I was lucky enough to taste this dish at a potluck dinner party. This salad combines roasted potatoes, green beans, onions, and garlic with a rosemary-flavored vinaigrette. It is so satisfying it could easily be served as a main course, along with a good loaf of bread. Adriana Gailing, a cook for Masseno's Cafe in Exeter, New Hampshire, was generous enough to pass her recipe along.

1¹/₂ pounds small new potatoes, cut into quarters

1 large Vidalia or red onion, cut into wedges about ¹/₄-inch thick

³/₄ cup extra virgin olive oil

3 tablespoons finely chopped fresh rosemary

Salt and freshly ground black pepper

1 head garlic, unpeeled

1 pound green beans, ends trimmed

¹/₄ cup balsamic vinegar

¹/₂ cup Calamata olives, pitted and cut in half

Preheat the oven to 425 degrees.

Place the potatoes and onion in a medium–size roasting pan or ovenproof skillet and drizzle with 3 tablespoons of the oil. Sprinkle with 1¹/₂ tablespoons of the rosemary, add salt and pepper to taste, and toss to coat.

Cut ¹/₂ inch from the top of the garlic head, exposing the cloves, and drizzle with 1 tablespoon of the oil. Wrap the garlic in a double layer of aluminum foil.

Roast the potatoes and onion, stirring occasionally, for 45 minutes. Roast the garlic along with the potatoes and onion until tender, 30 to 45 minutes. Remove the garlic from the oven and let cool. When the garlic is cool enough to handle, gently squeeze the pulp from each clove into a small bowl and set aside.

Meanwhile, bring a pot of lightly salted water to a boil. Add the beans and cook for 1 minute, then drain and rinse in cold water. Drain thoroughly and set aside. Add these blanched beans to the roasting pan with the potatoes and onion during the last 10 minutes of roasting to brown lightly.

Prepare the vinaigrette: Combine the vinegar and the remaining 1¹/₂ tablespoons of rosemary in a small bowl. Slowly add ¹/₂ cup of the oil while stirring with a whisk. Add salt and pepper to taste.

Combine the roasted vegetables, garlic, and olives in a large bowl. Add the vinaigrette and toss gently to combine. Season to taste. Serve in the bowl or transfer to a large serving platter. Serve warm or at room temperature.

Makes 4 to 6 servings

Roasted Potato Salad
with Olive Puree Vinaigrette

A few tablespoons of black olive puree mixed into a vinaigrette adds a dramatic flavor to roasted potatoes. The potatoes are tossed with the vinaigrette while they're still warm so they absorb the most flavor. The salad is then tossed with chopped celery, cucumber, radishes, and fresh herbs and surrounded with pitted black olives. The presentation is as dramatic as the taste.

2 tablespoons olive puree or tapenade (see Note)

Salt and freshly ground black pepper

2^1/$_2$ tablespoons balsamic vinegar

5 tablespoons flavored olive oil (pages 198 and 236) or good-quality olive oil

12 roasted small new potatoes or 6 medium-size potatoes from any of the recipes in this chapter

3 ribs celery, trimmed and finely chopped

1 large cucumber, peeled and finely chopped

6 large radishes, trimmed and thinly sliced

1 tablespoon chopped fresh chives or parsley

1 tablespoon chopped fresh thyme, rosemary, or oregano; or 1 teaspoon dried

1 cup pitted black Niçoise olives (optional)

In a small bowl, mix the olive puree, salt, and pepper. Add the vinegar and slowly whisk in the oil. Taste for seasoning.

Cut the potatoes into cubes—small or medium size, whichever you prefer. Place the potatoes in a medium-size bowl and toss with the vinaigrette. Add the celery, cucumber, radishes, chives or parsley, and thyme. Surround the salad with the olives. Taste for seasoning and serve warm or at room temperature.

Makes 6 servings

> **Note:** *Olive puree and tapenade (a pungent spread of black olives and capers from Provence) are available in specialty food shops.*

Herb-Crusted Goat Cheese

A small log of goat cheese is rolled in herbed breadcrumbs, drizzled with olive oil, and then roasted on a bed of fresh herbs—chives, tarragon, basil, or your favorite—until it just starts to melt. This dish makes a wonderful appetizer or first course. Serve it with a crusty loaf of bread or present it as a salad, placed on top of a mixture of greens lightly drizzled with a simple vinaigrette.

2¹⁄₂ tablespoons good-quality fruity olive oil or flavored oil (pages 198 and 236)

One 8-ounce log (about 6 inches long) soft or semi-firm goat cheese (chèvre) (see Note)

¹⁄₃ cup fresh or dry breadcrumbs

2 teaspoons chopped fresh tarragon or thyme; or ¹⁄₂ teaspoon dried

2 teaspoons chopped fresh rosemary; or ¹⁄₂ teaspoon dried

Salt and freshly ground black pepper

1 large bunch fresh chives or another herb (about 1 cup coarsely chopped)

Preheat the oven to 400 degrees.

Grease a small ovenproof skillet, small roasting pan, or shallow ovenproof casserole with 1 tablespoon of the oil.

Place 1 tablespoon of the oil in a small bowl, add the cheese, and coat all sides with the oil.

Mix the breadcrumbs with half of the tarragon and rosemary on a small plate and add the salt and pepper. Coat the oiled cheese on all sides with the seasoned breadcrumbs.

Place the fresh chives in the middle of the skillet and place the coated cheese on top. Drizzle with the remaining ¹⁄₂ tablespoon of oil, sprinkle the remaining tarragon and rosemary, and a generous grinding of pepper.

Roast the cheese until it begins to melt and get soft around the outside, 10 to 12 minutes.

Serve the cheese hot with toasted thin slices of French bread, or cut the cheese crosswise into 4 equal portions and serve with the herbs and oil from the pan on top of salad greens.

Makes 4 servings

> Note: *Goat cheese is available in specialty food shops and some supermarkets.*

Roast Chèvre with Tomatoes and Tapenade

When the goat cheese, tomatoes, and tapenade (olive puree) are roasting, don't be surprised if your kitchen smells like southern France. With a loaf of thinly sliced French or Italian bread and a fruity red wine, this makes a fabulous first course or hors d'oeuvre.

Here's another variation on this recipe: Surround the cheese with the tomato as well as 1 small leek, trimmed and thinly sliced, and 1 small red bell pepper, cored and chopped into small pieces, and proceed as directed below. The combination of colors—the green of the leek mixed with the red of the tomato and pepper against the whiteness of the cheese—is particularly striking.

Try the cheese with Provençal-Flavored Eye of Round Roast (page 14) or any of the roast lamb recipes.

2 teaspoons fruity olive oil

1 tablespoon chopped fresh rosemary

1 tablespoon chopped fresh sage

One 6-ounce log or oval soft goat cheese (chèvre) (see Note)

1 large ripe tomato, cut into chunks

1 tablespoon tapenade or olive puree (see Note)

¼ cup crusty bread cut into small cubes

Preheat the oven to 400 degrees.

Grease the bottom of a small ovenproof skillet or small roasting pan with 1 teaspoon of the oil. Place half of the rosemary and sage in the center of the skillet. Place the cheese on top and surround it with the tomato. Sprinkle the remaining oil and herbs on the cheese and top with the tapenade and then the bread cubes.

Roast the cheese and tomatoes until the cheese begins to melt and get soft around the outside and the tomatoes are soft, about 15 minutes.

Makes 4 servings

Note: *Tapenade, a pungent puree of black olives and capers from Provence, and goat cheese are available in specialty food shops and some supermarkets.*

Fruit

Roasted Pears with Grand Marnier–Cream Sauce

This elegant dessert is ideal for a cool winter's night. It can also be made with apples.

6 ripe Bosc or Anjou pears, peeled and cored (see Note)

1/3 cup water

3 tablespoons granulated sugar

1 cup heavy cream

3 tablespoons sour cream

2 tablespoons Grand Marnier or orange juice

1/3 cup light brown sugar

Preheat the oven to 350 degrees.

Stand the pears in a large roasting pan, pour in the water, and sprinkle with the granulated sugar.

Cover the pears with aluminum foil and roast, basting after 15 minutes, until they feel tender when pierced, about 45 minutes.

Remove the roasting pan from the oven and pour the pear juices into a small saucepan, keeping the pears in the roasting pan. Add the cream to the saucepan and simmer over moderately high heat until reduced to 1/2 cup, 8 to 10 minutes. Scrape the reduced cream into a bowl and let cool slightly. Mix the cooled cream with the sour cream and liqueur or orange juice, and set aside.

Preheat the broiler. Sift the brown sugar evenly over the pears and broil until the sugar is melted and bubbling, about 2 minutes. Place each pear on a serving plate and drizzle the cream sauce on top, or around the fruit.

Makes 6 servings

> Note: *Use a melon baller or small spoon to core the pears, working from the bottom of the fruit. Cut a thin slice off the bottom of the pears so they will stand in the pan.*

Roasted Figs with Pepper and Prosciutto

Fresh raw figs served with paper-thin slices of cured prosciutto ham and a sprinkling of black pepper is a favorite Italian antipasto. Here I take a twist on this classic and roast the figs and ham just until the figs start to soften. Serve these figs as a first course or an hors d'oeuvre with cocktails. You could also serve this on top of or alongside a mixed green salad.

1 tablespoon good-quality olive oil

4 paper-thin slices prosciutto, cut lengthwise into 4 strips

4 ripe fresh figs, peeled and cut lengthwise into quarters

Freshly ground black pepper

Preheat the oven to 400 degrees.

Grease the bottom of a small roasting pan or ovenproof skillet with half of the oil. Wrap a strip of prosciutto around each fig quarter and place in the pan. Sprinkle generously with the pepper.

Roast the figs until they are hot all the way through but not falling apart, 5 to 8 minutes, depending on the ripeness of the figs.

Makes 4 servings

Fresh Figs Roasted in Orange Juice

This simple recipe—fresh figs quickly roasted in orange juice, then the pan juices cooked with a splash of cream and chopped pine nuts—makes a quick, elegant summer or autumn dessert. For an extra-special touch, sprinkle a few fresh berries over the figs before serving. Serve hot or at room temperature.

Four fresh figs, ends trimmed

1/4 cup orange juice, fresh-squeezed or "old-fashioned" type with pulp

1 tablespoon heavy cream or crème fraîche

2 tablespoons chopped pine nuts

Fresh berries (optional)

Preheat the oven to 400 degrees.

Place the figs in a small nonreactive roasting pan or small ovenproof skillet and pour the orange juice on top. Roast the figs until tender, 6 to 8 minutes, depending on the size.

Remove the roasting pan from the oven, place the figs on a warm platter, and cut them lengthwise in half. Place the pan or skillet over high heat and add the cream and nuts. Simmer until thickened, about 5 minutes. Pour the hot sauce over the figs, sprinkle with a few fresh berries, if desired, and serve hot or at room temperature.

Makes 4 servings

Roasted Mango and Peach Chutney

Exotic, rich, and totally refreshing, this chutney takes about 20 minutes to make and it's ready to eat. The chutney keeps only about 24 hours. Serve it with roast pork, chicken, shrimp, fish, or beef or with curries.

1 large ripe peach, peeled, pitted, and cut into thick slices

1 ripe large mango, peeled, pitted, and cut into thick slices

1 tablespoon butter, cut into small pieces

1 tablespoon dry white wine

3 radishes, trimmed and coarsely chopped

1 cup chopped ripe tomato

2¹/₂ tablespoons peeled and chopped shallots; or 2 scallions, trimmed and chopped

Juice of 1 lime

¹/₄ cup light olive oil

Salt and freshly ground black pepper

1 tablespoon chopped fresh chives (optional)

1 to 2 teaspoons hot pepper sauce

Preheat the oven to 400 degrees.

Place the peach and mango slices in a small roasting pan or ovenproof skillet and dot with the butter.

Roast the fruit, gently stirring once or twice, until very soft and juicy, 10 to 15 minutes.

Remove the roasting pan from the oven and immediately pour in the wine, scraping up any browned juices. Let the fruit cool, then chop into big chunks.

Place the roasted fruit chunks along with the pan juices in a medium-size serving bowl and mix with the remaining ingredients. Season to taste, adding as much pepper sauce as you like. Serve cold or at room temperature.

Makes about 2 cups

Roasted Honeyed Bananas

This is a variation of honeyed bananas, a favorite Chinese dessert. The bananas are sliced lengthwise, dusted with ground cinnamon and ginger, and then topped with honey. Next they're roasted until golden brown and the juices are slightly caramelized. When cooked this way, bananas take on a buttery texture. They can be served for dessert, accompanied by a scoop of vanilla ice cream, or they can be served as a savory accompaniment to beef, curries, or pork dishes.

1 tablespoon plus 1 teaspoon unsalted butter

2 bananas, peeled and sliced lengthwise

Pinch ground cinnamon

Pinch ground ginger (optional)

1½ tablespoons honey (see Note)

Preheat the oven to 350 degrees.

Grease the bottom of a small roasting pan or small oven-proof skillet with the 1 teaspoon of the butter. Place the bananas in the pan and evenly sprinkle with the cinnamon and, if desired, the ginger.

Roast the bananas for 8 minutes. Remove the roasting pan from the oven, drizzle the honey evenly over the bananas, and dot with the remaining tablespoon of butter cut into small pieces. Continue roasting another 2 minutes.

Place the pan under the broiler and broil until the honey and butter look slightly caramelized and the bananas are golden brown, about 2 minutes. Serve hot with the pan juices poured on top.

Makes 2 servings

Note: *This is the type of dish that calls for a really flavorful, light-colored, flowery honey. Look for something special.*

Roasted Caribbean Banana Chutney

This is a thick, chunky condiment that is fabulous spread on slices of cold roast beef, lamb, or pork. It also goes well with curries, rice dishes, and seafood.

3 bananas, peeled and cut into 1-inch pieces

2 tablespoons plus 1 teaspoon olive oil

2 tablespoons light brown sugar

1 tablespoon butter, cut into small pieces

1/2 red bell pepper, cored and chopped

3 scallions, trimmed and chopped

About 1 tablespoon seeded and chopped jalapeño pepper; or several dashes of hot pepper sauce

Juice of 2 limes

Juice of 1 lemon

Preheat the oven to 400 degrees.

Place the bananas in a small roasting pan or ovenproof skillet and sprinkle with 1 teaspoon of the oil.

Roast the bananas for 10 minutes. Remove the roasting pan from the oven, sprinkle the bananas with the brown sugar, and dot with the butter. Continue roasting another 5 minutes.

Place the roasted bananas in a medium-size bowl and mix with the remaining oil and other ingredients. Taste for seasoning, adding more jalapeño if you like a spicier chutney. The chutney can be refrigerated, covered, for up to 24 hours.

Makes about 1 1/2 cups

Savory Roasted Apples

The idea of roasting apples with garlic and herbs comes from Deirdre Davis, author of *A Fresh Look At Saucing Foods.* It may take some getting used to, but once you taste this savory dish, you'll be convinced it's a wonderful idea. Serve the apples with roast poultry, game, pork, or beef; they make an especially good side dish for holiday meals.

2 tablespoons olive oil

1 large clove garlic, peeled and chopped

1 tablespoon chopped fresh parsley

1 teaspoon dried oregano

1 teaspoon dried thyme

$^1/_2$ cup fresh breadcrumbs

Salt and freshly ground black pepper

2 medium-size tart apples, such as Granny Smith

Preheat the oven to 350 degrees.

In a small bowl, combine the oil, garlic, herbs, breadcrumbs, salt, and pepper. Mix well with a fork to moisten all the crumbs evenly.

Cut the apples horizontally in half and remove the cores using a melon scooper or teaspoon. Do not peel them. Sprinkle the cored sides with salt and pepper. Spoon some of the crumb mixture into the cavity of each apple half.

Lightly grease a medium-size roasting pan, shallow casserole, or gratin dish. Place the apples in the dish and sprinkle any excess crumb mixture over the tops.

Roast the apples until they are tender but not mushy when pierced with the tip of a knife, 20 to 30 minutes. Broil the tops to brown if desired.

Makes 4 servings

Roasted Rhubarb with Brown Sugar Glaze

When the first stalks of rhubarb shoot out of the ground early each May, it is a sure sign that spring has arrived in Maine. And after a long, cold winter, it is one of the most welcome sights imaginable. This distinctly sour fruit (botanically speaking, it is actually a stem or a leaf) becomes buttery and silky in texture when roasted, and it is simply delicious topped with a sprinkling of brown sugar (to cut the tartness) and dotted with butter for added richness.

This is a great last-minute dessert that can be put together and roasted in about 20 minutes. You can serve the rhubarb on its own, but I especially recommend it spooned on top of a scoop of vanilla ice cream or drizzled with heavy cream.

2 cups rhubarb chunks (2-inch pieces)

1½ tablespoons unsalted butter, cut into tiny pieces

½ cup light brown sugar

About ½ cup heavy cream (optional)

Preheat the oven to 350 degrees.

Place the rhubarb in a small roasting pan, shallow flame-proof casserole, or gratin dish. Dot the rhubarb with the butter and sprinkle with half of the sugar.

Roast the rhubarb until soft when pierced, 10 to 12 minutes, depending on the thickness of the rhubarb.

Remove the roasting pan from the oven and preheat the broiler. Sprinkle the remaining sugar on the rhubarb and place under the broiler until the sugar has melted and formed a "crust" over the rhubarb, 3 to 5 minutes. Serve hot, at room temperature, or cold. Drizzle with heavy cream if desired.

Makes 4 servings

Chestnuts Roasting . . .

Chestnuts and roasting are two words that are inextricably linked in most people's minds. Roasted chestnuts, whether done over an open fire or in your kitchen oven, are indeed a holiday treat. When properly cooked, they are buttery, tender, and addictive. Roasting chestnuts can be tedious, but it's well worth the effort. Before roasting, you must carve a small "X" into the flat side of each nut, which can take time. This allows steam to escape, so that they don't explode during the roasting process. After they come out of the oven (or fire), they must be cooled before being peeled.

Preheat the oven to 400 degrees. Using a small sharp knife, make a small "X" in the flat side of each chestnut. Place the chestnuts on a baking sheet and roast until they begin to pop open through the opening, 12 to 15 minutes. Your kitchen will smell rich and nutty, which is a sign that the chestnuts are nearly done. Let cool slightly, peel off both the outer shell and the papery skin underneath, and eat. The roasted chestnuts are now also ready to be used in soups, stuffings, purees, mousses, puddings, and other recipes.

Roasted Waldorf Soup

This imaginative recipe comes from food writer Deirdre Davis of Ipswich, Massachusetts. All the ingredients of a Waldorf salad—celery, apples, and walnuts—are roasted and then blended together into a savory soup. This recipe can easily be doubled.

4 large ribs celery, trimmed and cut into 1-inch pieces

2 green apples, such as Granny Smith, peeled, cored, and cut into small pieces

2 cloves garlic, peeled and left whole

1/4 cup good-quality olive oil

Salt and freshly ground black pepper

About 2 tablespoons chopped walnuts

1 1/2 cups homemade chicken stock or low-sodium canned chicken broth

About 2 tablespoons sour cream

Preheat the oven to 400 degrees.

Place the celery, apples, and garlic in a small roasting pan or ovenproof skillet and toss with the oil, salt, and pepper.

Roast the mixture, stirring occasionally, until tender, about 30 minutes.

Place the walnuts on a baking sheet and roast at the same temperature until lightly toasted but not burned, about 5 minutes. Remove the baking sheet from the oven, let the walnuts cool, and set aside.

Working in batches if necessary, transfer the roasted celery and apple mixture to a blender and add 1 1/4 cups of the stock or broth. Puree until the soup is smooth.

Transfer the soup to a medium-size saucepan and warm over low heat. Add the remaining 1/4 cup stock or broth if the soup is too thick. Taste for seasoning and serve in cups or bowls, topped with a spoonful of sour cream and sprinkled with the toasted nuts.

Makes 4 servings

Fresh Roasted Pineapple with Caribbean Topping

According to Claudia Sansone, food writer for *Outbound Traveler* magazine and co-owner of the Wishing Well Fitness Spa, this is "pineapple reaching new heights." Fresh pineapple is cut into long strips, sprinkled with a Caribbean-style topping of lime zest, brown sugar, and grated coconut, and then roasted until tender. The pineapple is then placed under the broiler for a minute to crisp up the topping. Sansone suggests serving the pineapple as an appetizer, dessert, or snack, or as an accompaniment to other roasted or grilled foods.

One 3-pound pineapple

Grated zest of 1 lime

2 tablespoons light or dark brown sugar

3 tablespoons flaked sweetened coconut

Preheat the oven to 400 degrees.

Line a baking sheet with aluminum foil.

Slice off the top and bottom of the pineapple. Stand the pineapple on one cut end. Using a medium-size sharp knife, cut off the skin in long strips. Cut out the "eyes." Core the pineapple using a corer or cut the fruit in half lengthwise and cut a small V-shape in each half to remove the core. Cut each half lengthwise into 6 long strips.

Place the lime zest, brown sugar, and coconut in a food processor and process until well mixed, about 10 seconds. (This can also be done in a blender or you can finely chop the mixture by hand.) Place the mixture in a shallow bowl. Press the topping onto one side of each pineapple spear and place on a baking sheet with the topping side up.

Place on the upper rack of the oven and roast the pineapple for 10 minutes. Remove the baking pan from the oven and immediately turn on the broiler. Broil the pineapple for 1 minute to crisp up the topping. Serve warm.

Makes 6 servings

Sauces

Chinese Sesame-Chile-Lemon Dipping Sauce

This simple dipping sauce, inspired by my friend Valerie Jorgensen, wakes up the flavors of roasted or steamed asparagus. It's made with a little bit of Chinese chile paste (which gives it a rosy color and wide-awake taste), but if you prefer a spicier sauce, you can easily add more. This sauce also works well with steamed artichokes, roasted fish or potatoes, or roasted or steamed vegetables.

½ cup mayonnaise, homemade or bottled

½ cup plain low-fat yogurt

Juice of 1 large lemon

1 teaspoon Dijon mustard

½ to 1 teaspoon Chinese chile paste

1 teaspoon toasted sesame oil

1 scallion, trimmed and very thinly sliced

¼ cup chopped fresh parsley

Mix all the ingredients in a small bowl and taste for seasoning, adding more chile paste if desired. The sauce can be made ahead of time and refrigerated, covered, for several hours before serving.

Makes 1 cup

Green Sauce

This piquant sauce enlivens a wide variety of roasted foods. Made from capers, green bell pepper, parsley, and scallions, it goes particularly well with cold roast beef and Salt-Encrusted Roasted Shrimp (page 148).

½ cup cored and finely chopped green bell pepper

3 tablespoons finely chopped fresh parsley

3 tablespoons tiny capers

2 scallions, finely chopped

¼ cup good-quality olive oil

3 tablespoons red or white wine vinegar

Salt and freshly ground black pepper

In a small serving bowl, mix all the ingredients. Season to taste. Serve cold. The sauce can be refrigerated, covered, for up to 24 hours.

Makes about 1 cup

Yogurt Dill Sauce

This simple sauce goes well with roasted vegetable chips, such as Roasted Dilled Beet Chips (page 162) and Roasted Sweet Potato Chips (page 206). It also makes a nice dip for roasted shrimp or fish.

1 cup plain low-fat yogurt (see Note)

¹/₄ cup chopped fresh dill

1 tablespoon lemon juice

Dash hot red pepper sauce

Mix all the ingredients in a small bowl and season to taste. You can make this a mild, fresh-tasting sauce or a spicy one.

Makes 1 cup

Note: *If you want a thicker sauce, drain the yogurt in a colander lined with a piece of cheesecloth until all the whey (the thin milky substance) has drained, about 3 hours or overnight. Drain in the refrigerator.*

Raita (Cucumber-Yogurt Sauce)

This refreshing cucumber-yogurt sauce provides a good balance for any of the spicier roasts in this book. It's particularly good with Larisa's Indian Roast Chicken with Masala-Apple Stuffing (page 92).

1 cup plain low-fat yogurt (see Note, preceding recipe)

1 cup peeled and grated cucumber

Salt and freshly ground black pepper

1½ tablespoons chopped fresh mint; or 1 teaspoon dried (optional)

In a small bowl mix all the ingredients. Cover and refrigerate until ready to serve. The sauce keeps well for only 3 to 4 hours.

Makes about 1½ cups

Gingered Cranberry Sauce with Pineapple and Pecans

Each Thanksgiving I experiment with a different cranberry sauce. This recipe, an adaptation of Lucy's Cranberry-Orange-Maple Sauce that appeared in my first cookbook, *Condiments*, is the culmination of many versions tried over the years. It combines tangy cranberries with colorful slivers of orange zest, pungent ginger, juicy pineapple, and crunchy pecans.

It is sweet enough to be poured over ice cream or pound cake but not so sweet that you wouldn't want to serve it alongside every type of roast meat, poultry, or pork dish imaginable.

I like to make large quantities of this sauce (it's not much more work) and place it in old Mason jars to give to friends and family as a holiday gift.

2¹/₂ cups sugar

6 cups water

4 cups fresh cranberries, about 1 pound

1 cup orange juice, fresh-squeezed or "old-fashioned" type with pulp

6 tablespoons slivered orange zest

¹/₃ to ¹/₂ cup pure maple syrup

3 tablespoons peeled and grated ginger

1 medium-size ripe pineapple, peeled, cored (page 224), and diced

1¹/₂ cups shelled pecans, chopped

Mix the sugar and water in a large saucepan and bring to a boil over high heat. Reduce the heat to moderate and let this syrup simmer until slightly thickened, about 8 minutes. Add the cranberries and simmer until they begin to pop, about 5 minutes. Add the orange juice, orange zest, maple syrup to taste, ginger, and pineapple and simmer until the liquid is maroon-colored and the fruit has softened, another 3 minutes. Remove the pan from the heat and stir in the pecans. Let cool.

Spoon the sauce into clean jars, seal, and store in the refrigerator for about 2 weeks or freeze for about 2 months.

Makes about 10 cups

Aioli Sauce

This is the sauce for garlic lovers—rich and pungent, with real pow. Try this garlicky mayonnaise with roasted potatoes, vegetables, or chicken; or as a dip with roasted shrimp or fish. Why not spread some on black bread and top with paper-thin slices of cold roast beef, lamb, or pork?

This recipe calls for two or three cloves of garlic: two cloves will give you a strong garlicky flavor, and three will knock your socks off. Use your discretion.

2 or 3 large cloves garlic, peeled and chopped

Large pinch salt

1 large egg yolk, at room temperature

1/2 cup olive oil

1/4 cup mild vegetable oil

2 tablespoons lemon juice

Freshly ground black pepper

In a small wooden bowl or mortar, smash the garlic with the salt, using the back of a spoon or a pestle, until it makes a rough paste.

Place the egg yolk in a food processor or blender and process for a few seconds. Very slowly, add the oils in a thin, steady stream and process until thickened. Add the garlic paste and process until blended.

Scrape the mixture into a small bowl. Gently stir in the lemon juice and pepper. Taste for seasoning. The aioli can be refrigerated, covered, for about 4 days.

Makes about 3/4 cup

Horseradish Cream

This is a quick, simple sauce that is a classic accompaniment to roast beef. It's equally good served with roast lamb, pork, or chicken.

½ cup heavy cream, sour cream, or crème fraîche

2 to 3 tablespoons grated bottled horse-radish, drained

2 tablespoons trimmed and very thinly sliced scallion (optional)

Freshly ground black pepper

Whip the heavy cream until it holds stiff peaks. (Sour cream and crème fraîche don't need to be whipped.) Gently fold in the horseradish, scallion if desired, and pepper. Taste for seasoning. Serve cold. The sauce can be refrigerated, covered, for up to 3 hours.

Makes 4 to 6 servings

Moroccan Hot Sauce (Chermoula)

A musty, exotic sauce that enlivens the flavor of any roasted food—particularly poultry, lamb, beef, and pork—this is also wonderful drizzled over roasted vegetables, barbecued foods, or as a marinade for seafood or lamb.

¼ to ½ teaspoon cayenne pepper

½ teaspoon salt

3 cloves garlic, peeled and chopped

1½ teaspoons sweet Hungarian paprika

½ to 1 teaspoon ground cumin

½ cup chopped fresh cilantro (optional)

½ cup chopped fresh parsley

Juice of 1 lemon

2 tablespoons red wine vinegar

2½ tablespoons olive oil

Place the cayenne, salt, garlic, paprika, cumin, cilantro, and parsley in a food processor or blender and pulse until smooth. With the motor running, slowly add the lemon juice and vinegar and then the oil. Taste for seasoning and adjust, adding more cumin and/or cayenne to taste.

Makes about ½ cup

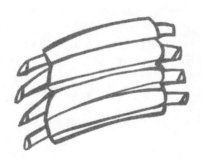

Apple-Mint Jelly

Unlike traditional mint jelly, which is loaded with sugar, this recipe, an adaptation of one from my first book, *Condiments*, is made by simply boiling a gallon of apple cider with a handful of fresh mint leaves until thick. The result is a minty apple-flavored jelly full of only natural ingredients—no added sugar, pectin, or preservatives.

You'll need to keep a close eye on the mixture toward the end of the cooking time. The jelly tends to thicken quickly. You want to avoid caramelizing the jelly or letting it get too thick.

This is the classic accompaniment to roast leg of lamb, but it goes equally well with roast chicken or pork. I also like to make a Cheddar cheese and cucumber sandwich on thinly sliced black bread with a dab of mint jelly. It may sound odd, but give it a try.

1 cup fresh mint leaves or several varieties of mint

1 gallon unsweetened fresh apple cider with no additives

Wrap the mint in a double layer of cheesecloth and close tightly with a knot.

Place the cider in a large heavy pot and bring to a boil over high heat. Reduce the heat to moderate and add the mint bundle. Let the cider cook over moderately low heat at a low, rolling boil until it reduces to 2 cups and coats the back of a spoon, about 2 hours. Press down on the cheesecloth every 30 minutes to extract the mint flavor.

Discard the mint bundle and pour the jelly into a sterilized canning or jelly jar, using a spatula to get the last bit of jelly out of the pot. Let cool to room temperature and seal the jars. The jelly will keep for about a month or can be processed and canned.

Makes 2 cups

Basic Vinaigrette

A vinaigrette is the simplest, most versatile salad dressing of all. It goes with everything from tossed greens and chicken salad to roasted vegetables and shrimp. The recipe doubles or triples easily.

1 tablespoon Dijon mustard

Salt and freshly ground black pepper

About 3 tablespoons good-quality red or white wine vinegar

About 6 tablespoons good-quality olive oil

In a small bowl, whisk together the mustard, salt, and pepper. Whisk in the vinegar and then the oil to form a smooth dressing. Taste for seasoning; add more vinegar if the dressing tastes too oily, more oil if the dressing is too tart. Vinaigrette can be refrigerated in a covered jar for up to 1 week. Shake or whisk to reemulsify.

Makes about ¹/₄ cup

Vinaigrette Variations

Garlic Vinaigrette: Mash 1 clove peeled garlic into the mustard, salt, and pepper until crushed. Proceed with Basic Vinaigrette.

Herb Vinaigrette: Add 1 tablespoon chopped fresh herb, one or more kinds, to the vinaigrette or use 1 teaspoon dried.

Creamy Vinaigrette: Add 1 tablespoon low-fat milk to the mustard, salt, and pepper. Proceed with Basic Vinaigrette.

Honey Vinaigrette: Add 1 to 2 teaspoons honey to the mustard, salt, and pepper. Proceed with Basic Vinaigrette.

Roasted Shallot and Rosemary Vinaigrette: Roast 2 shallots in a teaspoon of olive oil and a teaspoon of balsamic vinegar in a 350-degree oven for 10 to 15 minutes. Remove from the oven and finely chop the shallots. Add to the vinaigrette along with the pan juices.

Garlic-Fennel-Chile Oil

Allow this richly flavored oil to sit for two weeks in a warm, dry spot before using. Save an old wine bottle, rinse it well with soap and hot water, dry thoroughly, and use to store the oil.

This oil is delicious drizzled over roast chicken, lamb, pork, beef, potatoes, or vegetables. It can also be used in vinaigrettes, marinades, and barbecue sauces and for sautéing all manner of foods.

4 cups good-quality olive oil

1 tablespoon fennel seeds

6 cloves garlic, peeled and cut lengthwise in half

8 small dried red chile peppers

Place the oil in a clean bottle. Add the fennel seeds, garlic, and chile peppers and let sit 2 weeks before using. Store in a cool, dark spot or in the refrigerator. The oil should keep for about 2 months. Discard at the first sign of mold.

Makes 4 cups

Side Dishes

Creamed Spinach

You can't go wrong serving this classic comfort food with roast beef, pork, poultry, or fish. For some innovative variations on this classic, see the list below.

20 ounces fresh spinach or two 10-ounce bags, stemmed, thoroughly washed, but not dried

About 1/2 cup heavy cream

Salt and freshly ground black pepper

Freshly grated nutmeg

Preheat the oven to 300 degrees.

Put the spinach in a large pot with the water still clinging to the leaves. Cook over high heat until soft, about 5 minutes, stirring once or twice. Rinse under cold water, drain, and press all the water out of the leaves.

In a blender or food processor, puree the spinach with the cream, salt, pepper, and nutmeg. Taste for seasoning and adjust as needed.

Place the creamed spinach in a lightly greased small ovenproof casserole. Cover and roast until heated through and simmering, about 20 minutes.

Makes 4 servings

Creamed Spinach Variations

Place the creamed spinach in a lightly greased small ovenproof casserole and top with any of the following. Cover and heat the spinach in a 300-degree oven until heated through, about 20 minutes. Remove the lid during the last 5 minutes.

- 1/3 cup seasoned breadcrumbs
- 1/3 cup slivered almonds or chopped pecans or pine nuts
- 3 tablespoons pesto
- 2 tablespoons Roasted Garlic and Herb Butter (page 197)
- 1/3 cup Caramelized Honey Walnuts (page 249)
- 3 tablespoons olive puree

Sautéed Escarole

This is a simple, delicious way to cook fresh escarole or spinach.

1 teaspoon olive oil

1 clove garlic, chopped

1 pound fresh escarole or spinach, stemmed and thoroughly washed, but not dried

Salt and freshly ground black pepper

Heat the oil in a large skillet over moderate heat. Add the garlic and cook, stirring, 1 minute. Do not let the garlic brown. Add the escarole or spinach with the water still clinging to the leaves and cook, stirring constantly, until soft, about 8 minutes. If there is an excessive amount of water in the bottom of the pan, blot it up with a paper towel and continue cooking to evaporate the water. Add salt and pepper to taste.

Makes 2 to 3 servings

Spinach Soufflé Roll Stuffed with Roasted Red Peppers

The red and green colors of this soufflé make it perfect holiday fare. Although there are several steps involved in this dish, once the advance prep work is done, all you have to do at the last minute is beat the egg whites, fold them into the spinach, and bake. The soufflé pairs well with roast beef, pork, fish, or poultry dishes.

2 medium-size to large red bell peppers

1 pound fresh spinach, stemmed, thoroughly washed, but not dried

1 tablespoon butter or margarine

2 tablespoons olive oil or vegetable oil

1 large onion, peeled and thinly sliced

¼ teaspoon freshly grated nutmeg

Salt and freshly ground black pepper

Preheat the oven to 450 degrees.

Place the peppers on a piece of aluminum foil and roast, turning the peppers every few minutes, until blackened on all sides, about 15 minutes.

Remove the peppers from the oven and wrap tightly in the foil for about 5 minutes. Using a sharp knife or your fingers, peel off the blackened skin. Cut the peppers lengthwise in half and remove the seeds and core. Cut the peppers into thin strips and set aside.

Place the spinach in a large pot with the water still clinging to the leaves. Cook over high heat until soft, about 5 minutes, stirring once or twice. Rinse under cold water, drain, and press all the water out of the leaves. Finely chop the spinach and set aside.

Line the bottom and sides of a baking sheet or a large shallow baking dish with a single piece of wax paper, folding the paper to fit where needed. Butter the paper well and set aside.

In a large skillet, heat the butter or margarine and 1 tablespoon of the oil over moderate heat. Add the onion and cook, stirring occasionally, until soft, about 3 minutes. Add the chopped spinach and cook, stirring, another 2 minutes. Remove the skillet from the heat and add the nutmeg, salt, and pepper. Let cool slightly. (The recipe can be prepared to this point and refrigerated, covered, for a day.)

4 large eggs, separated

²/₃ cup grated Parmesan cheese

2 tablespoons trimmed and chopped
scallion or fresh chives

Preheat the oven to 400 degrees.

In a large bowl, whisk the egg whites until they hold soft peaks; do not overbeat.

Beat the yolks to mix and gradually stir them into the cooled spinach mixture. Gently fold the spinach mixture into the whisked egg whites. Using a thin-bladed spatula, spread this lightened spinach mixture on the prepared baking sheet. Sprinkle with half of the cheese.

Bake on the top shelf of the oven until the soufflé has risen and is firm to the touch, about 10 minutes.

Meanwhile, heat the remaining tablespoon of oil in a medium-size skillet over moderate heat. Add the pepper strips, scallion, salt, and pepper. Keep warm.

Remove the soufflé from the oven and gently flip it upside down onto another baking sheet or piece of wax paper. Peel off the paper from the soufflé and spread the warm peppers and scallion over the surface. Roll the soufflé up into a fat log shape, trim the ends evenly, and sprinkle with the remaining cheese. Serve immediately.

Makes 6 to 8 servings

Sautéed Pea Pods in Soy Butter

This is an extremely fast, simple way to cook fresh snow peas with a sophisticated flavor. They go well with a wide variety of roasted foods. I particularly like serving these peas with roast duck or a fish dish.

1 teaspoon vegetable oil

1/2 pound fresh snow peas, trimmed

1 teaspoon peeled and grated fresh ginger;
   or 1/4 teaspoon dried

1 tablespoon butter

1/2 tablespoon low-sodium soy sauce or
   tamari

In a large skillet, heat the oil over moderately high heat. Add the peas and half of the ginger and cook, stirring constantly, until crisp-tender, 3 to 5 minutes. Remove the peas to a platter. Add the butter and remaining ginger to the skillet and, as soon as the butter melts, add the soy sauce. Let cook for about 30 seconds and pour on top of the peas.

Makes 2 servings

Celery Rémoulade

This classic bistro dish is the French equivalent of coleslaw. Celery rémoulade is made from celeriac, a knobby root that is full of the fresh flavor of celery. Its main attraction, however, is its wonderful crunchy texture. The root is peeled and sliced into thin matchstick-size strips and then tossed with a mustardy-mayonnaise sauce flecked with pepper and parsley.

Serve this refreshing salad with roast poultry, meats, fish, or game. Or try it as a starter, as the French do, served on a bed of mixed greens and accompanied by a sprig of fresh parsley and a wedge of lemon.

Plan on letting the salad "marinate" for a minimum of 2 hours to allow the celeriac to soften.

One 1-pound celeriac (celery root)

$^1\!/_2$ cup chopped fresh parsley

$^1\!/_2$ cup mayonnaise

3 tablespoons Dijon mustard

1 teaspoon olive oil

1 tablespoon lemon juice

Salt and freshly ground black pepper

$^1\!/_2$ cup chopped walnuts (optional)

$^1\!/_4$ cup trimmed and finely chopped scallions or fresh chives (optional)

Peel the celeriac and cut it into quarters. Cut the quarters into very thin matchstick strips and place in a medium-size serving bowl. Stir in the parsley.

In a small bowl, mix together the mayonnaise, mustard, olive oil, lemon juice, salt, and pepper. Gently stir the sauce into the celeriac until it is thoroughly coated. Taste for seasoning. Stir in the walnuts and scallions if using. Cover and refrigerate for at least 2 hours or preferably overnight.

Makes 4 to 6 servings

Carrot and Parsley Salad

This is a thoroughly refreshing salad that takes just minutes to make. It complements any roast.

About 4 large carrots, peeled and grated (2¹/₂ cups)

4 scallions, trimmed and very thinly sliced

1 cup finely chopped fresh parsley

4¹/₂ tablespoons red wine vinegar

7 tablespoons good-quality olive oil

Salt and freshly ground black pepper

In a medium-size bowl, mix the carrots, scallions, and parsley. Stir in the vinegar and oil and season to taste with salt and pepper. Serve cold.

Makes 6 servings

Mashed Potatoes

An old-fashioned favorite that is loved by young and old, mashed potatoes can be served with just about any roasted food and can be made with endless variations. Add 3 to 4 cloves peeled whole garlic to the pot when you cook the potatoes and then mash them right in with the potatoes. Or finely chop roasted cloves of garlic and/or shallots and stir into the mashed potatoes. You can experiment by adding herbs and spices or flavored olive oil instead of traditional butter. Also try stirring in a tablespoon of horseradish (red horseradish with beets will add a brilliant pink color to the potatoes and keep your diners guessing). I like to stir grated Parmesan or a variety of other cheeses into mashed potatoes just before serving. You can also try this recipe with sweet potatoes and add a dash of grated nutmeg or ground ginger.

12 medium-size baking potatoes, peeled and quartered (see Note)

8 tablespoons (1 stick) butter

About 1 cup milk

Salt and freshly ground black pepper

Place the potatoes in a large pot of boiling water. Simmer over moderately high heat until they are tender but not falling apart, 15 to 25 minutes. Drain thoroughly.

Using a ricer or a potato masher, mash the potatoes in the pan over low heat. Add half of the butter and half of the milk and mash well until incorporated. Add the remaining butter and milk and season to taste with salt and pepper. Some lumps are desirable. If you like your potatoes moister add another $1/4$ cup milk.

Makes 8 servings

> Note: *Many cooks prefer to leave the potatoes unpeeled.*

Yorkshire Pudding

Dozens of recipes for this English pudding exist in cookbooks old and new; this is the one I have always used and the one that I find produces the most flavorful pudding. The trick is to preheat the pan so it's scorching hot, which causes the pudding to rise properly.

The pudding should be mixed and ready to go so that it can go in the oven as soon as you take out the Standing Rib Roast (page 18). As the meat sits, the pudding is cooked.

2 large eggs

1 cup milk

1 cup all-purpose flour, sifted

Salt and freshly ground black pepper

Beef drippings from the roast beef;
    or 1 tablespoon butter, melted

In a medium-size bowl, vigorously whisk the eggs until light. Add the milk and beat well. Gradually add the flour and stir until the batter is smooth. Season well with salt and pepper.

About 8 minutes before the roast beef is done, place a medium-size ovenproof skillet or shallow oblong pan in the oven for about 8 minutes at whatever temperature you are roasting the beef.

Remove the roast beef from the oven. Set the oven to 450 degrees. Remove the preheated pan from the oven and pour 2 to 3 tablespoons hot fat from the roast beef pan into the preheated pan. (Be careful: the fat will sizzle.) Immediately pour in the pudding batter and bake on the center shelf for 10 minutes. Reduce the oven temperature to 350 degrees and continue baking until the pudding has risen and is golden brown, about 10 minutes.

Cut the pudding into squares and pour some of the beef juices on top. Serve hot with roast beef.

Makes 6 servings

Spider Corn Cake

This is an exceptional corn bread, baked with a thin, custard-like layer on top. The recipe comes from my friend Penelope Brewster, owner of Ceres Street Bakery in Portsmouth, New Hampshire. This is an old Brewster family recipe, passed down from one generation to the next. Originally it was made in a spider pan, a black cast-iron skillet with "legs" that gave it a spiderlike appearance. You can use a regular cast-iron skillet or any thick, ovenproof skillet.

Serve the corn cake with roast chicken, vegetables, fish, or beef. Or indulge and serve it on its own, accompanied by some sweet butter and a cup of hot English tea.

1½ cups yellow cornmeal

½ cup sugar

½ cup all-purpose flour

2 teaspoons salt

1 cup buttermilk (see Note)

½ teaspoon baking soda

2 large eggs, beaten

2 cups milk

2 tablespoons butter, melted

Preheat the oven to 350 degrees. Lightly grease a large cast-iron skillet or ovenproof skillet.

In a large bowl, mix the cornmeal, sugar, flour, and salt. Add the buttermilk and baking soda and mix well. Add the eggs, 1 cup of the regular milk, and the melted butter to the batter and mix well.

Pour the batter into the prepared skillet and bake 10 minutes. Pour the remaining 1 cup of milk on top and continue baking until the cornbread is firm, about 35 minutes. Cut the cornbread into wedges and serve hot or at room temperature.

Makes 6 to 8 servings

Note: *Soured milk can be made by adding 1 tablespoon vinegar or lemon juice to 1 cup warm milk*

Herbed Pepper Popovers

These airy popovers are a treat with any roast, but they are particularly good served with a Standing Rib Roast (page 18).

3 large eggs

1¹/₂ cups milk

1¹/₂ cups all-purpose flour

2¹/₂ tablespoons butter, melted, plus
   additional for buttering

1 tablespoon chopped fresh rosemary;
   or ¹/₂ teaspoon dried

1 tablespoon chopped fresh thyme;
   or ¹/₂ teaspoon dried

Salt and freshly ground black pepper

Preheat the oven to 400 degrees. Butter a 12-cup muffin tin or popover cups.

In a medium-size bowl, whisk the eggs. Add the milk and beat thoroughly. Sift in the flour and stir. Add 1 tablespoon of the melted butter and the herbs, salt, and a generous grinding of pepper.

Fill the prepared cups two-thirds full with batter. Drizzle a little of the remaining melted butter into the center of each popover and bake 15 minutes. Reduce the oven temperature to 350 degrees. Bake until the popovers are golden brown and puffed up, 15 to 20 minutes. (Be careful not to open the oven during the cooking time.) Serve immediately.

Makes 12 popovers

Caramelized Honey Walnuts

These sticky, gooey walnuts are so irresistible they seem to disappear right before your eyes. Make a double batch to play it safe. Serve these walnuts with any roasted food. They're good sprinkled onto composed salads made with leftover roasted meat, pork, poultry, or fish (see Composed Salad of Roast Beef, Roasted Shallots, and Caramelized Honey Walnuts on page 28). You can also serve the walnuts with cocktails before dinner.

1 tablespoon butter

1 cup walnut halves

2½ tablespoons honey

1 teaspoon low-sodium soy sauce (optional)

In a medium-size skillet, melt the butter over moderately high heat. Add the walnuts and cook, stirring constantly to prevent burning, for 1 minute. Add the honey and soy sauce, if desired, and cook, stirring constantly, until the sauce thickens and thoroughly coats the nuts, 3 to 5 minutes.

Transfer the nut mixture to a large plate, separating the nuts so they don't clump together. Let them dry. Place the dried nuts in a tightly sealed jar or container and refrigerate for up a week. Bring to room temperature before serving.

Makes 1 cup

Bibliography

Behr, Edward. *The Artful Eater.* Atlantic Monthly Press, 1992.

Bridge, Fred, and Jean F. Tibbets. *The Well-Tooled Kitchen.* Hearst Books, 1991.

Child, Julia. *The Way to Cook.* Knopf, 1989.

Davis, Deirdre. *A Fresh Look at Saucing Foods.* Addison Wesley, 1993.

Graham, Kevin. *Simply Elegant.* Grove Weidenfeld, 1991.

Gunst, Kathy. *Condiments.* G.P. Putnam's Sons, 1984.

————. *Leftovers.* HarperCollins, 1991.

Hazan, Marcella. *The Classic Italian Cookbook.* Knopf, 1973.

Herbst, Sharon Tyler. *The Food Lover's Tiptionary.* Hearst Books, 1994.

Holt, Geraldine. *Recipes From a French Herb Garden.* Simon & Schuster, 1989.

Kennedy, Diana. *The Cuisines of Mexico.* Harper & Row, 1972.

Killeen, Johanne, and George Germon, *Cucina Simpatica.* HarperCollins, 1991.

Lang, Jenifer Harvey. *Larousse Gastronomique.* Crown Publishers, 1984.

London Cordon Bleu Cookery School. *Cordon Bleu Basic Cookery Methods.* B.P.C. Publishing Ltd, 1972.

Marshall, Lydie. *A Passion for Potatoes.* HarperCollins, 1992.

McGee, Harold. *The Curious Cook.* Collier Books, 1990.

Ortiz, Elizabeth Lambert. *The Encyclopedia of Herbs, Spices & Flavorings.* Dorling Kindersley, Inc., 1992.

Rosso, Julee, and Sheila Lukins. *The New Basics.* Workman Publishing, 1989.

Shulman, Martha Rose. *The Vegetarian Feast.* Harper & Row, 1979.

Webster's New Universal Unabridged Dictionary. Simon & Schuster, 1979.

Index